CLASS
STRUGGLE

Also by Jay Mathews

One Billion: A China Chronicle (with Linda Mathews)
Escalante: The Best Teacher in America
A Mother's Touch: The Tiffany Callo Story

CLASS
STRUGGLE

What's Wrong (and Right)
with America's Best
Public High Schools

Jay Mathews

TIMES 𝕿 BOOKS

RANDOM HOUSE

FOR LINDA

Grateful acknowledgment is made to A. P. Watt Ltd. on behalf of The National Trust for permission to reprint eight lines from "The White Man's Burden" by Rudyard Kipling. Reprinted by permission of A. P. Watt Ltd. on behalf of the National Trust.

Library of Congress Cataloging-in-Publication Data

Mathews, Jay
    Class struggle : what's wrong (and right) with America's best public high schools / Jay Mathews.
        p.   cm.
    Includes index.
    ISBN 0-8129-3140-8
    1. Upper class—Education (Secondary)—United States—Case studies.
2. Public schools—United States—Case studies.   3. Elite (Social sciences)—United States—Case studies.   4. Social status—United States—Case studies.
5. Mamaroneck High School (Mamaroneck, N.Y.)   I. Title.
LC4941.M38   1998
373.1826'21—dc21   97-27887

Text design: Levavi & Levavi

Random House website address: www.randomhouse.com

Printed in the United States of America on acid-free paper

9 8 7 6 5 4 3 2

First Paperback Edition

CONTENTS

MEASURING STICKS

MONEY

REACHING OUT

CONCLUSIONS

AFTERWORD

INTRODUCTION

Like many Americans, I assumed before I decided to write this book that I already knew why elite public high schools did so well. They had the strongest tax support, the most ambitious students, the wealthiest parents, the best-paid teachers, and the smallest classes. In schoolyard terms, they were a slam dunk.

But as I began to study them, it became obvious that for many of these schools, such assumptions were misplaced or not carefully examined. There were few scholarly studies of high-achieving schools. Journalists like me steered clear of them. We preferred to write about teachers and students in trouble, and how they found ways to teach and learn despite low expectations, poor equipment, and impoverished homes.

The deeper I went into this privileged world, the more I became convinced that it was time to examine not only our worst educational cases, but those we have always taken to be our best. We could, I thought, take apart the various devices that produced accomplished students in well-endowed schools and see if they might be reassembled cheaply in less affluent neighborhoods and have a similar impact. One favorite tool of elite schools, the Advanced Placement, or AP, program, was particularly promising. Not only had I seen it perform wonders at one of the poorest schools in the country, but it served as an excellent litmus test for affluent schools whose reputations exceeded their accomplishments.

Examining high-achieving schools also provided a useful counterweight to the oft-expressed view that public education does not work in America. If so many of these schools did so well, perhaps it was wrong to reflexively dismiss tax-supported institutions as irretrievably bureaucratic and old-fashioned.

The schools also have an intriguing and unexamined downside. Many of them suffer from the same kind of expectation gap I had encountered in low-achieving schools. Many students at rich schools, like poor ones, do not do as well as they could because they are not thought capable of doing very well. Teachers, counselors, and administrators try to make them comfortable rather than smart and then blame the sad results on inattentive parents, badly wired brains, cultural isolation, or some other fashionable excuse. Some of our best schools bar enthusiastic students from challenging courses, allow talent to fester in classes that do little more than fill time, and divide students by perceived intelligence despite few signs of any significant differences in their ability to learn. If we are going to make our best-known high schools, such as New Trier, Scarsdale, and Beverly Hills, models of secondary education, we have to know more about how snob appeal distorts learning.

Elite public schools have been created for the best and worst reasons. No one can quarrel with the desire to make standards high and put education at the center of children's lives. And as we shall see, some high-achieving schools have found ways to engage creatively a few of their lowest-achieving students. But these schools exist not only for high achievement, but because of the irresistible urge to set ourselves above others. Class and status yearnings have produced restrictive covenants, redlining, segregation, white flight, and other bits of elite school history that do not appear in the nicely printed brochures that the schools give prospective home buyers and college admissions offices.

Perhaps in districts where education is not a top priority, there are good reasons for putting the most motivated students in separate classes. If ill-endowed schools do not do so, the parents of their most ambitious students may take their children elsewhere. None of us has the power to delete with a few taps on the keyboard our ethnic and class biases. But it is much more difficult to justify pedagogical segregation in elite schools where there are no significant differences in the family backgrounds of the lower-track and upper-track children, and where the parents are unlikely to leave. When we divide children in these best of all possible educational enclaves, we expose the irrationality and impurity of our motives and reduce the chances for learning.

To write this book, I found a school in Westchester County, New York, Mamaroneck (pronounced Ma-MAIR-row-neck) High, whose administrators were willing to let me spend three years talking to students, parents, and educators. I visited seventy-five other schools throughout the country, particularly those in the four largest enclaves of elite public education: the New York suburban villages of Westchester and Long Island, Chicago's North Shore, the hills and beaches on the rim of the Los Angeles basin, and the Beltway suburbs of Washington, D.C. I collected information on thousands of other schools. In this book I tell stories about Mamaroneck entwined with what I hope are relevant tales from many of these other schools.

There is no satisfactorily precise definition of an elite public school. One of the strengths and, I think, one of the delights of the American education system is that local citizens decide what their schools are going to be like. Each school sees achievement and ambition in a slightly different way, although almost all embrace a national culture that worships high test scores, good grades, and placement in fine colleges. The schools ranked at the end of this book comprise only the uppermost slice of a much longer list. I assume about twenty-one hundred schools (or 10 percent of the twenty-one thousand public high schools in the country) can in some way be considered elite, based on the records of college recruiters who, in essence, decide which schools are going to have records of achievement that impress parents and taxpayers.

The public school students admitted to Yale's class of 2000 came from 966 different high schools. The public school boys admitted to the Harvard class of 1999 came from 619 schools, and the public school girls from 535 schools. Since many of the highest-achieving schools don't send students to Yale or Harvard every year, a figure of about two thousand elite schools seems reasonable. That is the number of public schools that get at least one student into Stanford every five years, university officials estimate, and that number appears to be increasing. If the growth of the Advanced Placement program is any indication, dozens of schools are joining the highest achievers every year, and adopting many of their good and, I suspect, some of their bad habits.

We ought to pay more attention to what happens in all of our high schools. Few of us appreciate how much our secondary school educations define us. Many of the politicians, industry leaders, and celebrities I have met as a journalist over the last thirty years mention their colleges in their official biographies and in interviews. When I began asking a few years ago where they went to high school, they often seemed surprised at the question. When I attempted to identify the high schools attended by the fifty state governors and the chairmen of the fifty largest American companies as background for this book, in nearly every case the information was not in the official biography and someone had to ask the boss where he or she went to school. Yet many Americans, I suspect, remember more about history, literature, and mathematics from what they learned in high school than from the narrower courses they took in college. For the majority of Americans who do not have college degrees, their high school experiences are even more important.

I found it reassuring that my survey of governors and corporate chairmen showed that opportunity is not confined to graduates of the best schools. Far more of the one hundred political leaders and executives spent their high school years in undistinguished rural schools than in the elite suburban schools examined in this book. Larry Breen, a vice principal at Greeley High in Chappaqua, New York, one of the most successful high schools in the country, noted that Greeley had produced few historical figures (with the possible exception of singer-actress Vanessa L. Williams) but that it gave the world "a lot of dentists who live in New Jersey."

I was impressed by the extraordinary range and rigor of these schools as much as I was bothered by the uneven way in which their gifts are dispensed. The instincts that lead many of us to seek out the best in public education do harm when the schools are organized in the same stratified way, with so little bearing on how children learn. Perhaps that should lead us to rethink those instincts, as difficult as that might be. We can start by considering this: When the best schools in the country cannot resist labeling some of their students as mediocre and denying them the most challenging courses, then all schools, no matter how ambitious and affluent, are in trouble.

FUNDAMENTALS

1

HARD AND SOFT

In 1991 Dan Hopkins received an 83 on his first report card in Algebra. To most students and most families at most schools in America, this would be fine. On the 100-point scale, 83 was a low B. It meant he could do better but he understood a large portion of what he had been taught.

The problem was that Hopkins, a wavy-haired boy who loved to swim, was not an ordinary student. He had exceptional academic talent, a sense of irony and grasp of subtlety that had enchanted teachers since he was seven. His parents were both physicians. He lived in Larchmont, New York, one of the wealthiest and best-educated communities on the planet. His grade would go on his permanent record at Mamaroneck High School, one of the top 1 percent of American secondary schools and a place where an 83 on a report card was frequently cause for alarm.

The unexpectedly low Algebra grade unsettled Hopkins's parents. Their reaction echoed in other households where disappointing marks in the 70s and 60s were given to children in the honors algebra course.

Hopkins himself said he was not so upset. An example of God's occasional extravagance, he was not only brilliant and athletic but also had several close friends, a wide range of other interests, and a flawless complexion. The grade meant he was not as good at mathematics as he had thought, but there were other ways to make his mark.

The parents did not take it so lightly. Within a few days, seventeen families had formed a committee to consider a response. If the Mamaroneck schools and teachers had imperfections, they were going to do something about them, and the quicker the better. This high plateau of American public education had been created for them with their money, invested in large mortgages and heavy real estate taxes so they could live in a prime school district. They were hoping to make explicit what up to then had been implicit: Anything or anyone in the school that significantly displeased them ought not to endure.

Joy Sarlo, a classmate of Hopkins, received a 92 in Graphic Arts at the end of the spring semester of her junior year in 1995. All her grades that year were in the 80s and 90s. That made her and her parents happy. Yet she wondered what the marks meant.

On many days the Graphic Arts course had been more of a circus than a learning experience. The class was small and noisy. Students discussed the upcoming football game at Harrison and the previous week's keg party in Sheldrake Woods while the teacher tried to steer the conversation toward color registers and printing techniques.

Other Sarlo classes, such as History and Mathematics, demanded more of her attention in class but still required very little homework, a total of no more than an hour a day. Graphic Arts had no homework at all. Her Photography class had no daily homework and, since she had taken an independent project option, only occasional meetings with the teacher.

She was a student with the same rights and responsibilities as 1,050 others at the school, but she had come to understand that Mamaroneck's expectations for her were different than for many of her classmates. Her father was a police officer for the village of Mamaroneck; her mother was a nurse. The Sarlos, John, Dawn, Joy, and her brother John, did not live in one of the large brick homes in the hills of the Ridgely neighborhood or in one of the $1 million bungalows with wraparound porches near Long Island Sound. Their home was a prefabricated three-story frame house her father had constructed for $95,000 on Madison Street in Mamaroneck's Washingtonville section, a neighborhood of low- and middle-income families known as the Flats.

Despite the school's low expectations of her, Sarlo was quick and bright. She could detect faulty reasoning. She had a lively interest in literature and art. She was a lifeguard and a cheerleader and probably knew more people on campus than any other student at the school. Occasionally a teacher would engage her full attention and successfully demand that she devote significant energies to a class. But that did not happen often. Usually she was passed along with grades just good enough to secure a place in one of New York's state universities. She did not feel she learned very much at Mamaroneck, despite its reputation.

That spring, just as she was completing the Graphic Arts course that earned her a 92, she attempted to turn in her final project in her art and studio photography course. She had been told this was the assignment on which her grade would depend. She went to the classroom. She went to the department office. The teacher could not be found.

She brought the photographs home and put them in a drawer in her living room. She had received passing marks, sometimes high ones, for courses in which she had done little work. She wondered what sort of grade she would get for no work at all.

Olga Telesford was a live-in housekeeper working for an elderly woman in Rye, the village north of Mamaroneck. In February 1991 she brought her son Samuel from Panama. She had no thought of what to do with him other than that she could not bear another year without him.

The boy was thirteen—handsome, athletic, and lively. He had never heard of the SAT. Cold winters, grade point averages, and the English language were all equally alien to him. One day he was playing soccer on a sunny field at the Escuela Jose Maria Torillos, his school near Panama City. The next day he was on an Ecuadorian Airlines flight to New York. Wearing only slacks, a T-shirt, and sneakers, he walked out of Kennedy International Airport and into an arctic blast of wind.

Although the neighboring communities of Mamaroneck and Larchmont had been early havens for Quakers and had a reputation in Westchester County for diversity, their residents were mostly white. A small number of African American families lived in the area, some of them descendants of Freedmen who had been there before the Civil War. Diplomatic and United Nations families added a few more dots of color.

The loosening of immigration restrictions in 1965 brought Asians and Latin Americans like the Telesfords to the school district. Some rented rooms in old wood-frame houses in the Mamaroneck Flats or in apartment buildings just off the Boston Post Road. By the time Samuel Telesford arrived, Mamaroneck High was about 10 percent Hispanic and 5 percent African American. He fit in both groups.

He was one more test of the idea that a school as advanced as Mamaroneck High could thrive no matter what ethnic mix it accepted. But the standards that the school set for most children were not initially extended to him.

Phil Restaino had grown up on 11th Street in Queens. He was the first member of his Italian American family to graduate from college. He had been fired from an early job teaching English in the Hudson River Valley town of New Berlin when a school board member objected to his use of the paperback novel *M*A*S*H* with a mildly risqué cover. But he had talent. He was hired at Mamaroneck within a few hours of his first visit.

He was slight and bespectacled, with graying hair hastily combed over a small head. He spoke softly in class and frequently gave the impression of being lost in thought. He could shut himself away in a corner for hours, playing with a new piece of software on a computer. In the classroom he was a magician, mixing themes and moods, stiffening the spines of frightened freshmen, and deflating bullying seniors.

He had begun as a traditional teacher. He stood at the board, writing important words and names and doing what he could to inspire interest. He remained at the center of the discussion, for fear of losing the thread and falling behind schedule. Then he began to be exposed to different teaching styles, particularly in the graduate school courses he took to earn his doctorate. At Mamaroneck High he encountered Duke Schirmer, a writing teacher who thought lecturing was a waste of time and began every period with a writing project to be turned in the next day. Schirmer scrambled about the room, challenging an ill-examined thought, mediating a disagreement between subject and predicate, praising a metaphor. Restaino thought that this approach would kill an ordinary teacher like himself, with too many students in his classes and too few minutes in the day. But when he counted heads, he discovered Schirmer often had more students than he did, sometimes as many as thirty in a class.

Restaino tried his own experiments, breaking each class into groups. Massed together, he discovered, adolescent humans were like a herd of grazing animals, dull and rude and given to senseless stampedes. Divided into small thinking parts they approached their lessons with some interest, if prodded by a teacher willing to dart from desk to desk with the persistence of a sheepdog.

Restaino began to think about ways to employ this insight to bring the blessings of learning to all students, not just those like Dan Hopkins, who, although a joy to teach, already had all the advantages.

2

BRAIN FARMS

Mamaroneck High School stretches across a low hill in a mixed commercial and residential section of Mamaroneck, New York, eighteen miles northeast of Manhattan. Its two- and three-story buildings, completed at different times over seven decades, show the Georgian influence on architects who wanted to associate the school with the stately lecture halls of the Ivy League.

Across from the school on the Boston Post Road—part of the historic route that linked the early colonies—are a few delicatessens and fast-food outlets. A tidy motel painted white and blue welcomes travelers. There are expensive homes nearby, but across Richbell Road at the southwest edge of the campus is a row of apartment buildings that houses retirees and Latin American immigrants.

Mamaroneck High is a well-run institution with talented, well-paid teachers and a higher percentage of students taking college-level courses than 99 percent of the high schools in the country. Like most public schools, it also has problem students and like most public facilities it needs repair. There are occasional fights in the halls and out on the sidewalks, although so far the school has been largely free of knives and guns. Some students use drugs, particularly marijuana and cocaine. Weekend beer parties are common.

The science laboratories are cramped and bear the scars of rough teenage use. Some classrooms are too cold to be used in winter. Several clocks do not work. Bathrooms need fixing. The three boilers, each sixty-six years old, break down repeatedly and were slated for replacement in a 1996 bond issue. No one has cemented over the words MAMARONECK JUNIOR HIGH SCHOOL carved in large Roman script on the school's Post Road building, even though it has been used exclusively as a high school since 1968.

Other high-achieving American high schools share this shopworn look. La Jolla High School produced all three of California's Westinghouse Science Talent Search Award winners in 1995, but its campus is indistinguishable from a thousand low-slung California high schools, with stained stucco and courtyards of brown grass. Richard Montgomery High School, with the strongest International Baccalaureate program in the country, is hidden behind a Marlo furniture store on Rockville Pike in the Maryland suburbs of Washington. Bellaire High, one of Houston's best, sits beside a neighborhood of small frame houses with some cars parked on threadbare lawns.

Not all elite high schools appear so modest. Whitman High of Bethesda, Maryland, is in a new building that, with its clean brick walls and aqua portals, looks like an upscale mall. The administrative offices of Scarsdale High resemble the executive wing of a Fortune 500 company, with oak paneling, maroon tweed carpets, and matching chairs. The airy, flag-draped lobby of Beverly Hills High would fit well at the United Nations building. The principal of New Trier High in Winnetka, Illinois, has a bigger office than some corporation presidents.

But those are exceptions. The worn-down look of most high-achieving schools fits well with their relative anonymity. They are usually unknown outside their own regions. Even their own teachers and students are often surprised to hear how well they are doing when compared to schools around the country. They have little time to worry about making national reputations and are commonly ignored by federal policy makers and university researchers. Their teachers and administrators have elevated the highest standards of American high schools to levels never reached before, but public recognition of this is rare. Immigrant parents from Taiwan, Korea, Iran, and India look for homes in these school districts. Their students are winning international academic competitions. Their graduates are populating the research and management offices of computer and biochemical industry leaders such as Microsoft and Intel, Pfizer and Merck. But all this occurs with little notice.

In the 1995 book *The Manufactured Crisis: Myths, Fraud and the Attack on America's Public Schools,* David C. Berliner and Bruce J. Biddle formulated an axiom that characterizes the most ambitious public high schools: "Regardless of what anyone claims about student and school characteristics, opportunity to learn is the most powerful predictor of student achievement." These schools offer not only large portions of mathematics, science, history, and English but many more exotic courses. Radnor High in Radnor, Pennsylvania, for example, offers 20th Century European Economic History as well as Saturday morning classes in Chinese. Souhegan High in Amherst, New Hampshire, has a one-year course in video production as well as a course in Native American Studies. Paradise Valley High in Phoenix has two years of Jazz Performing as well as Creative Writing. Murphy High in Mobile, Alabama, offers a course in probability and statistics as well as Advanced Placement History of Art.

Barrington High in Barrington, Illinois, has an interrelated arts program that uses teams of teachers to relate the study of art, music, theater, and architecture to the study of American literature. The Area Studies program shared by Beachwood High and Shaker Heights High near Cleveland concludes with a trip to Japan one year, and China the next. Bethesda–Chevy Chase High offers a science intern program for students who wish to work at the Armed Forces Radiobiology Research Institute, the National Heart, Lung and Blood Institute, the Carnegie Institute, or the National Institute of Mental Health. Berkeley High offers courses in

African American Literature, Asian Literature, and Women's Literature. Cardozo High in Bayside, New York, has established the DaVinci Science and Math Institute with opportunities for research in school as well as symposia, lectures, and summer institutes outside the school. Millburn High School in New Jersey offers three different levels of psychology courses, plus courses in oceanography, biochemistry, plant and animal behavior, and two fiction-writing seminars.

Brookline High in Brookline, Massachusetts, has a course called Senior Seminar: The Mind's Eye in which students are invited to explore the fuzzy border between "science and reality." According to the course catalog, they study "mind-brain dichotomy; brain biology and neuroscience; abstract and narrative models in mathematics, science, literature, politics and time." Credit for the course fulfills graduation requirements in either mathematics or English, whichever the student prefers.

Several studies have suggested that on average, American students are not performing at the same level as their foreign counterparts, but the reports obscure the variety of U.S. schools. When studies and contests focus on schools that emphasize achievement, American students jump to the front of the line. In 1994 the American team at the International Mathematical Olympiad in Hong Kong scored the first perfect score in the competition's thirty-five year history, with the U.S. contestants all from public schools: Ithaca High in New York, Stuyvesant in New York City, Montgomery Blair in Silver Spring, Maryland, Swampscott and Lexington Highs in Massachusetts, and the Illinois Mathematics and Science Academy in Aurora. A U.S. team finished second to China in the 1995 International Physics Olympiad in Canberra. Its members included students from La Jolla High, New Rochelle High, Los Alamos High, Lowell High in San Francisco, and special public schools for science and mathematics education in Oklahoma, Virginia, and North Carolina.

At teacher conferences and university seminars and congressional hearings discussing America's beleaguered public schools, places like Souhegan and Mamaroneck, Lexington and La Jolla are rarely mentioned, much less studied. Teachers nod when they hear the names of the few well-known schools, such as New Trier, Scarsdale, and Shaker Heights, or some of the entrance-by-examination schools such as Stuyvesant and Lowell. They are envied for the affluence and involvement of their families, the depth of their curricula, and the strength of their tax bases. But they are not considered useful examples of how the majority of U.S. schools might improve.

They are treated like peacocks in a chicken farm. Many educators say they are private schools masquerading as tax-supported institutions. The impression is that their students have few academic problems, their equipment is modern and plentiful, and their local taxpayers—eager to maintain real estate resale values—will pay whatever is necessary to maintain their reputations. Research has overlooked the way a few such schools have enlivened the educations of unmotivated students in circumstances not much more favorable than those at any school, and shown ways to make the Berliner-Biddle axiom real for all students. Scholars and journalists have also ignored the odd and potentially harmful ways these schools have stratified their students. There is a class system imposed, without much thought of how well labels such as honors, regular, and remedial fit the children involved.

Elite public schools draw energy from the most obvious, and most suspect, motivator—college admission. To the parents and the students involved, the schools have one function. They are brain farms. The parents plant their children in the school because it has a reputation for turning out well-regarded college applicants. Each child is nourished by skilled teachers to grow an intellect broad and adept enough to score well on the Scholastic Assessment Test (SAT)—once known as the Scholastic Aptitude Test—and overcome other hurdles of college enrollment.

Whether it is right for American teenagers to be herded in increasing numbers onto a college track has already been the subject of several studies, conferences, and magazine articles. For the purposes of this book, I accept the system as it is and try to convey how it affects the most academically ambitious schools. The administrators of such places say they are following the highest traditions of democratic education, but the reality is different.

At Mamaroneck, the College Information Center (CIC) is located at the school's fulcrum point, the enclosed overpass between the Post and Palmer sides of the school. Students pour in each day to sit at large tables, read from thousands of catalogs and course books, and chat with college recruiters who arrive by the dozen to recruit seniors. Many high-performing public schools, like their private school cousins, close for a week in early spring so that students can visit colleges, or go skiing if they have already made up their minds. Nearly all such schools print a graduation issue of the student newspaper that lists all seniors and which college each has decided to attend.

Such attention to college exacerbates the debate over how to treat less motivated students and whether to change the way courses are taught. Many parents and teachers at elite schools dislike change, and for good reason. Suggest a revision of the curriculum and they respond with valid rhetorical questions: Did Sabin fiddle with his vaccine after it saved millions from polio? Why should we alter a formula that has sent so many students to Amherst and Columbia and MIT?

3

MAMARONECK

The cover of the October 20, 1934, *Saturday Evening Post* is a Norman Rockwell painting. It shows a boy gazing at sailing ships from his perch on a weathervane in a seacoast town. He is the age Rockwell would have been when he attended Mamaroneck High. The picture evokes a small but ambitious town, looking out at the world more than it looks in on itself.

Rockwell loved the romantic side of American education: football games and flirtations and school plays. He did not think much of what went on in its classrooms. He left the high school in 1909, in the middle of his sophomore year, to pursue art studies at the National Academy School and the Art Students League in New York City.

From the start, Mamaroneck, like Rockwell, had big dreams. It nudged students in a very specific direction—toward college or secure employment, followed by well-considered marriage and professional prominence. It strived to stay well above the national average. It loved celebrities but barely tolerated rebels who might tarnish its reputation for upright excellence. It dragged students over the bumps of adolescence, just as schools did in other towns run by people who wanted their children to inherit their comfortable lives along with their eye color and religion.

In the spring of 1986 Jim Coffey, a worrier with a sense of humor, sat in his office thinking about his job. He was head counselor at Horace Greeley High School in Chappaqua, New York. The college application season had just ended, its residue of relief and disappointment cluttering his mind. He began to compose an essay for *The Journal of College Admissions*. It was entitled "What Do You Mean I Didn't Get In?" and began with a description of the Westchester town of Chappaqua:

> It is an environment where real estate agents sell homes and estates because of the school system. It is an environment where parents jockey for a pole position in life, expect more than the best for their children and pay for it. Likewise, they expect their sons and daughters to reach the same heights as Mom and Dad, perhaps an unreasonable pressure today given the changing employment structure in the country. Discussions about college begin in Lamaze classes for some, while the less anxious parents wait until elementary school.

Coffey had mixed feelings about the competition for college admission. There was no question that it motivated teenagers who appeared to have few other incentives. Suburban children had no threat of hunger or death to move them. The need to get into a good college, or be doomed to a life of mediocrity, was based on several false premises, but at least it persuaded many of them to do their homework.

The problem, Coffey thought, was that the worship of college and career often killed the joy of discovery. The pervasive desire to get into Princeton made it more difficult to nurture unorthodox talents that might mean more in the course of a lifetime than a 1500 on the SAT. It fueled parental ferocity and political favor trading. When college rejection letters arrived, Coffey noted, parents would invariably call a counselor "regarding the friend of a client who is on the Board of Trustees, the interested field hockey coach, or the third cousin whose boss donated a science building."

During Coffey's first year at Greeley, April 15—the day college letters arrived—fell on a school holiday. He blithely spent the day playing golf. When he returned home he found four telephone messages his wife had written down from the same parent. The last one said: "Mrs. B. had to be put to bed because her son had just received his third wait list letter in two days."

Coffey had known what he was getting into when he took the job at Greeley. He accepted most of its assumptions, but he thought there was a way to soften its traditions of hard competition and late nights and use them to deepen other aspects of high school life.

He was forty-six, a man of medium height with graying hair and a round, open face. His father had been a blue-collar worker, his mother a chef. He doted on children and institutions (such as the Boston Red Sox) that found themselves in trouble. He had grown up in Danbury, Connecticut, and graduated from Fairfield University, where he enjoyed the demands of a Jesuit education. After graduation he slid into teaching when the basketball coach at his old high school in Bethel, Connecticut, offered him a job as an assistant.

Many of the high school team members grew fond of loitering at the Coffey house after school, a blurring of life and work that his wife Ellie tolerated. Coffey moved into counseling. He took a job as director of guidance for the tiny school district of North Salem, New York, near the Connecticut border. He and Ellie raised two sons and learned much about children growing up. He tried new ways of steering the unmotivated through difficult courses. He organized a weekend camping trip for incoming ninth graders. The New York State School Counselors Association made him Counselor Administrator of the Year in 1984, and he was soon asked to become director of guidance at Greeley.

If North Salem High was the corporate equivalent of a neighborhood candy store, then Greeley High was Merrill Lynch. Few high schools boasted more accomplished students or were better known among professional educators. Greeley served a semi-rural portion of mid–Westchester County full of lawyers, accountants, and investment bankers. Each year 10 percent of the high school's seniors qualified as National Merit semifinalists. More than 90 percent of its graduates attended four-year colleges and universities.

Coffey took the Greeley job and adjusted. He became an assistant principal and then grew restless. Word reached him of an opening for a principal at Mamaroneck High School. He decided to apply.

In 1661 an English trader named John Richbell, reputed to be friendly with smugglers, bought a large swatch of land along Long Island Sound north of the Dutch colony of New Netherland, later to be called New York. He paid two Siwanoy Indian proprietors, Wappaquewam and Mahatahan, the sum of twenty-two winter coats, twelve shirts, fifteen hoes, fifteen hatchets, and three kettles. The name Mamaroneck, derived in part from an Indian word for "fresh water meeting the sea," was attached to one of the stunted peninsulas jutting into the Sound. The opportunity to log the thick forests and build a community less than a day's sail from New Netherland made it a bargain.

Public education in Mamaroneck began in 1704 with the appointment of a teacher who stayed four months each year. A one-room schoolhouse was built in 1733 near the Post Road, the meandering dirt highway that went, with some interruptions, all the way to Boston. In the nineteenth century Mamaroneck became a popular summer retreat from the heat and stench of New York. The next-door village of Larchmont, named by its founder for his Scottish gardener's favorite tree, had a splendid yacht club. New York businessmen built manors and large houses there. Theatrical stars like the Barrymores came for holidays. The area acquired a reputation for wealth and privilege, the first step toward a well-endowed school system.

In 1887 the school trustees built their first large school, equipped for grades one to eleven. It was a two-story brick building with steep roofs and a pointed cupola on a hill alongside the Post Road. Four teachers taught two hundred fifty students. The curriculum included English, literature, history, science, physical training, art, music, manners, and morals. The first high school graduating class, four young women, received diplomas in 1891.

As in other suburbs, the population mushroomed after World War I. In 1925 the district constructed its first separate high school, a building alongside Palmer Avenue that is still part of the school today. The new redbrick structure had a red-topped cupola and a broad entrance with white columns. In 1931 Mamaroneck Junior High School, for seventh through ninth graders, was constructed on the Post Road. An athletic field separated it from the high school on Palmer.

After World War II, Westchester County drew more young parents. In the late 1960s the district built a new junior high, the Hommocks, a few blocks south on the other side of the Post Road. The old junior high building became part of the high school, connected by a new enclosed walkway and library-gymnasium extension to make the large, rambling, notoriously inconvenient building that still houses grades nine through twelve and resembles, from the air, an amoeba about to split in two.

By the 1990s Mamaroneck, like other suburban schools influenced by falling birthrates, had shrunk from a 1970s peak of twenty-two hundred students to just over a thousand. It remained in the top rank of American high schools in SAT scores, college admissions, and Advanced Placement strength. Its teacher salaries had risen to more than $80,000 a year for 30-year veterans. It offered four years of Chinese. Its evening Russian language class took summer trips to St. Petersburg. The faculty included composers, published authors, and even a successful contractor.

The school's students and faculty were often modest about its exceptional status, and sometimes unaware of it. Other Westchester schools of national caliber, particularly Scarsdale, Greeley, and Bronxville, received more attention. Mamaroneck, despite its achievements, had a mild inferiority complex. But it was well known to university admissions officers. Most of its students were learning. The hockey team was still winning. At stressful times, most families could afford a relaxing weekend in Vermont or the Hamptons or on Cape Cod.

Among the students middle-brow American tastes prevailed. Questionnaires given to the freshman class in 1994 showed the favorite television programs were *Beverly Hills 90210* (life in a school whose real-life California model had an academic profile nearly identical to Mamaroneck's), *Melrose Place, Seinfeld,* and *Beavis and Butt-head.* Many said they were living in broken or re-constituted families. Few read newspapers regularly, but almost all identified AIDS, drugs, and violence as the biggest problems for their generation.

Parents told real estate agents they had come to Larchmont and Mamaroneck, which also had some affluent neighborhoods, because they liked the ethnic and religious mix. The school district was approximately one third Jewish, one third Protestant, and one third Catholic, more balanced than heavily Jewish Scarsdale or heavily Christian Bronxville and with significantly more blacks and Hispanics. Real estate taxes were somewhat lower than Scarsdale's, and the choice of housing was wider. The beach clubs and marina were attractive. The New Haven line train to New York stopped at both Larchmont and Mamaroneck stations.

Jim Wilbur, a chemical industry analyst for Smith Barney, and his wife Sandy, a composer and advertising consultant, researched the Westchester schools for three years before moving to Larchmont from Plainfield, New Jersey, in 1985. They liked their New Jersey home; it was spacious and relatively inexpensive. But property values had plummeted after the riots in Newark in the 1960s. The Plainfield schools were underfunded, and the Wilburs did not think they would improve in time for their children, Jason and Kristie.

Jim studied school budgets in the Westchester libraries. Sandy asked to see principals. She was Jewish. He was Protestant. They liked the balanced ethnic mix of Mamaroneck and Larchmont. Bronxville had a reputation, deserved or not, for anti-Semitism. Greeley had an intense academic atmosphere, augmented by an influx of Asian American students, that they thought might overwhelm Jason, who was shy and artistic. And it was too far north for a quick commute.

Once they decided on Mamaroneck, Sandy met her real estate agent on a Monday morning and by noon had picked a house. That evening she realized she could not even remember how many bathrooms it had. But the schools were good.

4

PARENTHOOD

Sandy Wilbur knew the Mamaroneck schools were not perfect. She heard parents complain about teachers devoting too little time to basic mathematics. The elementary schools' whole-language approach to reading had sparked rumors of illiterate sixth graders. But she had no complaints. The women and men who had taught her children had been consistently sensitive and energetic.

By middle school Kristie—a tall, blond athlete with some of her mother's musical talent—found herself near the top of her class. She had begun Chinese in the seventh grade. She was in the advanced science group. In the eighth grade she was permitted, along with twenty other students at the Hommocks, to start high school mathematics a year early. They began Course 1 Honors, the first-year algebra course usually reserved for the best ninth graders.

The class was assigned to a teacher who had taught at both the middle school and the high school. Wilbur assumed that Kristie was getting the best the system had to offer—all the accelerated advantages of a good private school at public school prices.

The first signs of distress puzzled her but raised no immediate alarm. Kristie disliked the teacher. She said she had difficulty understanding the woman's explanations and could not always decipher what she wrote on the board.

The teacher declined to discuss Kristie's complaints for this book, but her attorney suggested that the parents were unwilling to blame their children's difficulties on the children or themselves. No one denies that the parents reacted in an extraordinary way, a lesson in how important they are to the dynamics of such schools.

At first, Wilbur advised Kristie to have patience. The subject matter and the teacher were new to her daughter. She was certain the course would work out in time. Kristie continued to stew. Relations between the student and the teacher worsened. After one incident, Kristie was ejected from the class and came home crying.

Wilbur said she began to hear about problems with other students in the class. Another parent told Wilbur she had called the counseling office at the Hommocks, hoping to discuss the situation, but was politely rebuffed. It was a shame that this happened, the counselor reportedly said, but it was not surprising to see students, even as accomplished as these, act out at this age. The teacher was trying to establish some boundaries.

It was early in the school year. The parents who were concerned about the class had busy lives and thought it best to wait and see. They were urged to show restraint by many of their children, who had reached an age where parental involvement was as grating and embarrassing as a Jefferson Airplane LP.

Alice Prince tried to engage her son Dan Hopkins in conversation about the class.

"Danny, how's math?"

"Fine," he said. He acknowledged that Kristie Wilbur had clashed with the teacher, but that was it.

In November when the teacher gave out her first grades, many parents were unpleasantly surprised. Kristie received a 75, the lowest mathematics grade by far in her young life. Hopkins, who less than four years later would score a near perfect 1580 on his SATs, received an 83.

Sandy Wilbur knew many parents. The office for her music

composing and advertising consulting business was an upstairs room in her tidy Victorian home on Beach Avenue. Her daughter seemed to be the most upset and outspoken of the algebra students. Wilbur decided to call a meeting.

Parents of seventeen of the twenty students in the class gathered in her cheery living room, with green wallpaper and green upholstered couches. Wilbur said they agreed that there was a problem, but the solution was elusive.

Alice Prince was an associate professor of pediatrics at the College of Physicians and Surgeons at Columbia University. Her son had told her to butt out. He did not like pushy parents and had not raised her to be one. However, when the group discovered Prince spent much of her time writing research grants, she was elected to begin what became a testy correspondence with the school and the school district.

Linda Kalos, whose daughter Julie was in the class, was a school psychologist. She knew some of the administrators. She approached Rick North, the Hommocks principal. He said he would look into the situation. Told that some parents wanted to remove the teacher, North said he thought they ought to know that the mechanism for dismissal was set out by New York's Taylor Law, which had very specific requirements.

"Do you think we should complain to the school board?" Kalos asked.

"You obviously have that option," he said.

The parents continued to meet weekly in the Wilbur living room. Their letters and visits inched up the Mamaroneck chain of command.

In a one-minute telephone interview four years later, the teacher said that she became a target for notoriously aggressive parents whom she thought had a history of harassing teachers and summer camp directors. She promised to give a full account of what had transpired and why, but later changed her mind and declined several requests for further interviews and a request that she comment on a draft of this chapter that I sent her.

Her attorney told me in a letter that I was not being objective and was presenting only the point of view of some parents. He said some parents believed that their children could do no wrong and that their problems were someone else's fault.

The parents of some of the algebra students said they began to wonder if the district's ability to pay some of the highest salaries in the country was a mixed blessing. If veteran teachers were paid $80,000 a year for showing up and behaving themselves, what incentive was there for anyone to leave the system or to improve? Even when pushed, the laws requiring full documentation and lengthy hearings gave faculty members a great advantage, the parents said.

Several of the parents had professional degrees. Some had managed businesses for years. But they were not prepared for the intricacies of education labor law. In order for a teacher to be removed, they were told, there had to be proof of three years of misbehavior and incompetence. A teacher had to be allowed to confront these accusations in a series of conferences designed to cure his or her inadequacies, if there were any. Wilbur said she was told if the school tried to fire a teacher, the cost to the taxpayers in legal fees would be at least $80,000.

Norman Colb, the school superintendent, met with the parents. The meeting meandered over issues of adolescence and teachers' rights. Prince interpreted Colb's expressions of concern as a polite brushoff. She tried to tell him why she was concerned. "I have this kid who was going to be a scientist," she said. "He liked math and science, but now he says he's going to go to law school. He liked science, but now I think he's lost it."

The parents said they received no more satisfaction from Penny Oberg, a school board member who was also a professional educator, working as a counselor at Greeley High. They met with Oberg, who also had children in the school system, during her regularly scheduled school board office hours. The parents said that Oberg told them she was not prepared to discuss personnel issues with them.

Like many parents in such communities, they were self-conscious about their ambitions for their children. It was not dishonorable to want the best for their sons and daughters, but they realized their attitudes were rooted in a very arrogant assumption.

They had done well in life. Many of them were graduates of very selective schools—Sandy Wilbur had gone to Sarah Lawrence, Prince and Kalos to Wellesley. They remembered their A-laden high school report cards and high SAT scores. If Gregor Mendel was right, some of their genetic material had been passed on to their children. They assumed that if their child was having academic trouble, it was more likely the school's fault than theirs. Having spent so much to enroll their children in such schools, flaws were galling.

Prince's younger son Ben had struggled to read in the third grade. Prince saw the school psychologist. The woman told Prince that it was possible he was not getting enough stimulation at home, even though both Prince and her husband carried on dinner table conversation with their sons that would have impressed the Kennedys.

There were already two strikes against Prince: Ben's teacher had told the psychologist that Ben made his own lunch, and on the day the psychologist had called Ben in for a chat, the boy was not wearing socks.

Prince was then an assistant professor at Columbia, struggling for tenure. This woman was telling her she was neglecting her son. Back at her office, still shaking with rage, she received a call from the reading teacher, who wanted Prince to know that no one else thought she was a lousy mother. They were going to arrange tests for Ben that would provide a proper diagnosis. After doing so, they followed up with a careful selection of teachers for Ben that made Prince feel much better.

Except that occasionally, when Ben thought his mother was threatening inappropriate sanctions for some mischief, he would wonder out loud if he ought to go to school the next day without socks.

The parents confronting their doubts about the algebra teacher said they felt a measure of this guilt. They asked the school administrators if another teacher could take the class, or at least help those students who felt they needed assistance. They asked if special tutoring sessions could be held after school. They asked if the Parent Teacher Student Association would hold a districtwide conference on what they called "incompetence in the schools."

Any changes in teaching assignments or working conditions had to wait six weeks for a reply from union representatives, they said they were told. The parents felt as if they were rowing in a vat of syrup, first placing hope in expressions of interest from adminis- trators and then realizing that nothing was happening.

In February Colb invited a half dozen of the parents to a meet- ing at the school boardroom in the high school's Post building. He said the process had gotten to a point where he could act. First, he had something the parents considered bad news: the teacher would continue to teach Course 1 to the end of the school year. Then he offered what he hoped would be received as good news: The teacher would be closely monitored by the Hommocks mathe- matics department chair. That supervisor would sit in her class and observe one day a week. He would work with her on her technique and motivational skills. He would make himself available to any students needing extra help.

The parents said Colb told them he knew some of them had younger children and wanted to assure them that the teacher would not be teaching the honors course next year. They were still not happy, they said, but he asked them to help make the arrange- ment work. He urged them to encourage their children to stop fo- cusing on their complaints and take advantage of the assistance being offered.

As June neared, Prince said she was urged by several parents to make sure Colb understood how dissatisfied they were. She wrote a letter she hoped would keep the memory of their experi- ence alive, at least within the confines of the superintendent's of- fice. She said in part:

It is apparent that parents will have to take a much more active and public role . . . It was clearly our error to be placated by promises of change. We mistakenly thought that the organized impact of 17 parents of a single class would be sufficient to prompt a productive response by the school administration. There are obviously similar issues at other schools in the district. We will be actively discussing our experiences with our peers and will select more effective methods to prod the administration into dealing with these unpleasant personnel issues in a meaningful fashion.

The letter had no appreciable impact on the superintendent. Although he respected the insights of the parents, he believed it very poor practice to let them set teacher assignments. Such a practice might satisfy some parents in the short run, he thought, but it would also produce a number of other results that would be exceptionally destructive. He had concluded that the teacher performed at a level well above that required by statute to dismiss a tenured teacher and that the district's course of action in her case was appropriate, responsive, and legal.

Some students thought the teacher improved as the class went on. The department chair filled in some gaps for them. Grades went up, giving some parents the guilty feeling of a beauty pageant contestant awarded first prize after accusing the judges of negligence. The teacher's attorney said she did not inflate grades. The fact that the parents and students accepted the higher grades without complaint, he said, suggested they agreed there had been an improvement in performance.

Lorna Minor, the head of the teacher's union at the time, Hommocks Principal Rick North, school board member Penny Oberg, and Superintendent Colb declined to comment in detail on the case. Without the teacher's own testimony, it is impossible to know what happened in the class, but the specifics of the teacher's performance were in some ways less important than the intense parental involvement she inspired.

Set aside any conclusions about what really happened in Course 1. Imagine for a moment an advanced algebra class taught not in Mamaroneck, but in the South Bronx. What if a group of bright inner-city students from poor families had trouble understanding their lessons in the first weeks? Many would have taken it to mean that they were not as good at mathematics as they had thought they were. And that would have been that—a permanent stain on their sense of themselves, leading them to turn away from a subject that might have led them to careers in banking or physics or engineering. Their inner-city parents, scarred by similar problems when they were young, would have been unlikely to protest. It is hard to imagine them meeting for several weeks, petitioning the school board and the superintendent.

A 1996 book, *Beyond the Classroom: Why School Reform Has Failed and What Parents Need to Do,* noted that twenty thousand teenagers surveyed at nine different schools said their families and attitudes formed outside of school had much to do with their success or failure inside. Nearly one third said their parents had no idea what they were doing in school, and more than half said they could bring home grades of C or worse without their parents becoming upset.

That was not the way it worked at Mamaroneck High. It was a fine school, with exceptional teachers and rigorous courses. But its pride and ambition began at home, with mothers and fathers who only occasionally set foot inside the school. Without them, the high school would be a calmer, less stressful, and far less successful place. If that meant that teachers would be hurt, that was, to many parents' way of thinking, just too bad.

5

THE EXPERIMENT

As aggressive and influential as parents might be, they rarely inspire fundamental changes at schools like Mamaroneck. They have purchased a quality education for their children at a high price and are not quick to embrace those who say there is something wrong with it. When Mamaroneck risked making changes—and it did so more than most schools—they were almost always the work of innovative educators like Principal Coffey and teachers Phil Restaino and John Esposito.

In the spring of 1993, Restaino and Esposito were restless members of the English department with a yearning to mix history with science, English with mathematics, a tasty curricular stew. They reserved room D251, the big lecture classroom at the north end of the Palmer building, and called an informal teachers' meeting to discuss the idea.

They were acting on their own, with the eager if carefully muted support of Coffey and the new Mamaroneck superintendent, Mary Anne Mays, who had been hired after Colb quit to run a private school in California. The previous summer Coffey had sent three teachers to Brown University for a two-week workshop sponsored by the Coalition of Essential Schools. Mays was an ad-

vocate of the reform-minded coalition, headed by Brown professor
Theodore Sizer. In the fall she used district funds to fly herself and
Coffey, along with Restaino and two other teachers, to Louisville,
Kentucky, for the coalition's national conference.

At a pasta dinner at Restaino's house in Mamaroneck after the
Louisville conference, the group wondered how they might use
what they had learned about restructuring schools. Coffey had already prepared the ground for a curricular shift by bringing in two
consultants, Pat Carini and Heidi Hayes Jacobs, to talk to the faculty about mixing disciplines and changing routines.

Carini had conducted a series of seminars in the school library.
She encouraged teachers to discuss their dream projects, ideas they
thought were impossible to realize in a seven-period day. She presented research on the impact of students preparing their own
lessons for class presentation and crossing course lines: mixing
painting with computer graphics, autobiographies with quiz
shows, geography lessons with skits. Such devices produced a glue
that, several studies showed, attached history and literature more
firmly to some adolescent brains.

After several hours of food, wine, and pedagogical daydream-
ing at Restaino's house, Coffey made a suggestion. Why not try an
integrated approach in the ninth grade? The courses at that level
were simpler and more malleable, making it easier to mix science
with mathematics, social studies with English. The change would
help ease the often difficult transition from the Hommocks to the
high school.

Sizer's coalition had been recommending blending courses and
disciplines. Students would not be bored by physics, Sizer
thought, if they could see how Einstein's limits on the speed of
light in the twentieth century grew from Newton's and Leibniz's
calculus in the seventeenth century. Geography students studying
twentieth-century China would grasp the cultural devastation of
the Communist revolution more easily if their English teacher was
simultaneously taking them through Bette Bao Lord's memoir
Spring Moon.

The group at Restaino's dinner party applauded Coffey's idea,
but thought a cautious approach would be best. They agreed that

Coffey should indicate at the next faculty meeting his interest in an integrated ninth grade curriculum but leave it up to teachers to take the initiative. The meeting in D251 would be a modest first step.

Classroom teachers still ruled American schools, from the best to the worst. They responded to only the gentlest, least direct initiatives. Significant change could not be imposed from above. Wise reformers planted seeds and waited for something to grow.

When forty teachers—more than half the Mamaroneck faculty—showed up for the meeting, Esposito and Restaino were surprised and encouraged. Demolishing the ninth grade and rebuilding it on an entirely different model made sense to anyone who had spent time with Sizer's group. But the coalition's ideas had not sunk very deeply into American classrooms, particularly at high-achieving schools like Mamaroneck. And once the meeting began, many teachers expressed doubts. They were experienced educators who had found ways to help most of their students learn within the traditional system. Was it wise to hope for anything more? They were wary of education fads. They had encountered many ideas that seemed to have weight and texture when described, but disintegrated in the classroom. They reminded Esposito and Restaino that Regents examinations—tests required by the state in some subjects—were not geared to interdisciplinary offerings. They mentioned teachers' contract rules on scheduling and uncompensated planning time.

There was nothing new about what Esposito and Restaino were hoping to do. Individuation, the late-twentieth-century jargon for individual instruction, was the way African hunter-gatherers had taught their sons to sharpen spears half a million years before. The public schools in nineteenth- and early-twentieth-century America often operated on this very old model. Instructors in one-room village schools had to teach each child individually because there were so many different ages. Even when larger public schools and preparatory schools organized by grades became available, many affluent families employed tutors to teach their younger children or help the older ones with difficult subjects.

As urban and suburban schools grew large in the mid–twentieth century, the notion of preparing many more students for college became popular, and the European model of professor lecturers and student note takers took over. It was efficient. It was modern. It had a certain democratic aura: Everyone allegedly learned at the same pace, with no special privileges for the few.

But by the 1960s educational researchers began to detect signs of stagnation. The lecture system came under attack. Some educators experimented with open classrooms, particularly in elementary schools. Students were encouraged to spread out in a larger space that mixed several classes together. They played games or picked books from shelves and proceeded at their own pace. Some high school classes held meetings to decide what rules of behavior to observe and whether to be judged by a final test or a paper. It was noisy and chaotic, and in the hands of ordinary teachers failed to nurture students' thoughts. But other ideas, such as Mamaroneck's integrated ninth grade, bloomed in its place.

When Esposito first came to the high school he taught in D220, a small room with grimy windows looking out over the muddy practice field between the Palmer and Post buildings. He thought the long walk to the English department lounge at lunchtime was a waste of time, so he took his paper sack to the social studies lounge across the hall. He was a gregarious man, thrice married, with sharp, handsome features and a short beard turning gray. He found friends in the lounge and forged interdepartmental ties that became useful when he and Restaino began to look for recruits.

Denis Ahearn, white hair combed back, was an economics and history teacher who knew how to make students with different abilities focus on the same lesson. Mary Cronin, tall and intense, had a similar talent for moving teenagers along with humor and hard questions. Shannon Turner-Porter, an imposing woman who taught in the big lecture room D251, was very warm, and fearless before any audience.

A fourth social studies teacher, Ann Borsellino, also drew Esposito's attention. She was barely five feet tall, but had the voice and presence of a six-feet-six basketball coach. She had been a play-making guard at St. Thomas Aquinas College and had coached Mamaroneck basketball and softball after school. In the classroom she was funny and well attuned to the insecurities and blind spots of slower students.

She was also one of the few faculty members with team teaching experience. With mathematics teacher Frank Aiello and English teacher Janet Rogow she had given fifty sophomores each year, including Joy Sarlo, a taste of how their three subjects related to each other. Parents and students had praised the result, but the three teachers disbanded after three years, mostly because of exhaustion. Mamaroneck teachers knew that story. How could they be lured into a team-teaching project with five times as many students?

Esposito and Restaino looked for optimists like themselves. Borsellino was a natural. Ahearn, Cronin, and Turner-Porter signed up. A new English teacher, Linda Sherwood, was a possibility. She was still in her twenties, a Mamaroneck graduate who had a way with low-achieving girls. A part-time English teacher named Janice Landrum was also available. She was a former New York publicist with firm views on how good writing affected careers.

The idea had been to include mathematics and science in the mix, so they would have every main subject except foreign language. When the science-math recruiting failed, they settled for a two-department alliance. Coffey and Mays said to go ahead.

That left the parents. Team 9, as the interdisciplinary ninth grade program came to be called, had to be introduced with great delicacy. No Manhattan marketing director ever faced a tougher client presentation. If the Team 9 parents did not want to enlist their children as guinea pigs, the venture would not proceed.

Coffey and the Team 9 teachers chose the indirect approach. They held an evening panel discussion at the high school library for the next year's ninth grade parents. Hommocks teachers pointed out how their children had thrived in team-taught middle school classes. Team 9 teachers spoke of a smoother introduction to the ninth grade. The children would have more class time because the new English–social studies alliance allowed double periods, without the annoying class break in between. The students would do special projects and connect the disciplines in ways that would enrich the rest of their studies.

To finesse objections to mixing fast and slow students, the teachers promised an added attraction. Although there would be no honors sections, they would offer projects of extra difficulty to students who wanted an "advanced" designation next to their grade.

The pitch seemed to work, at least for the moment. Parents were accustomed to team teaching in the middle school. The group projects that would be part of the Team 9 approach were already common in the elementary schools. Coffey arranged for a dozen parents to form an advisory committee for Team 9. He told the teachers to get ready for fall.

It was a daunting assignment. They had to prepare a syllabus that would fill two hours a day for two hundred fifty students. They had to weave Asian, African, and Latin American history and culture—the state-required subjects for ninth grade global studies—into an equally varied English course. They had to improve ninth grade skills in writing, reading, and literary analysis that many parents thought had been damaged by an ill-advised move against phonics in the elementary grades.

Coffey had found enough money to pay every team member, plus an art teacher, a technology education teacher, and a foreign language teacher, for two weeks' preparation time over the summer. But it was clear to them it would take longer to overcome the widespread suspicion that the most ambitious experiments were the most likely to fail, and that a school as blessed as Mamaroneck would never stray far from the way it had always done things.

TOP AND
BOTTOM

6

FIGHT FOR HONORS

If Team 9 was a solution, what was the problem? Elite public schools have enormous strengths, but as the next few chapters illustrate, they have organized themselves in ways that provide neither the most challenging education for everyone nor the strongest motivation to do one's best.

When George Ehrenhaft, chair of the Mamaroneck English department, tried to eliminate the junior year honors course in 1992, he confronted a deep commitment to organizing students by their perceived abilities. Ehrenhaft was handsome and courtly, with graying hair and a doctorate from Columbia's Teachers College certain to please any Mamaroneck parent. He had headed the department for twenty years. Barron's enlisted him to write several of their guides to College Board tests. Other schools sought his advice. He had a gift for compromise and curricular finesse, but when he moved against the honors course, he knew he needed every bit of faculty allegiance and diplomatic skill. Even then he was risking a massacre.

Every department head wondered how to treat students of differing abilities and interests. Mamaroneck applied the usual method. It divided courses into different achievement levels, a system that harked back to the redbird, yellowbird, and bluebird groups that Mamaroneck parents remembered when they were learning to read in the first grade.

Required courses, like English, came in three varieties: honors, regular, and remedial. Sometimes the scholastic cantaloupe was sliced even more thinly, with an Advanced Placement class for the most ambitious students, a regular class for students who planned to take the Regents test, a regular class for those who would not take the Regents test, and a remedial class for those needing special help.

Few teachers or students questioned the arrangement. Parents of students in the upper-level classes demanded it. They wanted honors courses on their children's transcripts. Without that indication of exclusivity, they thought, how would Amherst or Michigan or Stanford know that Mamaroneck's program was worthy of notice? The notation on the transcript next to their child's grade was vital.

Ability grouping was an area of educational research that had acquired all the shared goals and collegiality of a punch in the nose. The academic combatants were so at odds they could not even agree on what to call what they were arguing about. Some insisted on calling it tracking, hence the title of UCLA professor Jeannie Oakes's landmark book *Keeping Track: How Schools Structure Equality.* "Tracking" had come to mean a system that stuck a child in the top track or bottom track of a school system and never let her out, something that all sides agreed was wrong.

"Ability grouping" was a more limited system of separating faster and slower children, with the assumption they could move from one group to another as their skills grew or eroded. Some educators did not like that term either, preferring something like "achievement grouping," which challenged the notion that children in lower tracks were not as able as others even when they achieved less.

Educational researchers had struggled for more than seventy-five years with the issue. Much of the argument rested on very thin evidence until 1976, when Gene V. Glass, president of the American Educational Research Association, proposed a way to resolve the debate with a method called meta-analysis—creating new insights from a comparison of old studies. Hundreds of reports were subjected to new statistical techniques and summarized to see what light they might shed on the controversy.

Much of this work never reached teachers. With papers to grade and college recommendations to write, they were as likely to read the latest abstracts in *Gifted Child Quarterly* or *The Journal of Experimental Education* as they were to have long, thoughtful conversations with their spouses on school nights.

Classes for gifted students in public schools dated back to at least 1891. In that year, the double-track plan developed in Cambridge, Massachusetts, put bright children into special classes that covered the work of six years in just four. The first large city to institute ability grouping in all grades was Detroit in 1919. Ability grouping lost favor in the progressive education movement of the 1930s, regained it after *Sputnik* went up in 1957, lost it again in the wake of the civil rights movement of the 1960s, and came back once more with the back-to-basics movement of the early 1980s. Then in 1985 Oakes presented research that suggested ability grouping not only was hurting children at the bottom of the scale but was also doing nothing for children at the top.

Many educators did not need Oakes to tell them their lower-track students were not progressing. In the mid-1980s many superintendents and principals began to discard arithmetic courses in high school and insist that every student take at least one year of algebra. Henry Gradillas, principal of Garfield High School in East Los Angeles, gleefully cut back on the home economics and vocational courses that had become dumping grounds for poor Hispanic students who, he thought, could handle academic classes.

With some exceptions, both the pro- and anti-ability-grouping forces came to agree that less motivated and less energetic children were not well taught in most lower-level classes. Those who opposed ability grouping said the neglected children could be saved by being mixed with higher-achieving students. They would be inspired by the better students and have access to the better teachers who usually taught honors classes.

The opposing group said better teaching, not mixing classes, was what students in academic trouble needed, as well as the chance to move up to the faster group the minute they showed they were able. This was particularly important in the elementary grades, where children could be inadvertently stuck on a lower track if the teachers were not careful.

On the subject of honors classes, the dueling researchers remained at odds. One side presented studies that appeared to show that quicker students gained very little from being placed by themselves in higher-level classes. The other side said the research was tainted, and cited studies that appeared to show that honors classes, if taught properly, deepened and broadened a student's grasp of a subject in a way that would not work in a mixed class. Some studies indicated that most honors classes offered little enrichment. This was read two ways: Pro-ability groupers said it meant the honors classes should be improved; anti-groupers said it meant the classes should be abolished.

A federal government plan to raise school standards—the America 2000 or Goals 2000 program—contributed to the debate. Both sides in the ability-grouping fight wanted standards raised as a way out of their quarrel. If the effort succeeded in making classes for lower-level students more challenging, then the guilt and discomfort that motivated teachers like Ehrenhaft to eliminate honors would likely recede.

Mamaroneck had some honors classes in the freshman and sophomore years. They were called "advanced" courses. About a third of the students applied and all of them were accepted. The heaviest weight of parental expectation and teenage angst came in the junior year. In the fall, college-bound juniors took the PSAT, then called the Preliminary Scholastic Aptitude Test. In the spring they took the SAT. Most of them were convinced—with little evidence to the contrary, despite what their counselors said—that it was the single most important measure of their chances of attending the college of their choice.

Half of the SAT tested verbal abilities, particularly reading comprehension and vocabulary. A strong English course in the junior year, with stacks of reading and frequent word quizzes, seemed essential. Parents of Mamaroneck students aiming for

Dartmouth or Vassar wanted their children in classes with only the best students. The competitive fire, they thought, would add to the pressure and make their children answer every last homework question and do every possible extra-credit assignment. Any attempt to water down the English curriculum in the junior year would not be welcome.

For a long time Ehrenhaft had supported ability grouping. In the spring of 1974 he had sophomores take a short screening test of their verbal abilities. The questions were similar to the SAT. He asked tenth grade teachers to recommend honors candidates based on writing ability, motivation, and classroom participation. With these results he cut the list of junior honors students in half. Parents immediately complained. One of the braver mothers called him directly. "How can you not put Jason in the honors class?" she said. "He's gotten such high grades, and I know there are kids who have been accepted with grades that aren't as good."

"I don't know Jason," Ehrenhaft said. "I have only these criteria to go by. If we're going to have an honors class, we have to set up certain admissions standards, and these are the standards that we use."

It was not a good year for English teachers. *Newsweek* had just published a cover story entitled "Why Johnny Can't Write." It described high school classes crumbling from the onslaught of television, dumbed-down textbooks, and the popular notion that, as the newsmagazine put it, "the only language activity worthy of the name is speech on the colloquial, slangy, even illiterate plane." Ehrenhaft did not think high school English instruction, particularly at Mamaroneck High, was in such peril, but he agreed that writing needed more emphasis. That was part of his reason for tightening the honors program. Teachers could accelerate the pace of writing exercises for the most able students, while focusing on common problems of grammar and vocabulary in the middle-level classes.

He began to worry about the remedial English classes. There were about as many of them as there were honors courses. They were slow moving and simplistic, and had more than their share of black and Hispanic students. Teachers assigned to them were frustrated by misbehavior and limited student interest, but this being Mamaroneck, such concerns were overlooked as attention fixed on college-bound students.

In 1983, Colb became superintendent. He was a tall, reform-minded former English teacher who had been working in wealthy Boston suburbs. He was very sensitive to issues of equity and fairness. At a parents' meeting early in his tenure, he was asked about complaints of children not being admitted to honors classes. Pleased to hear some interest in this, he promised that as long as he was superintendent no deserving student would be kept out. "If we have one hundred more kids who deserve to take the course, then we will add four more classes," he said. "If we have seventy-five kids, we will add three more classes." He persuaded the board to promise clear criteria for honors enrollment and enough classes to meet the demand.

Ehrenhaft thought Colb had no other purpose than to keep the parental barracudas at bay. His promise meant sections might become severely overcrowded. The term "deserving students" had no meaning—classes were of limited size, and there was always the risk of capable students being excluded. But the superintendent had spoken, so he created a waiting list for students with border-line credentials who still wanted honors. Some thought they had been unfairly evaluated. Others preferred the regular class but had bowed to pressure from parents and friends. If their work in their sophomore English classes showed notable improvement in the last few weeks of the school year, he added them to the honors program in the fall.

As the 1990s began, Ehrenhaft felt frustrated. His teachers were bursting with ideas for new courses—a survey of naturalist literature with perhaps a field trip to a national park; a publications course for all the students involved in the *Globe,* the *Mahiscan,* and the literary magazines *Calliope* and *Penpourri;* a workshop on dramatic writing for the budding screenwriters pouring into PACE (the Performing Arts Curriculum Experience); a class on coming-of-age literature. Somewhere along the line, the department had produced a new euphemism, "Contemporary Literature," to prettify the go-slow remedial classes. Some of them were little more than study halls. Wasn't it time to change?

Ehrenhaft accepted Colb's invitation to lighten his teaching load and spend a semester reviewing his department. He wrote to high-performing schools throughout the country: New Trier, Brookline, Shaker Heights, Whitman. Some were turning their eleventh and twelfth grade classes into literary bazaars, with a rich menu of courses from which students could choose. Could he do that? Would such courses appeal to both middle- and upper-level students? Could he include lower-level students also? The remedial classes had nothing but students who doubted their abilities and tried to change the subject—taunting the teacher, teasing each other, ignoring assignments. The conversation with the teacher was always about why they had not done the homework rather than how they might learn to do the homework.

Ehrenhaft had been able to reach some of these students in his own classes. But that was hard to do when he had nothing but hard cases. If he could sprinkle the more resistant students throughout his new curriculum, a few in each class, they would be easier to guide and more likely to soak up the enthusiasm of their classmates.

The best way to enliven the new courses, he thought, would be to eliminate the junior year honors classes. Would-be honors students would have to choose electives. Some would do dramatic writing. Some would sample the great books. Some would explore environmentalism and racism in literature. With no honors course, the best students would be scattered throughout the course list, heating the atmosphere and forcing teachers to keep instruction at a high level. He thought it would work, if he was not fired first. He thought about how he might prevent that.

In 1990 Ehrenhaft and his wife had Thanksgiving dinner in Falls Church, Virginia, with their friends Ira and Marti Kirschbaum. The Kirschbaums' daughter Sarah was home from Williams College. Ehrenhaft asked about her studies. She was majoring in theater. She had an honors project in one course. She said if she completed the extra work successfully, she would get an honors designation on her grade.

Ehrenhaft wondered if that might work in high school. If honors became something a student earned through extra work, rather than an admission ticket bestowed for past merit, would not the motivation be stronger and the chances of ill will less?

This was a marked departure from the feelings he had had about the honors program at the beginning of his career at Mamaroneck. Then he had wanted to reduce, not increase, the number of students with an honors designation. His change of mind was so natural and gradual that when asked in 1995 if there was not a contradiction between the old Ehrenhaft and the new, he paused and thought about it for seventeen seconds before agreeing that there was.

In October 1992 he sent the department a memo on curricular changes he wanted to make in the fall of 1993. It was vintage Ehrenhaft—hopeful, positive, and respectful of opposing views.

> We've spent more than a year discussing changes, and now I believe it's time to move, even though not everyone in the department may welcome far-reaching change. Some people question—properly—the need for change. Because we're doing well, why bother? Others question whether some of the changes under discussion might not actually weaken the department's curriculum. Still others seem indifferent to change as long as their teaching lives won't be significantly altered. And then, there are those who, for a variety of reasons, embrace a change. In effect, departmental consensus remains out of reach for the present.

He wanted to abolish the tenth grade remedial programs, Contemporary Literature, Elements of Writing, and English 10B. English 10B would be turned into a special preparatory course taught by Restaino, who vowed to bring students up to a level where they could choose one of the new courses. Eleventh grade English would be broken up into several electives, including Millions of Years in the Making: Literature of the Outdoors and the Environment, New York Scene, plus a publications course, an independent reading course, and several others. The department would keep the standard eleventh grade course, Junior Composition and Literature, for those who wanted that structure, plus the other traditional junior courses: American Literature, British Literature, and Creative Writing. It would also preserve Project Prepare, a joint history-English course for fifteen students with unrealized potential taught by English teacher Harvey Ross and social studies teacher Richard Ciotti.

Ehrenhaft would go ahead and risk a lynching by abolishing the junior honors course, English 11H. "Students interested in an honors course will design and carry out an honors project in conjunction with their teacher or with an honors coordinator," he said. "Some juniors may take the English AP exam at the end of eleventh grade (Preparation for the AP could be an honors project)." The senior year would continue the menu of electives.

Coffey liked the idea but was not certain his department chair had the necessary support. He suggested Ehrenhaft present the idea to the school board. As usual, word of this change spread quickly to parents. The volunteer editors of the PTSA publication *Palmer to Post* heard reports that junior English honors was in trouble. They did not print such hot news, but they activated the grapevine.

Many parents felt the high school faculty did not share their commitment to excellence. Their suspicions were common to parents at high-achieving schools. They were highly paid professionals who attributed their success to hard work and risk taking. Many of them had excelled in honors courses when they were in high school. They felt their children had the genetic endowment and family encouragement to do the same.

Their children's teachers, on the other hand, often came from different backgrounds. Most had not attended ultraselective colleges. A well-educated Larchmont mother told me that she liked Coffey but still could not understand why the district had recruited someone as principal whose degree was from Fairfield University. The Jesuit school in Connecticut was fine, she said, but her sons were aiming at the Ivy League and she thought the principal should reflect that.

Mamaroneck teacher salaries were far above the national average but still below the incomes of most of the parents. Many of the teachers did not share the parents' view that the nation's social and economic divisions were the result of healthy competition. The teachers belonged to a union. Once, when a clash with the school board left them working without a contract, they had discussed using the teacher's version of the atomic bomb—a refusal to fill out college recommendation forms. Many of them did not want to teach Advanced Placement courses—they did not care for the public scrutiny or the pressure.

Some parents thought they detected efforts to remove the notion of winners and losers, the core of their life experience, from the classrooms where their children spent much of the day. They were particularly suspicious of Ehrenhaft and Colb and their interest in classes that mixed ability levels. Those parents who had their own abilities awakened by good teaching appreciated Ehrenhaft's concerns for average students. But for many parents he might as well have been discussing bias against yak herders in Inner Mongolia.

By mid-December the parents were ready to fight. More than one hundred people appeared at the board session to hear Ehrenhaft's proposal. The conference room became so crowded the board moved the meeting to the band rehearsal room. All seven board members were there. Colb told the gathering that he admired the high school's effort to find a solution to a significant educational issue and saw it as an example of the wisdom and intelligence waiting to be tapped by the state's plan to decentralize educational decision-making. As Coffey introduced Ehrenhaft he tried to lighten the atmosphere. "This is just my second year here," the principal said, "and it may be my last year if I keep going out a limb like this."

Ehrenhaft outlined the changes. Board members asked questions. Some said they agreed that students of different abilities should interact. One board member said she liked the concept of an honors option but wondered if it might be broadened. If the idea of an independent study project was good for the most ambitious students, why not encourage the less able students to try it also?

But eliminating 11H, several board members said, was going too far. They said they were concerned that the more able English students might not be stimulated enough in classes full of average students. One board member asked if some of the elective courses could not be designated honors electives, so students who wished to be in a class with just their Ivy-bound peers could do so.

The audience was invited to comment, unleashing the final dose of acid on Ehrenhaft's frail seedlings. Karen Bell, one of the first to speak, was a lawyer whose daughter Catherine was, by most accounts, the best English student in the sophomore class. Bell had already organized a letter-writing campaign against the change and wanted the board to understand her reasons. She complimented Ehrenhaft and his department for demonstrating creativity in their approach but, she said, she did not want her daughter to suffer from the uncertainties of an experimental program. She reminded the board that "you have promised to provide our students with an education commensurate with their abilities."

Naomi Reice Buchwald, a slender U.S. Magistrate judge with long dark hair and a direct manner, had children just entering the high school, including one of the stars of the ninth grade. She said eliminating honors English would do a disservice to students who did not excel in mathematics and science, and who counted on a comparable honors track in English to develop and display their talents in that field. Breaking the English program into electives, she said, would also end the tradition of exposing each student to a common core of traditional great literature, which she felt was essential to a well-balanced education.

Cheryl Lewy, mother of Marshall Lewy, a budding playwright destined for Harvard, also asked that the board preserve the old system. Lewy was the elected mayor of Larchmont, a slim woman with a mass of curly hair who knew all the board members and had a keen sense of what parents valued most. She told the board that many people thought the ninth and tenth grade global studies classes had already been diluted to accommodate students of mixed abilities and they did not want that to happen to junior year English.

Some parents and students spoke in support of the mixed classes, but they were a minority. Jordan Snedcof, a dark-haired sophomore who served in the student senate, had taken honors classes and understood why some students preferred them, but he liked the choices Ehrenhaft offered. He did not think the new system could work unless the best students spread themselves throughout the department. He thought the honors option was a good compromise. Like Ehrenhaft, he was bothered by what was happening in some of the ordinary classes. Teachers found it difficult to coax good work from students who distrusted their own abilities. They adjusted their teaching for the slowest and least interested in the class, making everything as banal as a sixth grade hygiene lesson. The result was ennui and alienation, and less learning.

Snedcof thought some teachers were too dependent on the labels the counseling staff attached to students near the bottom of the class, including the school's ethnic minorities. They did not realize how bright and engaging many of them were. Snedcof was not aware of Harvard psychologist Howard Gardner's work on different forms of intelligence in the young, some academic, some artistic, some social, some athletic. But he knew that students who lacked motivation could still be very bright. "We had a good discussion in Global Studies today," he said. "I learned something from one student, and this is a student who got an 80 in his last exam. Just because you get an 80 on an exam and aren't in the honors program doesn't mean you can't do well in an honors program, or be a valid part of the discussion."

Several adults in the audience, including Ehrenhaft, remembered the comment years later, but it had no impact on the majority, and Ehrenhaft knew how to read a crowd.

The meeting ended. Ehrenhaft and Coffey went home, but Colb spoke to the board members in private before he left. The next day Colb called Coffey. "It's your call, Jim. But the board is divided. The community is divided. You think it over. I'll support you and George if you decide to go ahead."

Coffey repeated the message to Ehrenhaft. "It's your decision, George," he said. "You can do it, but I advise you not to."

Ehrenhaft understood. He did not want to return to the 1970s and invite months of poisonous dialogue with parents. He thought about another compromise. He would have to keep 11H, but why junk the electives? If his goal was to coax an interest in literature out of the slower students, courses that addressed special interests might do that even if he was not able to force honor students to take them. The point was to chip away the rust at the bottom of the system. He could still break up the remedial courses and send those students into the mainstream, where they had a chance of learning something new.

There was also no need, he realized, to drop the honors option. What better way to ease the strain of deciding who should get honors than to turn that decision back to the students? Anyone could get honors credit if she or he agreed to do an honors project in addition to the regular course work. Some of the more accomplished students might be so enchanted by this alternative that they would take one of the electives instead of 11H.

The modified plan went forward. Ehrenhaft was delighted to see twenty students take the honors option instead of the honors course. They included not only students who missed the 11H cutoff but students in 11H who wanted to do an extra honors project because it interested them.

The notion that teenagers could be their own best teachers intrigued Ehrenhaft. He looked for other ways to spread the idea, while remembering that any threat to the idea of honors grades would be quickly and decisively squashed, no matter how well considered. Mamaroneck had been built by parents and school board members who wanted their children, and themselves, to feel they had been set above the average, and that emotional and political need was more powerful than the instincts of teachers about how children learned.

7

GAME OF LEVELS

Ehrenhaft knew that Mamaroneck's love of exclusivity could never match what he encountered at New Trier High School, nine hundred miles west of New York. Few secondary schools are as well known as that collection of redbrick buildings stretched over a large suburban block of Winnetka, Illinois, near the shores of Lake Michigan. Among its graduates are film stars Charlton Heston and Ann-Margret, as well as thousands of men and women in the upper reaches of law, medicine, and academia in the United States. It has a reputation for excellence that stretches back to its opening in 1901.

New Trier has nearly three thousand students, almost all from affluent families with at least one college-educated parent. The communities of Glencoe, Kenilworth, Wilmette, Winnetka, Northfield, and small sections of Glenview and Northbrook send students to New Trier, along with tax dollars that allow the school to keep class sizes small despite the large student population.

When Ehrenhaft visited the school in 1992 as part of an evaluation team, it had just acquired a new principal, Dianna M. Lindsay. She was a short, well-dressed woman who had had a splendid career as an assistant principal, principal, and superintendent in several suburban Ohio districts. She took the New Trier job even though she had a serious philosophical objection to the way its courses were allotted.

She believed in stretching weaker students by moving them into classes with stronger students. New Trier was, by contrast, one of the most stratified high schools in the country. Every department was organized like a wedding cake, from level 5, for Advanced Placement courses, down to level 1 for students who needed remedial work. Some New Trier teachers were unhappy with the arrangement, but it was tightly woven into the school's course catalog and the expectations of parents and students.

New Trier had a culture that celebrated, even more than most high-achieving schools, the joy of staying ahead of one's neighbor. Although it sometimes produced some ugliness, such as the night New Trier students taunted their working-class opponents at a basketball game in Peoria, nearly everyone acknowledged it was a way to keep energetic young members of the American upper and upper middle classes properly motivated.

New Trier's defenders pointed out that the level system did not deserve to be called a tracking system. Tracking meant sticking a student at one level and insisting that he stay there for all of his courses, even if the quality of his work changed. A student who was level 2 in English at New Trier might also be level 4 in mathematics. Students were rated on the basis of test scores, teacher recommendations, and interviews. If a student's parent thought she was in the wrong level, she would be moved.

Lindsay had seen what such a system did to lower-level classes. They were deprived of the school sparkplugs willing to show some enthusiasm for the subject matter. The lower levels had so many unmotivated students that it was a struggle each day to win their attention and enthusiasm.

The mood at level 2 was not improved by the grade-weighting system. It gave much more credit on the grade-point average—crucial for college admissions—to students in the upper levels. A student who received an A in a level 2 course was given the standard 4 points, but an A was worth 6 points in a level 4 course and 7.2 points in a level 5. Even a B in a level 4 course, with 4.5 points, was worth more than a level 2 A. Someone who slept late, missed homework, and did only C work in a level 5 course still received 3.6 points, more than the 3-point B for which some level 2 students worked very hard.

The school had attempted to put the best face on the situation with what could be construed as euphemistic titles for each level. Level 1 was "general," level 2 was "college preparatory," level 3 was "accelerated," level 4 was "honors" and level 5 was "Advanced Placement." Lindsay wondered how likely it was that individual parents would push against the weight of professional opinion and ask that their child be moved up. The school insisted the parent sign a statement that read, "I understand that the teacher and department chair concerned do not endorse this change because of my child's academic predictors and current achievement. Therefore, I assume full responsibility for the consequences of this placement." The parent was also barred from insisting on a change in the middle of the year, when the student's ability to handle the work might be most evident.

During her first year Lindsay acted like a cultural anthropologist, soaking up local color, double-checking data. The school was so large, she felt more like the president of a multinational corporation. There were layers of administrators between her and the students. She tried to break through the barriers by teaching a history class and developing a circle of student friends.

Whenever Lindsay wondered if the students could connect emotionally with their teachers on such a large campus, she remembered the adviser system. Each entering ninth grader was assigned an adviser who did not change, barring transfer, death, or some other unusual circumstance, during the student's four years at New Trier. More than 40 percent of the faculty served as advisers, meeting daily from 8:10 to 8:35 A.M. with about twenty-five students each. They would tell jokes, exchange gossip, sift academic choices, and celebrate successes. Teachers stopped advisees in the hallway to check for problems, welcomed them to their classes for consultation, and—in a New Trier tradition dating back to 1928—visited all of their advisees at their homes in the first few months of the freshman year. The program kept a large school from becoming too cold and distant. In addition to the small class sizes, it gave many students an anchor against the paranoia and edginess that could not be avoided in such a competitive place.

The course catalog was rich with electives, and the teachers unusually skilled in communicating with different kinds of learners. Why then, Lindsay wondered, was it necessary to divide students into ability levels? Could not every learner find a course that would stimulate his or her interest and best work? Lindsay found that supporters of the system were so determined to segregate children into different ability groups that they measured achievement results on a scale applicable only to New Trier. Most schools place students scoring above the 90th percentile on national tests in honors courses, but at New Trier half the student body scored at that level. She told a friend "it was like saying to everyone who is going to graduate school, well, that's fine, but I still have to give some of you Cs, Ds, and Fs."

She was joined in her second year by a new superintendent, Hank Bangser, a former history teacher and assistant principal at New Trier. Bangser had graduated from Mamaroneck High in 1966 and knew the rhythms of elite public schools. He was tall and gregarious, with a smile as winning as Lindsay's. He was less critical of the level system than she was but agreed that it was time for a major study of all of the school's traditional practices. New Trier's regular evaluation by the North Central Association, a regional accrediting group, was due. Lindsay and Bangser decided to do something different.

Usually two dozen educators were invited to visit the school under North Central's direction. They looked around, interviewed staff and students, and wrote what was invariably a friendly report. For the October 1992 evaluation, New Trier organized the equivalent of the D-Day invasion, an assessment scheme of greater size, prominence, and intensity than had ever been attempted, as far as the participants knew, at any American high school.

Bangser and Lindsay invited one hundred seventeen educators, including Ehrenhaft, Scarsdale principal Judy Fox, and dozens of other teachers and administrators from universities and other high schools. They came from Greeley, Bronxville, Shaker Heights, Bexley, Edina, Stevenson, Glenbrook South, Naperville North, Beaverton, Darien, Evanston Township, Oak Park–River Forest, Barrington, Highland Park—an honor roll of the high school elite. Rooms, food, and transportation for the three-day visit cost nearly $40,000, but New Trier had the money and the integrity to want an honest review and not a love letter.

Ehrenhaft recalled that his brigade of the evaluating army loved the enthusiasm of the students they met, the clean, graffiti-free campus, and the candor of the English faculty, who argued vehemently over modern versus classical texts in front of their evaluators. But he and many other team members could not abide the level system, and attacked it in several of their reports.

A group led by John McConnell, of Glenbrook South High in Glenview, Illinois, said the level system in the mathematics department was "out of control" and did "more to serve the status needs of the parents and to perform a sorting of students for college entrance than to provide for individual differences." It called for "a fundamental analysis" of the system's assumptions and implications. The visitors were particularly disturbed that the level system fed off flawed middle school selection procedures for seventh grade algebra that "disqualify a large number of talented youth who are prepared to study algebra." To their astonishment, they found no female students in seventh grade algebra that year, although the class was tiny and could not be considered representative.

The science team noted "interesting, even heroic, efforts to enhance learning in these lower-level classes, yet the size of the classes and the limited space within the rooms make it difficult to carry out these efforts to full effect." The English team that included Ehrenhaft, about to make his own assault on English 11H at Mamaroneck, recommended the department "examine the issue of detracking with fresh eyes, perhaps with the assistance of an outside consultant." The evaluators' summary report said "the leveling system encourages the perception that the solution to instructional problems is to change the level of the student rather than modifying curriculum and instruction."

Bangser recommended and the school board authorized a strategic planning process to address the North Central reports, on a scale even larger than the visiting mega-committee. Over two hundred educators and community volunteers worked on eight task forces, with the school board holding fifteen public meetings of at least two hours each. When it became clear that the level system was under review, parents became involved. Letters supporting the system appeared in the local Pioneer Press weeklies and in the mailboxes of school board members. Parents spoke at hearings and in conferences with Principal Lindsay.

She was not surprised at the reaction. Many parents believed they had succeeded in their careers because they had been tracked in elementary and high school with other highly motivated children. Lindsay wondered if any of them would change their minds about the level system once they saw what happened to those of their children who did not inherit their motivation or their maturation rate.

Ben Daverman, a soccer and hockey star who was elected president of the New Trier student government, often found himself in level 3 classes. He thought they were challenging if he chose to make them so, but some of his classmates were so frustrated at being kept out of the higher levels that they turned off their intellectual engines and just sat.

He felt some of the same resentment. Unlike many elite schools, New Trier still kept class ranks. At the end of the first semester of Daverman's junior year, a period he knew would strongly influence how colleges perceived him, he ranked 100th in his class. He vowed to devote every available shred of time and energy to raising his second-semester grades. He did every extra-credit project. He participated enthusiastically in class discussions. He studied for exams even when the spring breezes were whispering to him to come outside and kick around a soccer ball.

At the end of the second semester he checked his ranking to see how many places he had climbed. The answer was: not a single one. Everyone above him had also been running at full speed. He was still number 100.

Lindsay's plan to detrack the school got no further than Daver-

man's class rank. In 1995 she accepted a job as principal of Wor-
thington Kilbourne High School, a new school in Columbus. It
would plug her back into the Ohio pension system.

The New Trier task forces' 190-page final report was published in May 1995. The level system, although tarnished, survived.
Bangser and a majority of faculty, parents, and school board members concluded it would work if managed carefully. The bottom
level of special education students and others with severe learning
problems was whittled down to no more than two dozen students.
The rest were moved to higher levels. For seniors at least, levels 4
and 5 became the same level, since departments did not offer a
level 4 honors class in the senior year when there was a level 5 Advanced Placement class.

Bangser and the school board trimmed the margins of the
grade-weighting system, reducing the weight of an Advanced
Placement grade of A from 7.2 to 5.67 and making other adjust-
ments. They proposed doing more to motivate students in level 2
and level 3 classes and changing, but not eliminating, the class
rank system for the class of 2000. Beginning in that year, colleges
would be told which tenth of the class a student was in but not his
or her precise rank.

It still seemed to Lindsay that a phenomenally gifted school
was covering its warts with blue ribbons when it ought to have
them removed. What would happen to the students who accepted
the notion that they were mediocre and then discovered years later
that they had talents that in any other school brought praise and
satisfaction? What of those with mild temperaments and uninter-
ested parents who could never summon the fortitude to ask to be
advanced to a higher level?

Wesley Baumann, the associate principal who assumed the
principalship when Lindsay left, said he shared some of her concerns even though he remained a strong supporter of the level system. "Often at New Trier the students themselves don't realize
how good they are," he said. "And it is hard to convince them until
they have left and gone to college and then it's, 'Oh, my gosh, I am
pretty good.'"

When Lindsay first arrived at New Trier, she found the level system so embedded that the middle schools helped promote it. They gave their own tests and made their own recommendations, making sure that each child's file was delivered to the high school with a level number neatly attached. Lindsay told them to stop. There were some complaints, but what she remembered were the parents who thanked her for insisting that low-level students be encouraged to push the limits. Her action delayed the level assignments by only a few months, but at least they were based on assessments by people at the high school she knew.

Back in Ohio, she made certain her new school avoided ability grouping wherever possible. But all she could do for New Trier was watch the task forces gingerly put the issue aside, as if it were a treasured if unsightly heirloom that they could not bear to throw away.

8

TAKING A BREAK

Teachers Phil Restaino and Shannon Turner-Porter held their first ninth grade class together in Turner-Porter's oversized D251. It was the largest classroom in the school, a lecture hall with risers in the back that had been used for the first gathering of teachers interested in Team 9.

Over the summer the team had created a plan for taking the entire ninth grade on a virtual trip around the world—a few weeks in China, a few weeks in Japan, a few weeks in Africa, and so on. The social studies teachers would introduce history, sociology, and geography. The English teachers would offer readings relevant to each part of the world, while also teaching Shakespeare, Dunne, Rostand, and other writers demanded by the standard curriculum.

The idea was to encourage students to relate what they were learning to their own lives. During the Africa unit, some students would be issued internal passports, similar to those carried by South African blacks under apartheid, and be required to show them to teachers they passed in the halls. Each student worked toward a final project, an autobiography incorporating all the narrative and analytical techniques learned in both Social Studies and English, to be presented with imaginative illustrations.

Several times during the year they would be required to make presentations—read a poem, perform a play, or present a report. In some cases, they would be teaching small parts of the courses. Teachers would help them develop lesson plans. One by one they would take the rest of the class through the intricacies of the Japanese tea ceremony or the justification for the bombing of Hiroshima, with videotapes, games, and costumes to hold their audience's attention.

The opening exercise for Restaino's and Turner-Porter's students was the same for the entire grade. Each student was assigned a partner. They were asked to interview each other, looking for personal characteristics. They were to return the next day and present to the class a visual presentation—a collage formed from magazine scraps, newspaper headlines, or their own artwork—representing their partner. This gave them a taste of public speaking and, at the same time, introduced some of the themes they would have to address in their autobiographies.

Many of the interviews were awkward, the social gaps sometimes wide. A Mamaroneck cabdriver's daughter was paired with a Larchmont lawyer's son. She asked her questions, using suggestions distributed at the beginning of the class, in a tentative voice. The boy was not much better. He wrote down her one- or two-word answers to the same questions without seeking any elaboration.

The next day, some of the presentations were lively; some were sterile and very short. The idea was to loosen the rules of expression. When the students presented their detailed autobiographies at the end of the school year, their teachers hoped they would go in several directions: words, pictures, graphs, poems, novellas, cartoons, videos, recordings. Team 9 believed in Howard Gardner's theory of different kinds of intelligence. In mixing students of varying abilities, they did not want to leave a single skill unexplored.

As for having students teach certain lessons during the year, the theory was that a student asked to frame a subject in his or her own words would absorb it more readily than listening to the same information from a teacher's mouth. Some educators argued that a student was more likely to listen to what a fellow student was presenting than what a teacher had to say.

The team members had doubts about how well this would work. The social studies teachers were concerned about coverage. Would such a patchwork of student presentations, projects, and occasional teacher explanations prepare the freshman class adequately for the Global Studies Regents test? What had been an orderly march of topics under the old system was to become a scramble. Pasted in the students' memories would be a splendid presentation on internment camps, a mediocre discussion of Buddhism, and a hopeless report on Japanese education. Several topics would not be discussed at all, at least not by students. The possible subject areas outnumbered the students available to address them.

Classes went to the library, the two-period arrangement allowing them more time to hunt for sources and citations. The team gave each student a guide to preparing the fact sheet leading to his or her presentation:

> You'll hand out your fact sheet to classmates the day before your presentation, so that they'll have a chance to familiarize themselves with your topic before your lesson. . . .
>
> There are six steps to take to prepare your fact sheet.
>
> Organize and edit your notes. Look over all the notes you've taken. Put them in a logical order and re-read them. Take notes from your notes, leaving out repetitions. Look also for gaps. Are there questions you have not answered, points that are unclear? You may need to do some "spot" research to fill in those gaps.
>
> Make an outline. How can you communicate your multiple pages in just two? Outline first! What are the most important facts and concepts you want to get across? What order is necessary or best?
>
> Start writing. Now that you know what you want to say and in what order, writing is easy. Just get the facts down first, from beginning to end.
>
> Take a break! No, I'm not kidding. You need to plan to walk away from your writing for a while. You need to give your eyes time to see what you've written without knowing what you meant to say.
>
> Get creative. While your fact sheet is "on hold," think about

how you can make it visually appealing, enticing, entertaining. If you are fluent with computers, you're lucky. Play with fonts, graphics. But a great form without great content is just that. Think creatively about the words you'll use. Consider humor, drama. But do not forget, your prime purpose is communication. If your document is funny but unclear, you and the class will lose out.

Re-read and revise. Go back and read your draft fact sheet. Is it clear? Would it have explained your topic to you two weeks ago, before you knew your topic? Have you used any vocabulary that needs explanation? Could another student use your fact sheet to study your topics for a quiz?

If you follow these six steps, there's no doubt you will succeed. If you have any questions, please see your teachers for further help.

From the fact sheets the students moved to presentations. Denis Ahearn and Janice Landrum, teaching another section of the course, told their students: "The most important thing to ask yourself is this: What is my main objective? Once you decide this, then you can plan the rest of your lesson plan."

They advised the presenters to have their materials ready. "Are there any special activities included in your plan? Are you going to role-play? Are you going to ask well-developed questions? Do you expect students to participate in your lesson? How? Perhaps you intend to share something you actually created. Or do you intend to ask for some class participation? Are you going to give a demonstration? In short, it is best to try to include at least some members of the class in your plan."

They emphasized experimentation, with the teachers to be viewed as resources rather than as judges. The last section of the Team 9 guide was called "Scope and Sequence." The teachers tried to demystify it:

Big words, eh? Relax! "Scope and sequence" simply refers to your "game plan" for your lesson. What is the most important information you intend to share with the class regarding your topic? This is considered the "scope" of your lesson. You can't share everything you learned. Make these important decisions carefully. Share information which is essential to your topic.

How do you intend to start your presentation? What will follow next? How will you close your presentation? Your knowledge
must be presented in a logical order or sequence. In many cases
your topic dictates the sequence of your lesson. However, that
shouldn't keep you from being creative.

All lesson plans need polish. Complete the lesson plan and
bring it to class on Thursday. I'll look it over and offer suggestions.

The presentations appealed to youthful imaginations. The
quicker students liked the chance to experiment. The others saw a
way to exploit talents for playacting, art, and video making.

But some were likely to stumble. Like every other American
high school, Mamaroneck had a significant number of special education students who did not usually participate in programs as
strenuous as this one. There was a special room, a haven on the
second floor of the Palmer building, where Sandra Weinman, a
Team 9 special education teacher, could work with them. The team
members agreed that the resource room was a good idea, but regularly warned themselves against dividing the class into ability
groups and leaving special education students off in a corner.

"I'm not comfortable isolating the kids," Restaino said at a
team meeting.

"Agreed!" Mary Cronin said.

". . . but we have to do something to address the needs of these
kids," he continued. "We have to go to their parents. I think it's a
big deal."

Ahearn said he had been dubious about putting students with
extreme learning disabilities in regular classes until two girls in his
economics class changed his mind. "Their first few papers were
unintelligible," he said. "But I have to tell you, when I was presented with their work last May, it was phenomenal, the progress."

Landrum wrinkled her nose and named one of the special ed
students in her class. "I can't give her a passing grade in English if
she can't read."

Restaino agreed. "We can't do it. We have to worry about our
credibility."

Ann Borsellino blamed family circumstances. One girl from

what had been a comfortable Larchmont family had a job every day after school because her parents had divorced and her father was not paying child support.

"But there are kids who just don't have the skill," Cronin added.

Landrum nodded. "I think we know more about these kids than the counselors."

"The counselors have lists of the at-risk kids, and they have resources," Restaino said. "But what we have to get back to is having a strategy to meet the kids' needs and not violate any philosophy of not isolating kids."

Mamaroneck had not fallen into the habits of some schools that created special education programs outside the school to segregate students from poor families. Still, enough students were sent off to Mamaroneck's special education rooms to make teachers like Restaino uncomfortable. Team 9 had been created, in part, to prove that those divisions were not essential for learning, that they could be overcome, and that students could learn more about their world, and in more useful fashion, if they worked through the subject matter together. It was so at odds with what the school usually practiced that none of the participants was certain it would work.

9

TOGETHER IN THE DARK

The moment of class consciousness material-
ized unexpectedly, as if Karl Marx were making a brief appearance
in the Palmer building. Restaino moved to squelch it.

His Team 9 class had, with his permission, slipped into an
undisciplined if passionate discussion of the O. J. Simpson trial. A
Larchmont girl said she had read about the culture of violence that
infected low-income neighborhoods. She said that was the sort of
place Simpson grew up and that she understood how that might
affect him.

A boy from the Flats snorted. "Sure you do," he said, the
words low and almost inaudible.

"Shut up, John," Restaino said sharply. "Keep quiet." He
called on someone else.

Most elite high schools have some income differences, as Mamaroneck does. It is difficult to find a community like Scarsdale or
Winnetka where almost no one is poor. It is also hard to tell, just
from looking, which students are rich and which are not. American teenagers of all social strata wear more or less the same clothing. For boys winter garb is sweatshirts, baggy jackets, and jeans.
The denims are one or two sizes too large in keeping with the

urban fashion made popular by MTV. Girls in winter don the same costume: jeans, sweatshirts, and jackets, with wealthier girls adding fine sweaters and expensive boots. In summer everyone wears T-shirts or polo shirts and shorts. Some girls wear sundresses, tank tops, and jeans, particularly if they are trying to impress someone.

Just how comfortably minorities have assimilated into Mamaroneck is a matter of debate. Some of them, particularly students from middle-class homes, mix in well. Some African American and Latin American students stick together, appropriating a section of the Palmer-to-Post corridor near the library for conversation and listening to music. The Mamaroneck schools have survived occasional outbreaks of anti-Semitism, anti-Catholicism, racism, sexism, and other forms of prejudice, some of them quite awful. A Ryeneck parent who paid tuition to send his daughter to Mamaroneck High had neighbors who joked about Italians chasing the Jews out of Mamaroneck at sundown. Someone had scrawled anti-Semitic slogans on the Larchmont village library and nine private homes in 1996. Public meetings were held. Mamaroneck students like Rachel Lissy, a talented actor, made moving speeches.

As diverse as they are, most Mamaroneck students are, like those at other high-performing schools, united by the assumption that they are there to prepare for college. Peer pressure works in favor of classroom life. The academically competitive children of academically competitive parents set the tone.

Mamaroneck teachers and counselors say about a third of the student body are hard-core academics, no matter how nonchalant they appear. Another third are distracted by adolescent pastimes—cars and sports and romance and alcohol—but have college-conscious parents and homes full of books. These students do a significant amount of schoolwork in spite of themselves.

The last third are from families without strong college traditions. School counselors think they are the most susceptible to the lure of parties and after-school jobs and teenage angst, even if many of them are as serious about college as their wealthy friends. A few teachers and counselors write them off early, giving them an excuse to revel in their defiance of the nerds. Teachers who seek out such students say they often are more thoughtful and interesting than many of the children who had 1400s on their SATs.

Restaino tried to have himself assigned courses with a heavy load of the least ambitious students. Until Ehrenhaft began to break up remedial courses, these children were consigned to low-end English courses with names like Developmental Reading. The students were coaxed to do just enough work to hoist themselves to the next rung of a very low ladder.

Restaino looked for books they might enjoy and topics on which they could write with some confidence. He had no special curriculum to guide him and no extra help. The classes were almost always small, perhaps no more than a dozen students, a blessing of a well-endowed school.

One of his elective courses was Contemporary Short Stories. He worked with each student, starting with newspaper stories or magazines about sports figures and moving briskly into literature. He had them write journals about their daily lives—football games, barhopping on North Avenue, hanging out at the Nautilus Diner. He asked them to compose short essays about what they were reading. He wanted them to examine what irked them about writers' pretensions and what truths they discovered that excited them. He asked them to talk in class about what they were reading. He assigned them small research projects and asked them to present their results to the class. He looked for tricks that would force them to offer their thoughts to the world.

He walked around the room, engaging each student as best he could. He asked questions. What was going on? What were they thinking about? The conversation did not necessarily have to be about school, although he might steer it in that direction.

He experimented with contracts. Each was a promise to complete a project—a few pages of journal written, a few stories read—by a certain date. On that date he would talk to the student. Here is what you said you would do, and here is what you did. How do you explain the difference? How do you want to adjust your work habits or your expectations so that you can do what you promised?

It worked for some students. They strayed into O. Henry and

O'Hara and Le Guin and Bradbury. For most, however, he was too late. Many students saw his approach as a con game and knew they could evade it if they wished.

Among his pedagogical tools was an appreciation of the terrors of the senior year's last semester. The college-bound strivers fretted over which schools would accept them. The noncollege kids wondered, at least to themselves, what they were going to do with the rest of their lives. He used this as leverage on students like Tony, a model of genial apathy. Tony was the youngest of twelve children. As far as Restaino could tell, Tony's parents had spent their last ounce of energy and resolve on his older siblings and so had let Tony do anything he wished. Tony told Restaino he had the greatest parents in the world.

"Well," Restaino said one day, stopping at the boy's desk. "It's March. That mean anything to you?"

"Yeah," Tony said with a smile. "I'm out of here in three months."

"Then what?"

"Well, then I'm going to party."

"You've been doing that for a long, long time."

"After I party, I'm going to party some more and then some more."

"And what's going to happen after that?"

The boy paused. He did not like his classroom daydreams interrupted, but he knew how persistent Restaino was. The man would not go away unless he addressed the question.

"I don't know," Tony said pensively. "I'll look around."

The hook was set. "Well, what are you going to look around doing?"

"I don't know."

"You can write. You know that? You really have an ability to make things clear on the page. Let's say you did a little bit more work here. Maybe there's a dispatching job, or a clerical job in one of the brokerage firms. You could do something. I could write a recommendation. Maybe even some courses at Westchester Community."

The boy nodded. Restaino proposed an assignment. Perhaps

Tony would do it, perhaps he would not. Restaino let the words sink in and waited to see where they led.

In the classroom, the ambitious habits of the affluent, book-smart majority ruled. Outside of the school building, the social and economic class divisions were still there but blurred by tastes in recreation and entertainment that crossed class lines. Athletic teams included all cliques and ethnic groups, the football and hockey teams being unusually rich in the children of blue-collar families. When Marshall Lewy—his father an investment banker, his mother the mayor of Larchmont—starred as a football tackle, he was everyone's favorite example of how social classes mixed at Mamaroneck. But on that squad he was more the exception than the rule.

Drugs also attracted students from varying social strata. Some self-appointed couriers made regular runs to the Bronx to buy marijuana. There were cocaine and harder drugs, but consumption of narcotics was minuscule compared to alcohol. In a Students Against Drunk Driving (SADD) survey conducted in 1995, 46 per-cent of Mamaroneck students said they thought there was a drink-ing problem at the school. Twenty-eight percent said they had knowingly let someone drive under the influence of alcohol. Twelve percent had driven under the influence themselves.

This was standard for high-performing schools, indeed for all suburban schools. Money, leisure time, and ill-disguised parental fondness for alcohol made it a favorite adolescent pastime. The urge crossed all class and ethnic barriers. At beer parties in the Mamaroneck hills it was usually too dark to tell who was who.

For one November keg party convened in the Sheldrake Woods, the invitations were issued word-of-mouth by the girls' field hockey team. The woods were a long, narrow stand of trees and brush marking the division between two hilly neighborhoods near the Bonnie Briar Country Club. Street parking was conve-nient, but unless one knew precisely where the party was, it was difficult to find.

The neighbors were not happy about the gatherings. They called the police when the din became loud enough to be heard over the chatter of their television sets. The Mamaroneck town police followed a ritual. They sent a car over at 10:00 P.M., usually an hour after they party had begun, and asked the celebrants to leave, which they almost always did.

As I approached the party, I wondered how the guests avoided serious injury. Almost no light reached the woods from the streets or the houses. There was no discernible path from Bonnie Way, where a home owner's basketball court offered access to the woods and to the small rise several hundred yards away where a beer keg had been opened.

Four youths guided me to the spot. They appeared to have no trouble keeping on their feet, despite an obstacle course of roots, pits, leaves, dirt, and rocks. Nor were they bothered by the 40-degree temperature. From fifty yards the buzz of teenage conversation was quite audible, but I saw nothing but a slightly darker mass in the middle of the thick gray murk ahead.

I climbed the hillock without breaking a limb. Once on top, it was not much easier to see. A girl in a padded jacket accepted my admission fee, two dollars. If I had planned to drink, it would have been a dollar more. She had to assure me that the bills I had given her were the correct denomination. It was too dark for me to tell.

About one hundred adolescents, wearing jeans and heavy coats or jackets, stood close together. They drank beer from paper cups. I could not see the keg but was told it was somewhere in the back of the throng.

I had expected loud talk and perhaps some roughhousing. I saw instead the teenage equivalent of a Larchmont cocktail party, the guests enjoying light conversation as if they were in a Tudor mansion with a caterer at hand. I saw boys and girls, hockey stars and National Merit semifinalists, fast students and slow. Joy Sarlo was there with several of her girlfriends. Mike Lisa, the senior class president and future Annapolis midshipman, lifted a cup of brew. The *Globe* staff, including Debbie Schoeneman and Matt Wexler, were present.

All went well until 10:00 P.M. when a report rippled through the crowd that police had been sighted. The revelers faded away, bound for home or one of the Post Road diners.

In 1995 police throughout Westchester County decided to

crack down on teenage drinking. The Scarsdale police blocked all exits from the rear parking lot of the Quaker Ridge Elementary School during a keg party and gave breath tests to young drivers trying to leave. In Mamaroneck, police invaded the Sheldrake Woods in force an hour earlier than usual and made thirteen arrests, provoking an immediate reaction from the *Globe*. "There was no warning given," complained reporter Kerry Constabile, "and a few arrested students said that only about half the students involved had had anything to drink, and it was only a minuscule amount at that. In addition, a few of the arrested attendees were just passing through to greet people and were not causing any disturbance."

Those "detained"—the police said they were not arresting anyone—were charged with trespassing and told to call their parents. Each was fined four hours of community service.

Several people who were not there claimed to have been. Tales of the Great Bust circulated for weeks. The most prevalent rumor was that the police had arrested more people than they wanted to because the first few youths they caught were black. The rumor implied they needed a broader sampling of the teenage community to spread the word of their displeasure. That was fine, both real and claimed participants said. They were all in it together.

MAKING THE GRADE

Grades are a popular tool for dividing students into ability groups. At elite schools, many students, parents, and teachers believe two contradictory things about good grades: (1) they are easier to earn than they once were, and (2) the struggle to acquire them has made school more stressful than it ought to be.

Classroom grades remain an important factor in college admissions. Many colleges complain that pass-fail systems, homework-free courses, grade weighting, and grade inflation have made it more difficult to calibrate the value of grades at many schools. But the only other readily available tool for identifying the best students, the SAT, has become less useful for the most selective universities, because the College Board adjusted the scoring system in 1995 and made the highest SAT scores, from 1400 to 1600, much more common than before.

One school's grading system is often different from another's. Individual teacher assessments also vary widely. Grade inflation is real: Several studies show a higher percentage of As and Bs on high school and college report cards. Parents have good reason to wonder if their children are working as hard for their grades as they did at that age, yet schools like Mamaroneck remain far above the average in tying grades to effort. Any student taking an AP course is unquestionably being asked to do more than her parents ever did.

Steve Pass transferred to Mamaroneck from Brooklyn's South Shore High when he was a sophomore. South Shore was a large school in a changing neighborhood that tried to keep its most ambitious students from moving or transferring to private schools by putting them in an academically oriented school within the school. It was called the Scholars Institute and included children who had been in honors classes since elementary school. Pass's grades in the program were consistently in the 90s.

When he transferred to Mamaroneck, his parents assumed he would adjust to the new school's standards. He did, but the process was painful. Despite the elite status of his South Shore classes, Mamaroneck was so far ahead that in Pass's first few months his mathematics and English grades dipped into the 70s.

A lean boy with black hair and a passion for baseball, Pass had special talents. His father worked with computers. Pass's own technological skills were so advanced that by the end of his sophomore year Nick Cucchiarella, head of the vocational studies department, was depending on him to debug programs in the computer lab. School secretaries asked him to fix their word processing systems. By his junior year he was back in the 90s in mathematics, and in the 80s and 90s in English, a bright student forced to do better by jumping into a tougher league.

Even with its relatively high standards, Mamaroneck permitted wild divergence in grading practice among teachers. The hardline approach was represented by Cliff Gill, who would retire without regret in 1996. He taught his mathematics classes the same way for thirty-six years, through the new math, the return to basics, critical thinking, and a dozen other educational fads he did not care for. He believed that all children could learn at a very high level if they had the proper motivation, something strong enough to cut through the teenage devotion to watching television and talking on the telephone. He understood that the majority of his students already worried that lackluster grades in his class might limit their college choices. Those who did not care so much about college had other fears that could be exploited.

He conducted the first few weeks of ninth grade algebra like a Marine boot camp at Parris Island, an impression augmented by his crew cut and loud voice. In fact, he had no military background and was a sophisticated man with a wealthy upbringing. "I'm here to do a job and for that job I'm paid a sum of money," he told his ninth graders. "You are here to do a job also, and you better do it as if you are paid. You are not paid in money right now, but you are paid in points, and those points gather and accumulate into a transcript that is going to get you into some school that is going to get you a further education that is going to get you a job that is going to pay money.

"This is your job. It is your job to pay attention and your job to do your homework." Those who did not do their job, he said, would regret it. "If the homework is not done, or not done to my satisfaction, you get a zero. If you get a second zero, it is five points off the report card grade. A third zero, five more points off," he said. "In class, there are no hats. There is no gum chewing. There are none of the things that I imagine are allowed to go on in all the other classrooms."

At the other end of the disciplinary scale was Don Phillips, at six-feet-six the school's tallest teacher. He taught in Mamaroneck's School Within a School (SWAS) from 1971 to 1982 and so liked its avant-garde assessment policies—teachers gave detailed evaluations, not grades—that when he returned to the regular faculty he refused to recalibrate himself. He became, in his own words, the Great Grade Inflator. If a student with poor writing skills did his best on a paper, Phillips was inclined to give him just as high a grade as a future screenwriter who turned out a prose poem. About 90 percent of his grades in Changing Times—a seminar on public issues in Hollywood films—and in Russian History were 90 and above. No one asked him to toughen his approach, although he detected some collegial disapproval, which he attributed to jealousy. His courses attracted scores of students, perhaps as much for his sense of fun as for his grading system. That left fewer customers for other teachers' favorite elective courses.

Another faculty maverick, Fred Levine in the science department, graded his Advanced Placement Physics course pass-drop.

If a student was not going to pass, he could escape without any grade at all. There was no mention of this in the course catalog. Coffey did not object. Most of Levine's students were seniors who would not have bothered with the course if it did not interest them. Levine saw no reason to waste time figuring grade averages for students who would be scored on the AP examination anyway, even if several members of the class, with no grades to motivate them, did poorly on the test.

Many Mamaroneck students felt they were entitled to respectable grades for what some educators might consider mediocre work. When Harvey-Ann Ross, an inventive member of the English department, asked students in her Public Speaking class what sort of work they thought should earn a grade in the 90s, the answers bore marks of the self-esteem movement.

A girl declared that a student should achieve a grade in the high 90s for doing "more than what the teacher asked for." A grade in the low 90s, she said, was "for someone who has done the work but maybe is bothered by getting up there and speaking." Ross asked her what she meant by "more work than the teacher asked for." "You can tell when they have put more work in than you asked for," the girl replied. "I think a low 80s grade would be for someone who did the work, but didn't put too much into it, just did it to get by."

Another girl said she agreed in general but thought her class-mate was too harsh in punishing a minor case of sloth. "Maybe they knew they didn't do the best that they could," she said, "but giving a grade in the low 80s just discourages them."

Several students said grades ought to be used to buoy student spirits. Graders, they said, should not make too much of individual differences. "Dan presented his speech extremely well," said one boy. "I don't think he should get a lesser grade than somebody who had more information."

"The grade should be based on how much someone has improved," said a girl. "I am still a little nervous when I get up there, but I think I improved on my delivery."

"I think effort in the class is more important," a boy said. "How hard you try, how much work you put into it—that should be important."

Some American teachers accept the notion of an A for effort. Some do not. Much of the desire to soften the process is motivated by a widespread, if likely erroneous, impression that there is less and less room for success in the world, that teenagers in school are playing a zero-sum game.

By the late 1980s, the inconsistencies in high school grading, enthusiastically aggravated throughout the country by teachers like Phillips and Levine, had persuaded many educators to strive for something more predictable and less confusing that could set a consistent high standard. One method was the rubric, originally a liturgical term that had come to mean a set of written standards for each grade, from A to F. A rubric was designed to tell each child what was expected of her, rather than force her to measure herself against the work of the teacher's pet tacked on the classroom bulletin board. By the mid-1990s rubrics had taken hold at Mamaroneck, particularly in art courses and in Team 9.

A huge rubric dominated the wall of art classroom D238. It said students who received grades from 90 to 100 would be those who did "more than required" and had work of "unusual quality in design and construction." A grade in the 80s meant the student had done "the required amount of work" and provided "good quality." The student who received a grade in the 70s had "met the requirements" and done work "satisfactory in design and construction." Those graded in the 60s, the lowest marks explained on the chart, had "not used class time to best advantage" and submitted work that was "incomplete and carelessly done."

The Team 9 teachers went much further. They fashioned rubrics that described what was required for every phase of every project. Their rubric for the student-as-scholar portion of their China project provided thirty different descriptions of work that ranged from A to U, the grade for failing work below 65.

The categories looked odd to some parents, particularly the descriptions of C or D work. They read like invitations to do poorly, but educational researchers said that that was not the case at all. Heidi Hayes Jacobs, a nationally prominent consultant based in Rye, New York, encouraged rubrics at Mamaroneck and other schools as a way to spare students the dizziness of six teachers with six different standards.

Jacobs said that as she explored standards and assessments with students across the country, the differences leapt out at her. She would ask a student, "Do you have to write complete sentences in your papers for science class?" The answer would invariably be, "It depends on which teacher you have."

Teachers giving grades, she argued, should follow the example of television analysts reviewing the performance of the New York Knickerbockers basketball team. They gave an overall postgame assessment of the team's performance but buttressed it with their opinion of the power forward's work on the boards, the shooting guard's 3-point percentage, the center's free-throw consistency, and the point guard's assists. Grades, Jacobs said, were multitrait, not single trait, and ought to be presented as such. Rubrics forced teachers to assess students on certain criteria—the opposite of grading on the curve, when each mark was dependent on how well everyone else in the class did.

College admissions officers rarely saw the rubrics, only the grade point average, usually on a 100-point scale or a 4-point scale. The 1995–96 Mamaroneck High School profile, a guide for both colleges and prospective Mamaroneck parents, placed the grade point averages of 231 graduating seniors on a bar graph. It showed 26.4 percent with averages in the 90s, 51.4 percent in the 80s, 19 percent in the 70s, and 3 percent in the 60s.

That rough division of one fourth As and one half Bs occurs in most high-performing American secondary schools. Since most schools grade on a curve that adjusts for the relative ability of the students, many schools with low achievement levels report As and Bs in these and even larger proportions. Several studies show that low-achieving schools give much higher grades than schools like Mamaroneck to students who otherwise score the same on nationally standardized tests. A January 1994 report by Judith Anderson of the U.S. Education Department's Office of Research concluded that "students in high poverty schools (those where more than 75 percent of students receive free or reduced price lunch) who received mostly A's in English got about the same reading score as did the 'C' and 'D' students in the most affluent schools."

M. Donald Thomas, a former superintendent of schools in Salt

Lake City, said audits of about two thousand schools conducted for SchoolMatch, a private school-rating service based in Westerville, Ohio, showed "a close relationship between low student achievement and high grade point averages." He said when teachers at such schools were asked why they inflated their grades, most said that "they don't want to have problems with the students or parents," although most studies show that low-income, low-achieving students are *less* likely to have parents who would object. In some urban schools with very low scores on standardized achievement tests, Thomas said, he found teachers giving 30 percent of the students As and nearly everyone else Bs just for showing up.

Worries about grade inflation in high-achieving schools seem trivial by comparison. Parents at such schools can be fairly confident that their children, when measured against the full range of American students, are earning their marks. Of Scarsdale High students taking English in 1992 to 1993, 24.8 percent received As and 55.6 percent received Bs. (C grades made up 15.6 percent, Ds 2.5 percent, and Fs 1.4 percent). About 25 percent of the 1996 graduating class at Andover High in Bloomfield Hills, Michigan, had A averages and about 48 percent B averages. Berkeley High in Berkeley, California, had about 25 percent of its 1996 seniors with A averages and 43 percent with B averages. Bountiful High in Bountiful, Utah, was, as its name suggests, more generous. It calculated 35 percent of its students had A averages over a ten-year period.

If grade inflation adversely affects learning, it is probably from the increasing use of weighted grading systems that give extra points for honors or AP course grades. Advocates of this system say it lures students into more difficult courses, but there is evidence of abuse. Several schools in the Midwest began to alter their weighting systems in the 1990s because the weights were so high for honors courses they seemed unfair to students in regular courses. Ty Wilde, a student at Naperville North High in Naperville, Illinois, said she found many of her classmates making crucial course decisions—taking Latin, for instance, instead of Spanish—not because of their interest in the subject matter but because Latin was the only language to give extra weight to third-year grades.

Some elite schools have tried to lessen the negative impact of grades by abolishing the tradition of high school senior academic ranks. The change is motivated in part by fears of unfair college competition. By 1993, according to a survey by the National Association of Secondary School Principals, 159 out of 2,175 high schools had abolished class ranking, most of them high-achieving schools like Scarsdale and Great Neck North.

Such schools no longer needed to tell colleges how their students ranked because admissions directors already assumed their top twenty or thirty students were at least as good if not better than the valedictorians of less-favored schools. Colleges like Stanford, Yale, and Harvard had enough staff to read each application three or four times. They knew the relative quality of the high schools and gave great weight to the content of the courses and to extracurricular activities and interview results. Class rank rarely became an issue, except in cases where they admitted a musician or an athlete or strong African American applicant or an alumnus's child who was not at the top of the class. If, at the same time, they rejected an applicant with better grades from the same school, they would either reconsider their decision to reject the higher-ranked candidate or brace themselves for complaints.

As class rank grows less popular, so does the tradition of a class valedictorian. This bothers traditionalists and educators who feel that the highest academic attainment ought to receive school recognition, as athletic skill and beauty do. But picking a number one always invites trouble, as Mamaroneck seniors discovered in 1994.

Matt Koppel, scheduled to graduate in 1995, became impatient with school at the beginning of his sophomore year. An unconventional thinker with long, unruly hair, he whizzed through science and mathematics courses, devoured John Perlman's poetry class and enthralled Myrna Thomas, the science research teacher, with a project on the immune response in tomato plants. He decided to dispense with his junior year and move directly to senior year and, as quickly as possible, graduation and college. He had taken some high school courses at the Hommocks. He added summer and extracurricular work. He not only had enough credits to graduate early but had the highest grade point average in his new, and until then unsuspecting, graduating class.

Members of the class of '94 were not happy when they heard that a stranger was going to make the valedictory address. Not only was Koppel an interloper, but he had earned the honor while risking his grade point average in fewer courses than they had. And that was not all. The next highest grade point average belonged to Toni Rainone, a hard worker who, nonetheless, had taken only one AP course in four years. Some students suggested the school adopt the practice of other high-achieving schools and grant extra weight to honors and AP courses in calculating grade point averages. Koppel was mildly annoyed at the complaints. Rainone said whatever happened was fine with her.

Coffey, as principal, struggled with the issue. He listened to several seniors. They told him they could not honestly deny Koppel the honor, given his brilliance, but was he the right person to give the speech? Coffey had sat through enough graduation ceremonies to know that the best students were often not the best orators. He arranged a compromise. Koppel would speak, but there would be a competition for a second student speaker picked by faculty judges. Matt Oberg, son of school board member Penny Oberg, won with a humorous look at high school life. Koppel briefly objected when he learned that the last spot on the program would go to Oberg, not him, but the ceremony proceeded without unpleasantness. Rainone was declared co-salutorian along with David Edelstein, the strongest of the four-year seniors on the AP track. The next year seniors chose a graduation speaker by ballot.

Other elite schools have turned away from individual honors. Stevenson High in Lincolnshire, Illinois, and Eleanor Roosevelt High in Greenbelt, Maryland, no longer pick valedictorians. Vestavia Hills High outside Birmingham, Alabama, has adopted a popular alternative: All graduates with grade point averages of 4.0 or above (often more than thirty students) are presented with an engraved plaque testifying to the achievement and are listed in the graduation program.

The self-esteem movement takes some blame for this turn away from individual honors, but there is no need to fear a loss of confidence among the students who place second or third at places like Vestavia Hills. The teachers and principals involved know how important grades, and their influences on colleges, are in motivating students. These administrators do nothing to dilute the power of grades on the transcript, but at a certain point, in their view, the selection of an academic king or queen based on odd weights and decimal points becomes petty and intrusive. They think they and their students have better things to do with their time.

High school students rarely let a day pass without an argument about grades, but they have no consistent view of what should be done about them. Some say that grading differences should be softened or abolished. Some feel they should be tightened.

The *New Trier News* published two conflicting articles on a plan to introduce pluses and minuses, with different grade points for each, to what had been a straight letter-grade system. One student, Jake Larrimore, argued that under the new system "every final, every project, discussion, paper, and test would bear a disproportionate weight" because students would begin to fret when they received an A-minus rather than an A. The other student, Lynda Yast, said the new system would allow teachers to "give either an A-minus or B-plus to those that fall in the hazy 89 percent range without changing their GPAs very much, whereas right now, the difference between an A and B is great. Students whose grades fall in that range would no longer be torn between the lure of the higher grade and the fear of the lower one."

At Mamaroneck, Dan Hopkins decried in a *Globe* editorial a culture in which "the most important aspect of school, the learning, is largely eclipsed by the corresponding number." But Michael Lisa, president of the Mamaroneck class of 1995, said he considered such talk little better than nursery-school prattle. Lisa was a short, muscular football lineman and linebacker who would eventually win admission to the Naval Academy. Every signal he decoded from the world at large told him that grades were very important and ought not to be obscured without reason.

He hated the geography teacher who jokingly called him a "dumb jock" and gave him only nine out of ten points on a quiz in which he thought he had missed none. He chided the teacher of his second-year mathematics course for slowing the pace to accommodate some students. "This is a waste of time, this is garbage," he told the instructor. "Look at what Japan is doing. Look at them. They have a curriculum three times harder than this."

He was frustrated by a history teacher who promised severe penalties for work not done in time, but gave a B to a student who turned in a paper two weeks late. He had heard people say that grades were easier to get than they used to be. He did not think that applied to him. He worked hard for his grades. "My job is to go to school, and you get paid in points," he said, repeating the Gill axiom.

If it was easier, he said, it was because "the kids are a little bit smarter. They know how to cheat. They know how to cheat, and they don't get caught."

CHEATING

Dan Hopkins heard the question but ignored it. He was passing out the second half of the Advanced Placement U.S. History examination in the Post cafeteria. He was more concerned with finishing his chore and getting back to his seat than he was in interpreting whispers.

It was May 15, 1995. Mamaroneck's test takers were among 132,015 students taking the U.S. History test, more heavily subscribed than any other AP examination except English Literature and Composition. The room had long tables and cafeteria chairs for the fifty-three students taking the three-hour examination. The test takers were widely spaced but could talk to one another during breaks. The proctor had chosen Hopkins to pass out the tests because he was sitting in front.

What Hopkins heard was: "Hey, when was the march on Washington?" He was not sure if the boy who spoke was talking to him or to a seat mate. At AP examinations, nervous chatter was common before the proctor started the test. Hopkins heard one or two other people exchanging views on the civil rights movement. He shrugged it off.

It was only when Hopkins opened his test booklet at the proctor's signal and read the questions that he began to worry about what he had heard. The first thing he saw on the examination was a famous 1963 news photograph of a civil rights demonstrator in Birmingham, Alabama, being attacked by a police dog. The photograph was one of several items the students were asked to inspect before answering the test's document-based question: "Analyze the changes that occurred during the 1960s in the goals, strategies, and support of the movement for African American civil rights." Hopkins began thinking about his answer and tried to push aside distracting speculations about how anyone might have gotten an advance look at the test.

A century ago the handling of cheating was a simple matter in American schools. Students were punished if caught. Expulsion, suspension, caning, failure of the course—the sanctions varied, but the principle was the same: Cheating and copying were wrong and demanded harsh discipline.

This adherence to traditional values survived more or less intact into the 1960s, when some educators began to notice a slackening of interest in the matter. Cheating prevention became progressively less important in the 1970s and 1980s. Many teachers were annoyed that they even had to deal with it. This was especially true in the nation's best public schools. Teachers enjoyed educating such highly motivated children. They did not think their students would betray their trust. Corwith Hansen, a mathematics teacher who became an assistant principal at Scarsdale High, had classes full of children so wonderful that, he said, "they just stopped your heart." If he gave them a test, he assumed they were not going to cheat, for no other reason, he said, than they were such great kids.

Nonetheless, cheating continued. There were no surveys to indicate if college-conscious suburban students were more likely to copy answers than less ambitious and more distracted urban children, but faculty and administrators who worked in both places thought that was so. Several surveys suggested a collapse of classroom ethics. Honor appeared to have lost importance because, for many students at elite public schools, to fall behind in the American contest for excellence was too awful to contemplate, no matter what the cost to their integrity.

A survey by New York State United Teachers, an affiliate of the American Federation of Teachers, asked local union presidents in 1994 and 1995 how frequently they encountered cheating in their classrooms. Six percent said it was constant and pervasive, 26 percent said frequent, and 55 percent said occasional, with only 13 percent saying it was rare. The problem was more severe at the secondary school level: Eight percent reported constant and pervasive cheating, 32 percent frequent, 49 percent occasional, and only 11 percent rare. Eighty-two percent of the New York teachers surveyed thought incidents of cheating had increased in their secondary schools in the past five years.

Students—particularly the college-bound—reported even higher rates. In 1995, *Who's Who Among American High School Students* released a survey of 3,351 high school students aged sixteen to eighteen. All had at least B averages. Seventy-six percent said they had cheated at least once. Eighty-nine percent said they thought cheating was common at their school but rarely detected or disciplined. Ninety-four percent of those who said they cheated also said they were not caught. Of those who were caught, only 5 percent said they were punished.

Yet in many favored high schools it was the students, not the teachers or administrators, who raised the cheating issue. Unlike their parents, they knew what was going on in the classrooms. They knew their fellow students better than their teachers did, and were not so burdened with fears of offending the young. In 1995 two students on the Scarsdale High School governance committee told their astonished adult colleagues that cheating had become common and that noncheating students felt abused by the practice. The faculty, they said, was at fault. Many teachers did not bother to proctor their own examinations. Some left the room for the hour to sip coffee in the teachers' lounge.

By the mid-1990s cheating had become a frequent topic in elite school newspapers. The *Three Penny Press* at Bellaire High in Houston blamed it on careless teachers in advanced courses. The *Tribune* at Greeley High said college pressure and vague rules confused the students. The *New Trier News* had an explanation from the school's AP psychology teacher, Tery Rodgers: lack of self-confidence, peer pressure, and "outcome-oriented" rather than "process-oriented" goals.

Paul Krouse, the *Who's Who* publisher, said much of the student concern over cheating appeared to stem from admiration for the same adults who were overlooking the problem. Eighty-three percent said they had a great deal of trust or confidence in their parents. They honored their teachers and worked hard for their grades. Yet the adults were not pushing them as hard as they felt they ought to be pushed to make ethical choices. They told the survey takers that they felt the greatest crisis facing the nation and their age group was a decline of moral and social values.

"Adolescence is a time to see how far you can push the boundaries and how much you can get away with," Krouse said. "If today's teens are not punished when they do something wrong or challenged to take their responsibilities more seriously, then their resulting poor attitudes and bad behaviors are only partially their fault."

The problem might be easier for schools to address if there were some agreement on what constitutes cheating. In the *Who's Who* survey, 66 percent said they had copied someone's homework, while 39 percent said they had cheated on a quiz or test. The New York teachers survey defined cheating as "looking at another student's paper during a test or quiz, copying from another student's homework, or plagiarizing," but few students would put those in the same category. Most teenagers agreed that copying during tests or plagiarizing published work was wrong, but copying a friend's homework fell into a gray area. Ninety-seven percent of students in a 1996 New Trier survey said looking at another student's exam was cheating, but only 46 percent applied the same label to asking someone from an earlier class what was on a test.

In 1993 Scarsdale High social studies teacher Ed Beach told his AP Government class that some students had submitted papers that seemed to be revised versions of papers they had done for U.S. History the year before. He thought plagiarizing one's own work was wrong, at least in the context of a project designed to encourage learning, but it was not expressly covered in the school rules. Use of siblings' old work raised more ticklish issues. No one would object if a student saved the scorecard from his first golf round below 80 or a picture from the junior prom. What was so wrong about saving an old paper and passing it on, for "reference," to a brother or sister? How different was this from their parents' and teachers' use of Cliffs Notes and other commercial study guides when they were in school?

Scarsdale held a series of faculty and student meetings on the issue in 1996 but reached no agreement on what constituted wrongdoing. English teacher Julie Leerburger's group decided cheating was "anything where students turn in work that is reported to be their own but really is not." Others demanded more specificity and fought over the explosive issue of ultrahelpful parents.

Many parents spent the equivalent of an inner-city family's annual income on real estate taxes that supported their local school. They had spent the equivalent of that same inner-city worker's lifetime income to buy a house in a good school district. If rewriting their child's English essay or paying a tutor to correct her physics homework moved the child closer to a good college, then given everything else they had invested, why hesitate? If the point of the exercise was that the child learn, could not some of the teaching come from the adults closest to her?

Corwith Hansen, the Scarsdale assistant principal, called this "positive collaboration." To him, it was both helpful to the student's understanding of what she was doing and unfair to other students who could not or would not seek similar support. But in Scarsdale everyone had access to such help, so was it a problem? Suppose a student had a father who was a professional writer and corrected all of his son's grammatical errors. Was that wrong? How different was that from the student who bought a computer program equipped to do the same thing? The College Board had already agreed to the use of graphing calculators on the AP Calculus examination. How could a teacher hold back the march of technology?

One student told Hansen that a private tutor "pregraded" a paper for him, allowing him to see and correct its flaws. "I had sort of a rough draft," another student told Hansen. "My dad took it to work and his secretary fixed it up and typed it out." Hansen hoped that parents would act more like teachers than editors. He thought a good rule was not to touch physically the student's work. Point or suggest or ask questions, such as: Is this punctuation correct? Do you understand this construction? Do you understand the rule that applies here?

The growing emphasis on cooperative learning, an important part of the reformers' creed, and the increasingly commercial character of American education made the ethics of school work even less clear. When Michael Roush was still teaching history at Mamaroneck, he constructed tests that he thought were "cheat-proof." A student could use his textbook or any other materials. The examination was always an exercise in analysis. For instance: Should assault weapons be legal in America? The students had to compose an argument based on their newly acquired historical perspective. Roush was less interested in what his students remembered than how adept they were in using that information.

Roush applied the same rules to homework. Like a few other teachers around the country, he encouraged his students to compare notes. Roush told his class that law students studied in groups, parceling out sections of an assignment and reporting back what they had learned to one another. He was still congratulating himself on this refined approach when he received homework assignments from two students that were almost word-for-word identical.

He scolded them. "But wait a minute, Mr. Roush," one said. "You said we could cooperate on this." They had a point. He had gotten ahead of himself. He had to reconsider his message. He wanted them to help each other, and yet give him their individual thoughts. How realistic was that?

In 1996 the Greeley faculty wrestled with a similarly ambiguous violation arising from a fourth-year French examination. The teacher had been using a series of taped lessons as oral exercises. She assumed the materials were available only to teachers. To guide preparation for the final examination, she told her students that an oral section would be based on a tape in that same series, one they had not heard.

The Greeley students were not only bright but resourceful. After calling several Westchester bookstores, one student found the tape the teacher was going to play. Eight students used it to prepare for the test, saying nothing to the teacher about it. When word of this got out after the examination, the students and their parents were called in, one family at a time, for a conference with the assistant principal. They were told they had used unauthorized materials and had kept it a secret. It was cheating, the teacher said, because not everyone in the class had access to it.

The participants heatedly disagreed. "The principal and vice principals are all wrong," one student told the *Greeley Tribune.* "They accused us of things we didn't do, like stealing the tape." Parents said they were proud of their children for taking initiative. Every day Greeley teachers encouraged them to think independently and take intellectual risks. *Tribune* sports editor Matt Danzig backed the students in a lead editorial: "The teacher probably did not intend to have the students go out and buy the tape. However, it is absolutely ridiculous to expect students to second-guess the intentions of their teacher. If a social studies teacher told her students that the midterm would have a section on the map of the United States, would that teacher really expect her students not to go and study the map? . . . One might question the morality of the use of an aid that supplied actual answers to the test, but that's as far as the 'wrongdoing' of these students goes. Nothing can be labeled as 'cheating' just because it can be viewed as immoral. These students might have felt that theirs was not the most virtuous of actions, but if they were told not to do what they did, they might not have done it."

The Greeley administrators retreated when they saw how little support they had from parents. At the beginning of the controversy, the school had threatened to suspend all eight miscreants. That was whittled down to a zero grade, but only on the oral portion of the test. It was a penalty that, not coincidentally, did not significantly affect anyone's final grade.

By the 1990s American teachers had grown accustomed to such compromises, another reason for them not to take firm stands on ethics. Henry Gradillas, who had run both inner-city and suburban schools in California, described a corrosive routine. The teacher gave the cheater a zero on the test. The parents complained to the principal, who tried to ease the tension with a compromise—perhaps half credit or a chance for the child to retake the test. The teacher felt betrayed and was much less willing to apply firm sanctions next time.

Was it the pressure for top performance at college-crazed high schools that made suburban students prone to cheat? Was it the fault of unscrupulous students or weak-kneed faculty? Danzig blamed it on the lust for sparkling high school transcripts. "Within the Greeley community," he said, "there have always been problems with cheating. The competitive nature of our academic environment almost forces kids to feel that they need to succeed at all costs."

Other students considered this a very thin argument that obscured other motives: teenage sloth and derring-do, laziness mixed with the irresistible urge to see what one could get away with. Mamaroneck student and *Globe* co-editor Debbie Schoeneman said most of the cheating she observed, from copying homework to peeking at answers, had little bearing on the student's grade or chances for college. A friend of hers once missed several mathematics tests and was allowed to take each one during a free period. He sat down with math-oriented friends at the school library, showed them the test, and wrote down their answers. He would have done fine without the help, she said, but he relished the thrill of breaking the rules.

Since there was no way to drain off the hormones that produced such behavior, Schoeneman and her friends, unlike some of their Scarsdale counterparts, preferred to live with it. They wanted no part of a plan that would force teachers to withdraw gestures of trust. Schoeneman occasionally struggled in AP Biology, but she loved the teacher, Barbara LaPine, for letting her take a makeup test alone in the classroom.

The prevalent faculty notion that cheating was little more than an irritating distraction pervaded Mamaroneck's investigation of the AP American History test. Hopkins did not at first report what he had heard. It did not seem to him that anyone had gotten an advantage. The few students who happened to have been involved had begged for help. They had apparently been tipped off only minutes before and had little time to prepare a good answer.

Nevertheless, word of the incident eventually reached Richard Ciotti, the social studies chair. He was told that some students might have peeked at the second section of the test during the first section of the three-hour examination. During the ten-minute break they had allegedly discussed how to handle the civil rights movement question they had seen. Ciotti reported this to Coffey and the administrator in charge of the Post building, Anne Garcia-Marruz. Ciotti asked the two AP U.S. History teachers, Lorna Minor and Kathy Donnison, to look into it.

Minor and Donnison kept a close eye on students when they gave their own tests. They cracked down on miscreants. Once, when Donnison heard a hint of someone copying homework, she swapped files with Minor and discovered two girls, one in each of their classes, had submitted identical essays. Both students were given zeroes.

The two teachers raised the matter of the AP test in their classes and asked that anyone who knew something speak to them afterward. Hopkins told Minor what he had heard. There were other vague accounts, but nothing that pointed a finger at anyone. A *Globe* reporter, David Berkowitz, interviewed student witnesses who said supervision had been light and opportunities for mischief abundant. There was only one proctor, a substitute teacher, in the gym. Talking was allowed during the break. For the free response question to have leaked out, someone would have had to break the seal of the essay booklet during the break, open the booklet, and read the questions. The proctor said he saw nothing of the sort, but there were fifty-three students in the room.

For a week the junior class talked of little else. This was a community where nearly every teenager had a telephone in his or her bedroom. The exchange of accusations and speculation continued well past midnight for several days. Names of possible conspirators were exchanged. Fear mounted that all of their test results would be thrown out, and they would have to take the test again the next year or abandon dreams of 5s, the highest possible AP score, on their transcripts.

In a school district as small and closely knit as Mamaroneck, age groups acquired labels, some dating back to grade school. One class became known as rebels, another was thought to be artistic, another athletic. The class of 1996, Hopkins and Sarlo and their friends, had been known since elementary school as the Little Darlings. They were sweet and polite and conscientious, always doing their homework and never talking back. A cheating scandal would tarnish their halos.

Garcia-Marruz conducted a two-week investigation. She was a slim, energetic woman who had taught French at the highly selective Hunter College High School in Manhattan before coming to Mamaroneck. She called in all fifty-three test takers, one by one, consulting a seating chart of the Post cafeteria as she asked what they had seen or heard. Hopkins told his story again but did not identify anyone. There were no confessions. Garcia-Marruz had no evidence that would allow her to take action against any particular person.

Minor and Donnison, seeing so little evidence of an actual violation, concluded there had not been one. Both of them were seasoned AP watchers with a talent for predicting questions that might be on the test. They had been warning of a civil rights question for several years. Some students, they decided, must have remembered that admonition in the nervous moments before part two and sought some last-minute help in case the question came up. It was a fluke, they thought, not a felony.

Coffey called the Educational Testing Service. The nonprofit corporation was housed in low-slung buildings in the middle of four hundred acres of undulating meadows and scattered woods outside Princeton, New Jersey. ETS officials were accustomed to dealing with cheating accusations, but found it difficult to make their policy toward such incidents understood. They were not in the business of catching criminals. There was no ETS jail to which they could send the guilty. Their only concern was: Had each student been given a fair and equitable chance to show what he or she knew?

If Coffey had had names of the offenders, ETS might have voided the results for those students. But if those same young people had sent in their $72 to take the AP U.S. History test the following year, ETS would have put them on the list, no questions asked. Coffey's information was so vague, with so little significance for the outcome of the test, that they politely told him to forget about it.

He called a meeting of all AP U.S. History students after school. Several dozen wedged themselves into the English department teacher's lounge. Coffey said he wanted to bring the matter to a close. He thanked Garcia-Marruz for her efforts and said no one could produce any hard evidence of what had happened or who had done it. Donnison spoke with passion on the importance of honor in any academic setting and asked them to reflect on their behavior.

The results of the examination were impressive, as usual. AP test scores were 5, 4, 3, 2, or 1, the equivalent of A, B, C, D, and F. Anyone who received a 3, 4, or 5 was usually eligible for college credit. On this test Mamaroneck students had seventeen 5s, eighteen 4s, nine 3s, and nine 2s. Eighty-three percent of the students had passing scores.

At Coffey's urging, a faculty committee drafted a new policy on cheating, short and direct. Cheating was "representing someone else's work as your own." The policy was that "a student who cheats on any class assignment, test, quiz, lab, or project will receive a grade of zero for that work. Parents will be notified and a conference will be held with the unit principal, teacher, student, and parents. . . . A student who has a second incident of cheating in the same course will automatically receive a grade of 50 for the quarter."

Globe reporter Mandi Schweitzer asked teachers and students what they thought of that. Most said they agreed. Schweitzer then illustrated the gap between reality and good intentions. One teacher told Schweitzer how proud and happy she was that she had never encountered any cheating in her class. Schweitzer was only a ninth grader, but even she knew the teacher's confidence was misplaced. She found two students, whom she declined to identify, who said they had cheated on each of the teacher's last three examinations.

Both were very bright, with excellent marks even when they didn't cheat. Why had they done it? "It was just easier," one of them said.

LOOKING DOWN

CHOICES

While Mamaroneck teachers and administrators strive to bring the school's many blessings to every student, some students are treated differently from others. There is nothing unusual about this. American educators have always tailored lessons and lectures to the perceived strengths and interests of their audiences. As a rule, the most obviously ambitious students from the most affluent families have gotten the hardest lessons. Less ambitious students from poorer families have been treated more gently.

The differences have arisen from the kindest motives, but the results have been uneven. Some students have done extraordinary work in classes designed for those with unusual intellectual gifts. Some students have become bored and disenchanted in easier courses designed to save them from allegedly poisonous frustration. The next few chapters examine the split-level character of elite public education and its impact on the assigning of classes, how those classes are taught, and what happens when choices must be made because of tightened budgets.

It took some time for Fitton "Samuel" Telesford, the young immigrant from Panama, to understand what the distinctions at

Mamaroneck meant to him. His mother installed him, by himself, in a single room in a boardinghouse on Mt. Pleasant Avenue, across the street from a liquor store and a laundromat. The rent was $300 a month. His mother's live-in job had no room for him so she saw him only one day a week. He cooked on a hot plate. In September 1992, a month before his fourteenth birthday, he enrolled at Mamaroneck with a feeble command of English, little experience with American social customs, and no previous connection with anyone at the school.

Andrea Yizar, a Panamanian-born counselor, enrolled him in the English as a Second Language (ESL) class. He took a basic mathematics course as well as Health and Physical Education. The football coach coaxed him onto the junior varsity. He was only five-feet-seven, but he had thick, well-muscled thighs and could hit hard.

Classroom acquaintances liked him. He asked to be called Samuel, pronounced "sam-well" in the Spanish fashion. He also answered to Sam or Sammie, and to "Turtle," a nickname from his infancy, when he crawled with great energy. His favorite places were sports fields, restaurants, and his mother's church, a little white building in New Rochelle used by a small Pentecostal denomination, believers in the Bible Way.

School was often difficult. Teachers gave lectures he did not understand. The textbooks were dense. He began to snap at instructors who pushed him to improve. He muttered about the psychic pain inflicted on him by detention room monitors and remedial reading teachers.

The school's response was to assign him to the Choices program, a series of computer-training classes designed for slower students. A counselor told his mother this might be best for a boy unlikely to blossom in Mamaroneck's academic hothouse. She signed the papers. Telesford, respectful of her wishes, went along. The program forced him to drop two afternoon courses, General Science and U.S. History. He boarded a small yellow school bus on the Post Road side of the school each day at 12:15 P.M. for a twenty-minute ride to Port Chester. The same bus brought him back by 3:15.

The Choices facility was full of Apple computers, but Telesford discovered he had little love for it. He had spent enough time in the United States to see that computers were the future, but the program seemed designed for children with learning disabilities. The teachers spoke slowly and repeated themselves often. To Telesford they were as boring as the 40-yard windsprints at football practice. Each afternoon, tapping the keys and struggling to stay awake, he wondered if the course was too easy. Mamaroneck High was difficult, but he thought he was beginning to understand how he might succeed there. He had friends on the football team who had as much trouble in class as he had had.

Michael Roush, then the social studies department chairman, had been the teacher of the afternoon history class that Telesford had been forced to drop. He missed the boy's warm, teasing demeanor. He had once been a rebellious teenager himself, growing up in Kansas, and liked Telesford's ambition. Telesford had been slow to catch on in History, but before he transferred he had been picking up some of the themes of the course and demonstrating some insight in his papers and classroom comments.

One afternoon Roush used a free period to drive to Port Chester and visit Telesford at the Choices facility. Roush noticed that the pace of the computer class was geologic. After a few minutes Telesford confessed that he was sorry to have dropped History. "Why is that?" Roush asked.

The boy had figured out the system. Like every high-achieving high school, Mamaroneck let some students slide through. New York was the only state with a long history of subject-area tests for high school graduation, but it was a race with very low hurdles. The most difficult examinations were the Regents examinations, which an average Mamaroneck student could pass without much effort. Below that were the Regents Competency Tests (RCTs), about as challenging as a seventh grade midterm.

Telesford was being asked to take none of those. If he stayed with the Choices program, he would receive a non-Regents diploma. It would allow him to participate in graduation and enroll at Westchester Community College, but he would have to do well there before any university would accept him. The Choices administrators hoped their graduates would find clerical work, although such jobs were not always available.

"I want to take courses that will make me get my regular diploma," Telesford said.

Roush said he would see what he could do. He asked Telesford if he understood this would mean extra years at Mamaroneck. The boy nodded.

Olga Telesford said she wanted what her son wanted, and signed the papers returning him to the regular program. To help him concentrate on his studies, she found a job that did not require her to live with her employers. She moved the two of them into a two-story wood-frame rooming house, also on Mount Pleasant Avenue in the commercial district. Mother and son were stuffed with all their belongings into a fifteen-by-twelve-foot bedroom that rented for $400 a month. The space was almost completely filled by their twin beds, two chests of drawers, clothes hanging on open racks, and a broken television set sitting atop a broken VCR. For some human companionship Telesford was willing to sacrifice his privacy at a time when adolescents craved it most, even if he had to sleep in the same room as his mother.

Wanting to be cautious, Telesford's advisers enrolled him in Team 9's new ninth grade English and social science course. He would be among freshmen, but the teachers were good and, Roush thought, imaginative enough to keep him engaged. The state of New York did not ask the level of English courses he took, as long as he took four years of English. He planned to repeat American History the following year and complete his graduation requirements the year after that.

Without Roush's personal intervention, Telesford would have likely been off the academic track permanently, with everyone involved thinking it was best for him. Returning to the main campus did not ensure he would escape further well-meaning negligence. Easy paths were also available to Mamaroneck students who spoke English fluently and had no ethnic disadvantages to speak of.

GRAPHIC ILLUSTRATION

Joy Sarlo strolled into Myron Tannenbaum's Graphics 2/3 class in room B274 of the Post building. Conversation was, as usual for Graphics 2/3, at a feverish pitch. Sarlo traded gossip for a few minutes and then stuck her head out of the window to threaten two ninth graders who were standing near the low brick wall at the front of the school. That was junior class territory and they had to be warned. It was 1:40 P.M. The lesson was supposed have begun ten minutes before.

Mamaroneck's course catalog described Graphics 2/3 this way:

"Venturing into the entire world of today's graphic communications techniques, you will experience computer graphic applications, silk-screen printing, airbrush art, and black-and-white photography. Color separation, offset printing, half-tone technology, and desktop publishing will be some of the projects that will challenge you throughout the graphics arts program."

Room B274 had been Tannenbaum's professional home for twenty-four years. He had a doctorate in education, but treated students as equals and was universally known as Mr. T, or to favorites like Sarlo just T. His equipment was outdated, with no money in the budget to replace it, but during the thirty-five-minute class little of it was used. About fifteen minutes were devoted to instruction in darkroom techniques, during which Tannenbaum demonstrated a way of transferring decals to T-shirts and the pitfalls of poor technique.

The other twenty minutes were spent in happy conversation. Tannenbaum, in a green shop coat, occasionally added a comment. There were only twelve students, but they made a great deal of noise, even when Tannenbaum was trying to present a lesson. They traded insults, planned weekend leisure activities, and discussed clothing purchases.

Five minutes into the class period, Tannenbaum had tried to impose order. "Frank, come on in," he said to a boy lingering in the hall. "We've got a tight schedule today. We got early dismissal."

"Ohmigod," Sarlo said, ignoring Tannenbaum. She spoke to the one of the two other girls in the class. "I tried on Sandy's dress. It looked so good. I don't understand how a hot pink dress can be so awesome."

Sarlo said she loved Tannenbaum. He in turn appreciated her high spirits and often deferred to her in class. She was slim with brown hair and a model's features, as well as athletic skills that made her a star cheerleader and a good lacrosse player. She was socially precocious, with a circle of friends that extended to every classroom and playing field at the school.

She had taken Mr. T's course every year she had been at Mamaroneck. So had her boyfriend, Chris Silo, a wide receiver on the football team. Silo had graduated the year before but was taking an extra year at a private school in Massachusetts in hopes of raising his SAT scores and adding muscle and playing time to win a college athletic scholarship.

The conversation continued at high volume while Tannenbaum went into the darkroom to arrange equipment. Sarlo and her friend Erin Campbell planned their own darkroom experiment. Campbell had bet a tall football player named Frank exactly $1 million that if Sarlo bit into a wintergreen Lifesaver in total darkness it would emit visible sparks.

Graphic and industrial arts and home economics classes had not fared well in the 1980s in the United States, particularly in urban schools with tight budgets. Some principals had done their best to remove both subjects from their curriculums. Shop and home ec, as they were called, appeared to be little more than dumping grounds for students that counselors thought could not handle difficult academic subjects.

At Mamaroneck and other elite schools, the same departments came under financial pressure but most of them survived. At Bellaire High outside Houston, principal Vivian Dailey marked a series of marketing and communication courses for extinction, but the district's assistant superintendent for vocational education overruled her. School board members and superintendents in college-obsessed communities saw such courses as emblems of their concern for the minority of students who did not care about the SAT. If they were a truly diverse school, they argued, then they had an obligation to offer vocational courses, even if they shivered at the thought of their own children enrolling in them.

Interest in such subjects was limited enough at Mamaroneck to allow all the vocational courses to fit in one department with a very long title: technology education, home and career skills, and psychology. Its chairman was Nick Cucchiarella, who had created a sophisticated architectural drafting course and had his own contracting business on the side.

Despite Cucchiarella's large ambitions, courses like Tannenbaum's put little pressure on students to achieve. There were no Regents tests in graphics. Colleges did not pay much attention to the grades Tannenbaum gave his students. No students bothered to seek outside tutoring to make sure their T-shirt designs were better than those of everyone else in the class.

Tannenbaum abhorred the traditional grading system. He thought it put more than enough pressure on his students in their academic subjects. He viewed his class as a respite from SAT chasing and mindless memorization. He wanted to introduce a few useful techniques at a comfortable pace. Sarlo thought this made sense. She wished that some of her other teachers would similarly let her have more time to absorb the subject matter.

In Cliff Gill's sophomore Regents Mathematics class, for instance, she had struggled with his insistence that homework be done on time and that all students maintain a steady pace. In one part of her mind, she knew that she needed to be pushed. At first she had been glad to get Gill. He played the ogre, but she was skilled at slaying dragons. In class she took his outbursts as what they were, bits of theater intended to motivate the meek and entertain the strong. Still, at the end of the first marking period she had a 65, barely passing. She could get through a class without fear, but she could not bluff her way through the complex homework and brain-squeezing tests. Gill listened to no excuses. He called home if you lagged. She did her mathematics homework first every night and then went back over it after doing her other assignments.

When she transferred out of Gill's class and into a non-Regents course, he called her a quitter. That infuriated her, but she noticed that her grade in the new course jumped to a 98. It helped her see how much she had learned in his class and how wide a spectrum of effort and reward the system accommodated.

Tannenbaum, she knew, would give her a good grade if she appeared regularly in class and at least sometimes listened when he spoke. Even if she did not pay much attention to him, she would suffer no penalty. He liked her. He rewarded students who were loyal to him and his neglected corner of the Post building. If she took Graphics again as a senior, she could become his student helper. Her boyfriend Silo had had the job the year before and she hoped to follow in his footsteps.

Tannenbaum was a pleasant man who liked teenagers and gave them enormous license in his classes, handling discipline problems his own way. On this day he managed, just barely, to hold his small audience's attention in the darkroom. "I got to show you a little problem with the project," he said. They were making a pattern for T-shirts bearing the Mamaroneck Tiger symbol, but the color was off.

He held up two alternative designs. "Which one is easier to do, guys?" he asked.

"Joe," he said to a student. "Set the camera for 5000/5000."

While Tannenbaum and the student adjusted the equipment,

the wintergreen experiment began. The sparks were not evident as Sarlo bit into the Lifesaver, but Campbell insisted she had seen something. She demanded her $1 millon.

Tannenbaum demonstrated how the different logos were reproduced. He remarked on the superior contrast in one sample. "That is the one that did work and the other is the one that didn't work, and we're going to find out why," he said.

"See this?" he said, holding up one logo. "Complete disaster." In the corner of the darkroom, the wintergreen argument continued, though softly.

"Make it 200 on both sides," Tannenbaum said.

"It's still too dark," Joe said.

"That's okay, because it's two colors the camera can film."

He encouraged the students to crowd closer and inspect the products. The noise level in the small room jumped as the wintergreen debate broke out again and other conversations resumed.

Tannenbaum watched as some of his students studied the equipment. He smiled at the noise. He assured me that such conviviality did not bother him. It was part of growing up in a town like Mamaroneck, where he also lived. "These kids have been together since they were little," he said.

He went back to the equipment and held up another sample. "Now we have done it again, and it is better," he said. "The problem we are having is very obvious. We can't separate the colors." He called several students by name to come up and look.

The bell rang. The darkroom door opened. The group filed out. There was no homework assignment. Sarlo and Campbell headed for their lockers. They found the few books they needed for other classes and headed home, the end of a busy day.

TRIMMING ORCHIDS

Mike Roush, promoted in 1995 to assistant principal in charge of curriculum, was proud of Mamaroneck's offerings. The school had 175 courses, including explorations of music arranging, the Lotus spreadsheet program, personnel management, New York City cultural attractions, sports fiction and nonfiction, jewelry making, Latin for the purpose of increasing English vocabulary, child psychology, forensic science, oceanography, gender issues in literature and history, architectural drawing on full-color computers, original scientific research, fashion design, television studio production, clay sculpture and ceramics, quest literature, and the films of Chaplin, Welles, Hitchcock, Lang, and Allen. Some critics called such variety the "shopping mall" approach to education. But Roush thought the rich choice intrigued students and energized faculty. It made parents feel their children were going off each morning to the equivalent of a small university. So when he was asked to trim the list, it was difficult to decide what to discard.

Other schools of Mamaroneck's caliber had similarly thick course catalogs. The lists of courses had grown in part because elite schools pushed so many students ahead of the usual high school pace and added so many periods to the day that they needed more courses to keep students occupied and interested. The catalogs also expanded because many teachers and administrators felt the core academic courses were too demanding and likely to break the spirit of students they considered ill equipped, by virtue of IQ or family background, to handle them. Thus soft electives like Graphics 2/3 remained and sometimes multiplied.

At Mamaroneck the more demanding part of the system produced students like Dan Hopkins, who was intensely interested in politics, international relations, science, and philosophy. On Saturday mornings he and his friends Justin Stein and John Halket drove down the Henry Hudson Parkway to Columbia University for two and a half hours of lectures on relativity, quantum mechanics, lasers, and optics. He attended Mamaroneck's Russian Academy on Tuesday and Thursday nights. And since the cream of the Mamaroneck course catalog was not enough for him, he began to arrange his own curriculum.

His sophomore Global Studies teacher David Stearns urged him to read a few history journals and think about preparing a scholarly paper for publication in the *Concord Review,* which specialized in student work. With the help of Stearns and AP American History teacher Lorna Minor, he scoured the Mamaroneck High and Larchmont libraries for the early work of the anti-Federalists who had constructed the Second Amendment. He then took the modern argument for the unconstitutionality of gun control laws and gently dismembered it, a limb at a time. He noted several court cases and commentary: *U.S.* v. *Cruikshank* 1876, *Presser* v. *Illinois* 1886, *Miller* v. *Texas* 1894, the report of the President's Commission on Law Enforcement and Administration of Justice 1965, the Gun Control Act of 1968.

He chided the author of a 1968 *National Review* piece for failing to quote the amendment's first clause, "A well regulated Militia, being necessary to the security of a free state. . . ." "The issue of crime is a modern issue," Hopkins said. "The Founding Fathers did not see the armed citizenry as a vehicle for crime prevention. And as this use of firearms was not considered an area where the federal government might encroach on the rights of its citizens, the

Founding Fathers probably would have omitted it even if crime had been an issue."

The paper was balanced, nuanced, thick with footnotes. It was fit to submit to any college Government course and had taken more time than the total amount of homework assigned in any of the lower-level Social Studies courses Hopkins had had. Yet it had been written with no course credit in mind. It represented the best of what a multilayered, well-funded public school could do, and showed how much difference there was in the expectations for Stearns's and Minor's history students and Tannenbaum's Graphics students.

There was no question that Roush's course-trimming work would have to make choices related to income and culture, the first-class courses for college-bound kids versus the second-class courses for the less ambitious. But in Roush's office on the Palmer building main corridor, where he kept a schedule board with course names written in different colors of marking pen, it seemed more complicated than that.

The largest class in the school was Russian History and Literature, a yearlong session for juniors and seniors team taught by George Ehrenhaft and Don Phillips. It had two sections, thirty-six students in first period and thirty-four in fifth. The smallest class was Frank Aiello's Basic Math course, just eight students. Aiello was the mathematics department chair. He created the course as a safety net for those who could not handle the algebra courses he wanted all first-year students to take. As the year went on, Roush and Aiello expected Basic Math's size to double as it absorbed casualties from algebra.

In normal times, and in most schools of this caliber, Roush would not have had to worry much about undersubscribed courses. But a narrow victory for the school budget in 1993 had changed the atmosphere. The school board's complaints about too many small, exotic courses had forced last-minute cancellations in the summer of 1994. The counselors had torn up their master schedule, causing heartburn and raised voices in faculty lounges. Coffey did not want that to happen again. He told Roush to set up a meeting in spring 1995 to clear the curricular underbrush before the new schedule was set.

In April Roush and Coffey met in the third-floor conference room near the principal's office with two school board members, including Oberg, and Ron Benizio, the veteran Palmer building principal. Because of the school's odd architecture, Mamaroneck had two administrators, the Post building principal and the Palmer building principal, serving under Coffey and responsible for maintenance, security, discipline, and other matters in their respective halves of the school.

Roush had a list of twelve courses for the fall 1995 term in which fewer than a dozen students had enrolled. Coffey wanted the committee to reach agreement on which should go and which should stay. If the cancellation of a course became an issue at a school board meeting or on the parent-student-faculty grapevine, they would at least have some mutual understanding of why they had done what they had done.

From the perspective of most American high schools, the Mamaroneck conferees were lords of a vast estate arguing over nothing more troublesome than the slaughter of a few diseased sheep. Even if the school had to cancel a few courses, its average class size of about twenty remained a source of envy, and several classes had fewer students than that. The Chinese language program rarely had more than a dozen in a section. Some of the higher-level mathematics courses, as well as Aiello's Basic Math, were very small.

Scholars of pedagogy once had lively debates about class size, but by the 1980s they had moved on to other things. Several studies, including landmark work by Gene V. Glass and Mary Lee Smith, had concluded that reducing the number of students in a class might have a modest effect on achievement, but only if the number could be pushed down to fifteen or below, where a single teacher might reasonably have time to work with each individual child. Few schools were likely to be able to afford such a student-teacher ratio unless they discovered oil under their basketball courts. Many university researchers responded to class-size questions by reflex: Changing the size of the class did not change achievement much, they said. Teachers had to learn how to manage better the class sizes they had.

This did not make much sense to teachers. They saw even a one-child reduction in class size as a chance to spend more time with the others. Many were delighted when new research appeared to support them, particularly the Student/Teacher Achievement Ratio project—Project STAR—in Tennessee. The four-year, $3 million study concluded that the smaller-class students outscored their larger-class friends on standardized tests. Poor inner-city children appeared to receive the greatest gains from the smaller class size, though the suburban and rural pupils also saw gains that seemed to hold up as the years went by.

The researchers said they were not certain such marginal size reductions would have as much impact in high schools. Individual attention had more impact on the very young, unresentful minds found in elementary schools. But the theory that students did better when there were fewer of them in each class seemed proven, and was an obvious source of strength for schools like Mamaroneck.

Mamaroneck courses with less than twelve students were, nonetheless, in trouble. The conferees quickly canceled three English courses on the undersubscribed list: British Literature, Sports Literature, and Holocaust Literature. British Lit had been offered several times in the past, but American Literature, Russian Literature, and AP English had lured away most of the juniors and seniors. Sports Lit and Holocaust Lit were new offerings that had not attracted enough students.

A general science course was dropped, a victim of a campaign to push reluctant freshmen into Regents Earth Science and Biology. Italian 3 was cut for attracting only three students, not surprising in a department that already offered French, Spanish, Russian, Chinese, and Latin. An Art History course also lost out, a casualty of a shift of students to Advanced Placement Studio Art.

In the business department, a course on marketing and a course on the Lotus computer software were dropped for lack of interest. The conferees also cut courses devoted to music theory, publications, food for fitness, and interior design.

There were few arguments about the decisions. The students had many alternatives. The only debate came at the end of the two-hour meeting when an Advanced Placement course was discussed. No school that wished to be known as a conduit to the *U.S. News and World Report* best colleges list would ever cut an AP course without a great deal of thought. And this was not just any AP course: It was Chemistry. Some Mamaroneck and Larchmont parents had the incorrect but nevertheless strong impression that their children would not be admitted to the premed program at any major university if they had not taken this course.

AP Chem had always been small. It was one of the most challenging courses in the catalog. Some years enrollment approached twenty students. Other years, like 1995, it dropped to a dozen. It was not clear why. Some medically inclined teenagers had apparently decided that their high school transcripts would look fine with just AP Biology. The portion of students passing the Biology test under teacher Barbara LaPine was a phenomenal 97 percent. Biology demanded less analytical skill in exchange for heavy memorization, easy for many Mamaroneck students. Those who wanted to become doctors knew they were going to have to endure one or two organic chemistry courses in college anyway. Why make themselves miserable in high school too?

The conferees knew that if they erased AP Chemistry they were guaranteed angry telephone calls, not only from the twelve students who had enrolled but from younger brothers and sisters and friends and their parents who would see this as a sign of curricular dry rot. Perhaps some irritated parents would call real estate agents in Chappaqua. Oberg had captured the community attitude aptly when Team 9 had presented the Sizer argument for fewer, deeper courses—"Less is more." "At Mamaroneck," she had said, "more is more."

The counterargument was also compelling. This was a school district proud of its diversity. How could they cut courses like Interior Design that energized a few children who otherwise did not like school, and at the same time save a course designed for Larchmont's future internists and oncologists? The college-bound students had more Advanced Placement and science options than they had time for. Why should the chairs always be arranged for their comfort?

Roush thought it was an equity issue. The conferees were taking away low-enrollment occupational courses and Sports Lit, say-

ing there was not enough student interest to justify them, and pro-
tecting an AP course. A kid was a kid. Learning was learning.
Were some people more equal than others in deciding what survived and what did not?

The committee members were all sympathetic to Roush's view.
They tossed AP Chemistry gently back and forth, a small bomb
with a hair trigger. The discussion ended where everyone expected
it would, no loud dissent, no surprises. Eleven courses were cut
from the schedule. AP Chemistry survived, with twelve students
enrolled. Mamaroneck might have flaws, but it was not going to
drop a course that served its principal clientele, no matter how few
of them might need it.

FLOORS AND CEILINGS

Linda Sherwood had to speak at Parents'
Night and she was concerned. Some parents had expressed doubts
about Team 9 mixing students of different speeds and motivations.
She anticipated many questions.

She thought Team 9 was reaching the point where it had to
overcome the historical tendencies of its school—different courses
and different expectations for different students—or surrender to
them. There had been far less parental resistance to Team 9 than
expected, little more than complaints about the summer reading
cutting into vacations, but Mamaroneck veterans had learned to
hedge their bets. The task had fallen to Team 9's youngest and least
experienced member to confront the issue directly at the largest
parent gathering of the year.

Sherwood had grown up in Mamaroneck. Her father had managed a bowling alley for many years, then finished high school and
college and became a computer programmer for Metropolitan
Life. Her mother worked as an office manager in New York City.
Sherwood had gone to the Academy of the Resurrection, a
parochial school in Rye, but by her freshman year in high school
found herself longing for something more. A teacher had awak-

ened in her an interest in literature, and her initial contacts with colleges indicated she had to strengthen her course load. Ten blocks from her home was Mamaroneck High School, with every course imaginable. Why not transfer? Her parents were skeptical. They did not like her moving beyond the orbit of their friends and family. She was insistent. A college counselor told them she would have a better chance of admission to a good college if she were enrolled at a better high school.

She switched in her junior year. She failed to win election to the football cheerleading squad, the price she paid for being a new girl, but by winter she was on the basketball cheerleading squad and plowing through the curriculum. She was pretty and gregarious. She made friends in every social category—Catholic, Jewish, Protestant, rich and poor.

She could not afford to go to anything but a state school, so she spent two years at the State University of New York (SUNY) Albany. She had fun, and matured a bit before transferring to Pace University in Westchester. There she studied seriously. She earned a master's degree at Columbia's Teachers College and worked as a researcher in a real estate appraisal office. An appraiser in the office, Steve Sherwood, told a friend, "I'm going to marry her," and he did.

They had two children. Her parents wanted a smaller place, and turned their house over to Linda and Steve. As Sherwood's children, Steven and Kayla, approached school age, she felt she was ready to go back to school too.

There was a one-class-a-day part-time opening in the Mamaroneck English department. She was the youngest of the twenty applicants, but Ehrenhaft liked her verve and intelligence. Coffey agreed to hire her. Her age was to her advantage. Most of the English teachers were in their forties and fifties. Coffey agreed with many parents that the school needed new blood.

Students took to Sherwood immediately. Some of them were the younger brothers and sisters of her own school friends. They did not seem very different from the students she knew when she was a student at Mamaroneck, except that the socially adept girls were now almost all sexually active, and their mothers knew it.

Children frustrated by the academic demands of a school catering to colleges came to her for help. The girls in particular used her as a confidante and, in a way, as a cheerleader. She told them about their hidden talents. She assured them the work was not as difficult as it seemed. She tried to give them a taste of the excitement in learning she had felt when she was their age.

Many other faculty members shared her distaste for the elitist character of honors classes and the often mediocre offerings for the less motivated or less prepared. Teachers with Ivy League degrees, like Ehrenhaft and Jon Murray, were just as determined as those from Catholic and state schools like Restaino and Ahearn to see how far children from noncollege families could go. They loathed remedial labels and low standards. The fewer levels there were, they thought, the more challenges.

Frank Aiello bridled at the pedagogical snobbery he encountered in the mathematics department. One of the calculus teachers openly dismissed the notion of teaching any lower-level course. Another teacher said to him, "I teach math, but don't ask me to teach a kid how to multiply." Aiello thought the mathematics he had taught in middle school was more important than anything his transcript-padding high school students would learn. He recalled the scene in the film *Peggy Sue Got Married* when actress Kathleen Turner, caught in a time warp, finds herself back in high school. In the middle of an obtuse algebra lesson she raises her hand. "Excuse me," she says, "but I have to say something. I know for a fact that you are never going to use this stuff when you grow up."

Teaching bright kids calculus was a snap, Aiello thought. Real teaching was getting the Italian kid from the Flats, a child like he had once been, to appreciate probabilities and estimation and be able without hesitation to add, subtract, multiply, and divide.

Unfortunately, few teachers had discovered how to serve both motivated and unmotivated students in the same class. Josh Hafetz, a member of the class of '95 who would go to Princeton, had been in several mixed-ability classes. He knew why so many of his friends were uncomfortable in them. In his sophomore Global Studies course the teacher, Nina Hurwitz, sister of future CIA director John Deutch, had to pry responses out of students who did not care about European geography. When she asked about Bosnia or Northern Ireland or Sicily, Hafetz was usually the only one to raise his hand. He read *The New York Times* each day. Several of his friends did the same. But they were sprinkled into classes full of MTV watchers. Some days he wondered if he was the only student in the class who read any daily newspaper at all.

As he grew older and encountered other courses, he began to realize he had misread the problem. It was not aptitude but attitude. Several classmates he would not have guessed were interested in current affairs did keep themselves current, often through television. The difficulty was they did not like speaking in class. They had the usual adolescent reasons. They did not want to look pushy. They did not want to risk the public embarrassment of being wrong.

Hafetz saw this in English teacher Mike DiGennaro's film class. He took the course because he was enthralled with movies and had dreams of being a screenwriter. He assumed the seniors with dim academic reputations were hoping for an easy B, but he discovered he was wrong. Many knew the film world as well as he did. They participated in class discussions and provided more insight and enthusiasm than he would have expected.

Sherwood thought such connections between A students and C students were being made in Team 9's classrooms, but she knew that many parents did not appreciate that. Some of them assumed that if a course was not divided into three ability levels, it was not giving their children proper stimulation.

Sherwood wanted to explain that Team 9 was seeking a middle way between the pro-ability groupers and the anti-ability groupers, something that experts like Joseph S. Renzulli of the Center for Talent Development at the University of Connecticut had been seeking for some time. He was a pro-ability grouper, but he praised Robert Slavin, an anti-ability grouper, for a proposal that sounded very much like what Team 9 was doing. Slavin said special projects that created excitement in honors classes could do the same for nonhonors students.

Jeannie Oakes, the UCLA professor leading the anti-ability grouping forces, suggested mobilizing the parents of lower-track students to change the system. This, she thought, was one way to counter the lack of generosity among the upper-track parents to whom Sherwood was going to have to aim her remarks. At one school Oakes studied, a special teacher paid by a gifted-students program adopted a plan similar to Ehrenhaft's, offering special projects to nongifted students who asked for them. The gifted-student parents reacted as if the teacher were stealing their children's lunches and giving them to beggars. One said, "It is our children that are generating this money. How dare you spend any time with these other children?"

Sherwood and Esposito faced two hundred parents at two different sessions that night in the Palmer cafeteria. Esposito spoke at the first session. He discussed the rationale behind the team's approach to literature and how social studies meshed with English. He was swamped with questions about how children would earn the advanced designation, the mark placed on their transcripts for special projects. Parents asked if the team approach was sufficiently challenging to the fastest students. Sherwood had to address the second session, due to start in six minutes. She had a few notes, but no clear idea of what she wanted to say. She resolved to go with her heart and let the rest take care of itself.

The sight of parents jammed into the room made her feel more comfortable, in a way. They were like her, pleased that their children had an opportunity to go to a splendid school and yet aware it was run by human beings. She began by telling them how much she was enjoying their children and how much they reminded her of her own two. She was intrigued by the differing rates of Steven's and Kayla's development. Had her audience noticed the same with their kids? "When children are just one and a half, some are crawling, some are walking, and some are running around the house," she said. "Some can't wait for the door to open so they can take off and soar across the yard.

"In the same way they don't develop at the same level at eighteen months, they don't develop the same way when they're fourteen years old," she said.

She explained Team 9's curriculum and the menu that gave each student a chance to choose from a list of research topics.

They could choose the regular program or, if they wanted to do in-depth work, the advanced designation. "It is like teaching them to walk," she said. "We build the floor, and we support the students there and talk to them a great deal. We teach them and encourage them, that is what we are doing.

"Some of them crawl across the floor with our help and support and encouragement, and some of them will walk across it with confidence, and others will need to soar," she said. She showed the parents the assignment sheet with the suggested extra work for the advanced designation. She did not go into great detail. That was where she thought Esposito had faltered; she wanted to make a larger point.

"We have built the floor," she said, sweeping her arm up, "but we have removed the ceiling. Those who want to soar, we give them all the room they need. . . . As you all know, you can't force a child to walk when they're not ready, and you also can't stop them once they are ready."

Her hands were shaking a bit, but she saw no unpleasant stares. Ahearn told her he had liked it. She was happy it was over and she could go home.

The next day Coffey stopped her in the hall. He had been getting telephone calls about her talk. Other compliments rolled in. She was driving to work when Peter Berendt, the unit principal for the Post building, spotted her as they stopped at a red light. He rolled down his window. "I just wanted to tell you," he said. "I got phone calls from parents. I heard you were spectacular on Parents' Night."

She thanked him and drove on to work, wondering if she would be able to teach the lesson to her students as well as she had promoted it with their parents.

MEASURING STICKS

A NEW TEST

Elite public high schools offer a number of statistics as evidence of their success. If they can show that more than 70 percent of their graduates go on to four-year colleges, or more than 5 percent of their seniors win National Merit citations, or at least a dozen or so each year are admitted to an Ivy League college, their status is secure. The Scholastic Assessment Test (SAT) is also a favorite measure. Schools whose students average above 1100 make parents very happy.

The next few chapters explore the nature of such measuring devices, and the sometimes false assumptions behind them. To begin with, none of the tests commonly used to define elite schools directly reflects the quality of classroom learning. The SAT is an arithmetic, vocabulary, and reading comprehension test. It addresses topics most test takers encounter before the ninth grade. What they have learned in high school is largely irrelevant to doing well on the SAT.

As a consequence, many educators in the last two decades have come to rely on a much less well known byproduct of the rise in college enrollment, the Advanced Placement (AP) test. It not only measures what has been taught but appears to inspire low-income students and provide a means of comparing the values and standards of one school or one student to another. AP has its flaws. It leaves little room for teacher choice of subject matter and often disrupts the senior year, but as a rallying banner for educators who want all schools, not just the richest ones, to perform at high, measurable standards, it has begun to come into its own.

In 1997 the College Board's AP program offered thirty-one different tests in eighteen disciplines, from art history to statistics. Like the SAT, it is a three-hour examination given mostly to high school juniors and seniors. Unlike the SAT, it measures what has been learned in high school classes, taught with the depth and pace of introductory college courses. More than 2,900 colleges and universities gave course credit for a grade of 5, 4, or 3 (the equivalent of a college A, B, or C) on an AP test, allowing students to save on tuition costs.

It is difficult to overemphasize the impact the AP program has had on high-achieving schools. In 1996 at Mamaroneck, 250 students, about a quarter of the student body, took 344 AP tests. The tests are principally responsible for a marked increase in the rigor of high school courses, as well as a sharp change in the rhythm of the school year and the rules for deciding who will be allowed into challenging courses and who will not.

It is not surprising to find that AP has such influence on Mamaroneck, given that the program was designed for elite schools. What is unexpected is how much nonelite schools have achieved by applying the same rigorous national standard.

The impetus for AP came at the turn of the century. The deans of Harvard College noticed that some of their freshmen had had such good prep school instruction that many introductory college courses bored them. A special examination was designed to determine which incoming freshmen might skip courses in certain fields. The test sites were revealing. Students could take the test in Cambridge, Massachusetts, where the university was located; Quincy, Massachusetts, an exclusive Boston suburb; or Paris, France, where many fortunate eighteen-year-olds spent their fathers' money on summer tours of the Continent.

Other colleges tried the idea, but it did not spread far. After

World War I, American educators focused on bringing the majority of American children into the public high school system. They had no time for special tests for bankers' children.

During World War II many universities designed crash courses for military personnel. The administrators were surprised at how quickly these uniformed students absorbed advanced science and foreign languages. After the war the schools began to experiment again with accelerated education, particularly after the Cold War persuaded administrators that the Soviets were surpassing Americans in the classroom. One of the most radical efforts was the Korean War–era preinduction scholarship, backed by the Ford Foundation's Fund for the Advancement of Education. Talented high school sophomores skipped their last two years of high school and entered college in order to get at least two years of a university education before being drafted. Twelve colleges participated, including Yale, Columbia, the University of Wisconsin, and the University of Chicago. At first the program was reserved for boys, but when regulations changed to protect undergraduates from the draft, girls were added.

As Scarsdale social studies teacher Eric Rothschild notes in his history of the AP program, this was not a universally popular idea. High school principals and superintendents detested colleges stealing their best students. The executive secretary of the National Association of Secondary School Principals called it "a bomb dropped on secondary education." High schools searched for ways to keep their brightest students so engaged they would not be tempted to leave early.

Harlan P. "Harpo" Hanson, later head of the College Board's AP program, became an assistant dean at Harvard shortly after the Korean War ended. He and his friends at other campuses had noticed a slump in achievement and motivation among many first-year college students, similar to what their predecessors had seen a half century before. Many students from elite high schools found their first-year college classes were plowing old ground. Their secondary schools had already given them extensive reading in historical documents and relativity theory and calculus and the works of Baldwin, Beckett, and Camus.

In May 1954 students from twenty-seven public and private secondary schools took the first experimental advanced placement tests, designed by ETS. The high school students did as well on the tests as freshmen at twelve colleges who had completed introductory courses. College professors began to write examinations in several subjects for the College Board. The effort acquired so much momentum, Rothschild notes, that even skeptics such as Charles R. Keller joined in.

Keller taught history at Williams College and was one of the original authors of the AP American History examination that became the centerpost of Rothschild's teaching career. Keller wrote his first AP test only a year after he tried to mount a revolt against the very notion of national examinations for high schools. The tests were an insult to local schools, he had said. High school faculties would be better off organizing themselves to certify the excellence of their students and persuade the colleges to accept that on faith. Asked about his rapid conversion, Keller pleaded abject pragmatism: "I thought things over, decided that since, no matter what, there was going to be a history examination, I might just as well be on hand to help work it out."

For a long time after its birth, AP was drenched in the scent of ivy-covered walls and sherry in the common room. It operated in a corner of American education so remote that on its tenth birthday the vast majority of American high school students—including me, then just graduated from Hillsdale High School in San Mateo, California—not only did not have access to the test but had never heard of it.

The College Board officials who run the program today do not like hearing it called elitist. In their 1996 AP guide they offer a rejoinder: "To insist that all students be exposed to the same curriculum appears unfair to those who have already learned it, as well as those who are not ready to learn it. Recognizing the differences in student preparation and motivation is realism, not elitism."

Nonetheless, AP program administrators cannot deny their test was originally designed to relieve the ennui of a few bright high school seniors in extremely wealthy or competitive schools. The one hundred four secondary schools who participated in the first official AP examinations in May 1956 included Andover, Exeter, Groton, Deerfield, and Cranbrook. Among public schools on the list were New Trier and the Bronx High School of Science.

At the beginning of the AP program, the College Board agreed that every AP test would be open to any student who wanted to take it. The College Board directors did not want high schools to think they could not participate if their students did not trace their lineage back to the Pilgrims. Some educators, however, thought opening the door so wide was pointless. Few expected AP to move beyond its privileged domain. One Harvard admissions officer guessed that one hundred twenty high schools might eventually participate. Hanson loved a wager and went out on a limb—he predicted the program would someday reach two hundred twenty schools.

Four decades later, AP is installed in almost twelve thousand schools—more than half of all the high schools in the country. In 1996, 843,423 AP tests were taken by 537,428 students. This is only 9 percent of high school juniors and seniors but recent history suggests there will be much more growth. Another program, the International Baccalaureate (IB), has brought its series of challenging courses and examinations to 299 American and Canadian schools. IB schools often encourage students to take AP examinations too, allowing the programs to stimulate each other.

One of the distinguishing features of the AP test is that, unlike the SAT, it must be graded in part by human beings. The first half of the test is multiple choice, scored by machines. The second half is free-response questions. Students write out their answers, usually in longhand with ballpoint pens. Their work is scored at summer reading sessions on college campuses where the scorers, high school and college teachers, combine elements of a turn-of-the-century sweatshop and a fraternity weekend.

AP has radically altered the school calendar at some elite schools. At Scarsdale so many seniors were left with so little to do after the mid-May AP examinations and so many other students seemed to yearn for out-of-school experiences that the school decided to excuse all seniors from further classes. They were enrolled instead in a senior options program, devised by a group of teachers led by Howard Rodstein with the support of Principal Judy Fox. The seniors could pursue internships at schools, businesses, and hospitals and give reports on their experiences, or take seminar courses on topics not found in the school catalog. Other schools designed their own option programs, but many resented having to adjust their calendars so radically for an AP program they did not control. Larry Breen, an assistant principal at Greeley, said he thought his faculty could create courses just as good, if not better, than the AP, and not have to shut down half the school in mid-May.

Despite the complaints and the growth in the fee ($73 for each test in 1997, or $51 for low-income students), demand for AP has continued to increase. Many of the new test takers are from schools in low-income neighborhoods, a trend that Hanson discerned in the 1980s and tried to accelerate. In 1987 Claire Liszt of the Mellon Foundation suggested a program to turn minority teachers into AP leaders. She offered a $250,000 two-year grant, followed by several extensions. Hanson and his colleague Phil Arbolino set up AP Summer Teaching Institutes for sixty minority and female instructors, eventually expanded to one hundred fifty a year.

Hollywood provided a boost with the 1988 release of *Stand and Deliver,* the only feature film ever to use a College Board examination as a central dramatic device. The movie told the story of Jaime Escalante, a Bolivian immigrant who installed an AP Calculus program at Garfield High School in East Los Angeles in 1978. The school was more than 95 percent Hispanic, its students the children of Mexican immigrants who had dropped out of elementary school. It seemed an unlikely place to introduce AP, but Escalante persisted. Accusations of cheating in 1982 gave him an unexpected burst of publicity. ETS suggested that fourteen of the eighteen Escalante students who took the AP calculus test that year had copied their answers. Twelve of the fourteen retook the test in difficult circumstances—they had just a weekend to review with no textbooks available. They passed again, confirming the strength of Escalante's program.

By 1987 he had 129 students taking the test, more than every

other high school in the country except two New York City selec-
tive-admission schools, Stuyvesant and Bronx Science; Alhambra
High, a suburban Los Angeles County school with a majority of
mathematics-conscious Asian American students; and Phillips
Academy at Andover. The film portrayed ETS and its staff as chilly
bureaucrats, unwilling to accept the notion that poor Mexican
American students could do so well on a test designed for prep
schools. But to the surprise of many at ETS headquarters, the film
became one of its most effective promotional devices. If barrio
children could successfully conquer AP calculus, why couldn't
everyone? Interest in AP began to grow exponentially. Arbolino
enlisted both Escalante and his principal at Garfield, Henry
Gradillas, as frequent College Board consultants and speakers
at national conferences, AP workshops, and Summer Teaching
Institutes.

The AP test became popular in Midwestern high schools
where the SAT had not made a dent because of the strength of the
competing American College Test (ACT) examination. South Carolina, Indiana, and Virginia passed laws requiring schools to offer
AP courses whenever students asked for them. South Carolina
agreed to pay the AP test fees for all students. Florida, Indiana,
Kentucky, and Minnesota passed substantial fee-subsidy laws.
New Mexico, Texas, and Wisconsin paid fees for poor students beyond the subsidy granted by the College Board. State programs
paid for teacher training in many states. California, South Carolina, West Virginia, and Wisconsin required that state universities
accept AP grades of 3 or higher for college credit or advanced
placement.

Almost all American colleges eventually agreed to accept AP
credit. Studies showed the high school courses were the equivalent
of college courses and had some advantages over the university environment. A college introductory history course meeting twice a
week had only ninety class sessions a year. A high school AP history
course meeting four or five times a week had twice as many. College
students listened passively to lectures in large halls and had to attend section meetings if they wanted feedback. AP students met in
classrooms with usually no more than twenty-five other students

and had to respond to teacher demands for answers and arguments nearly every day. College students were often required to take only a midterm and a final examination and perhaps write a paper or two. AP students were given weekly quizzes and asked to write many short essays in preparation for the AP test's document-based questions (DBQs), the heart of the free-response section.

Several urban schools adopted Escalante's methods. They drilled their AP classes as if they were football teams preparing for the homecoming game. San Antonio's Southside High, Phoenix's Tolleson High, Washington's Woodrow Wilson Senior High, and Chicago's Whitney Young Magnet High made AP participation a goal for every child in the school.

There were still AP critics. The test had the virtue of measuring the results of actual instruction, but some teachers thought it also retained the weaknesses of standardized tests. Dale Roberts, an AP English teacher at Carolina Day School in Asheville, North Carolina, wrote in the February 1995 *Teacher Magazine* that even though multiple-choice questions took up only 45 percent of the English AP test, that was still too much for him. He said the questions were often shallow and penalized bright students who saw complexities that the test designer—trying to distinguish good students from poor ones—did not want them to see. The two hours of the test given to writing essays was not long enough, Roberts said. He quoted Truman Capote: "That's not writing—that's typing." He suggested the test be scrapped in favor of portfolios of each student's best work, certified by his or her teacher. He cited a precedent: The AP Studio Art examination was already administered by portfolio.

An opinion piece in *ism,* the independent school management magazine, agreed that AP had flaws but said the program had become too powerful a marketing device to cast aside. "The offering of AP courses is perceived by parents as the measure of a successful college preparatory school," the article said. "After all, isn't placement in college your goal? Including AP courses in your curriculum (and the number you offer) gives you an edge over much of the competition and, in parents' eyes, is a measure of the excellence of your academic program."

That was too much for some educators. No matter how much AP might motivate students, its use as a merchandising tool for ambitious schools made them see red. They did not want to add to the income of a distant New York nonprofit organization, nor cede to a College Board committee of professors and teachers they did not know important decisions over what they would teach.

A few schools, like Hanover High in Hanover, New Hampshire, went so far as to impose a virtual ban on AP. A school of its size and academic strength would ordinarily give at least one hundred fifty AP tests a year. In 1995 it gave thirteen, mostly in calculus, with a few physics tests. According to Clarke Dustin, the school's guidance director, many students would have been happy to take APs in English, history, and foreign languages, but the departments involved discouraged this and made it possible for students to enroll instead in courses at Dartmouth College just down the street. The students received the requisite taste of a college course. College admissions officers admired their grit. But the Hanover faculty seemed less concerned about the quality of AP than they were about maintaining control over what their students were taught.

If AP maintains its depth and rigor, many educators think it could revitalize thousands of schools. Escalante showed that lower-level courses improved when AP courses were established, if for no other reason than the principal and department heads did not want to be embarrassed by not having enough juniors and seniors prepared for the AP courses.

The problem for elite schools is that as AP sheds its walnut-paneled past, it challenges the snob appeal at the core of such schools' existence. If students at disadvantaged schools like Garfield are being welcomed into AP courses, how could places like New Trier and Scarsdale tell their middle-level students—likely to be as well prepared as other schools' best—that they ought not take AP?

GATEKEEPING

Brian Levite's freshman year at Mamaroneck did not go well. He was more interested in Rollerblading and reading science fiction than he was in mathematics and science. There was some improvement his sophomore year, but his Global Studies course was still a chore.

His junior year, he hoped, would be different. He looked forward to taking AP American History. Despite his slow start, he had a B average and a demonstrated interest in public affairs. His freshman year he was copresident of Mamaroneck's chapter of Junior Statesmen of America (JSA), a club for students intrigued by American politics. The AP History classes were taught by Minor and Donnison, both lively, intelligent instructors. Many of his friends would be there. He was thinking of majoring in political science in college. A good grade in AP American History would be an encouraging start.

But first he had to pass a qualifying test. AP History was very popular. The social studies department liked to keep the class sizes below twenty to assure close attention to each student. The teachers did not want students in the course who were not capable of handling the material. The ninety-minute test was conducted after school in the big Palmer lecture room, D251. Levite had the flu that day. His temperature was 101 degrees.

The test asked the students to answer a document-based question. This was standard for AP History, but Levite had never seen one before. He had forty minutes to review a dozen documents and write about the impact of women and feminism on the French Revolution. He did his best, but his strongest memories of the test were of perspiring heavily and wishing he could leave.

He expected a letter over the summer telling him if he had qualified for AP. It never arrived. Late in August he called the school office. After being passed from one extension to another for a few minutes, he learned that he was scheduled for the regular American History course, not AP. The first day of school he went to see his counselor, who passed him on to Roush, then the social studies department chair.

Roush was polite but unmoved. He said the department did not want to dilute the AP classes with students for whom the heavy load of reading and analysis would be a struggle. That would be unfair, both to the overmatched students and to the others in the class who would have to doodle and daydream while their classmates caught up. Levite's qualifying test results were "disturbing," Roush said, although he did not tell Levite precisely what they were.

Roush said he did not want Levite to think he had no control over his fate, even if it seemed to Levite that that was exactly what he was saying. If Levite still yearned for an AP history course and if he performed well in the regular junior year course, he could take AP European History when he was a senior.

This was gatekeeping—faculty-room jargon for restricting certain courses to the most accomplished students. It occurred at Mamaroneck, although not as commonly as at many other elite schools. A Mamaroneck student with reasonable grades and a thirst for hard work could talk her way into some AP courses, although she risked being treated with skepticism by the teacher and condescension by her classmates.

Many places are more exclusive. My estimate, based on interviews at 75 schools, is that at least 20,000 students a year are denied admission to AP courses at elite public schools in the United States. Access to such courses at less ambitious schools appears in many cases to be even more restricted, although there are also not as many students at such schools eager to work that hard. I estimate that each year at least 100,000 American high school students who would have done well in AP are denied the opportunity to take the course or are not encouraged to enroll.

In the late 1990s, suburban New Jersey's Millburn High School, one of the strongest AP schools in the country, every year turned down several dozen students who wished to take AP courses. Principal Keith Neigel said the policy grew from the school's fear that if too many marginal students took the test, they would lower the school's pass rate and tarnish its reputation with colleges. At Scarsdale, English AP courses were open only to students with strong teacher recommendations. A student who was passed over could demand to be tested, but if he did not score well he was unlikely to be admitted no matter how deep his interest in Byron and Keats.

Scarsdale's AP U.S. History course was also carefully guarded in the face of a flood of applications inspired in part by the presence of Eric Rothschild. He was an inventive, captivating teacher who had been profiled in *The New York Times* and become a national figure in the AP movement. To be considered for his or other sections of AP History, however, students not only had to have excellent teacher recommendations from ninth and tenth grade social studies, but also pass an hourlong test demonstrating their ability to handle analytical work. In 1996 the test asked them to discuss the need for year-round schools and write an essay analyzing either a cartoon critical of President Clinton's Bosnia policy or a chart showing the differing political and social attitudes of New Yorkers of different income groups.

Saying no to eager students bothered Rothschild. For a few years he risked his health and sanity and offered the AP experience to students in the regular history classes. In his spare time he prepared and graded extra essay assignments for them. Just before the examination he held special weekend preparation sessions. One year fifty-one regular History students did the extra work and took the test. They received fifteen 4s, twenty-one 3s, and fifteen 2s.

But Scarsdale refused to open additional AP classes for this overflow. Rothschild and others worried that they could not guarantee top-quality teaching for so many students, and that with eighty-five students already enrolled they risked eroding the college-level quality of the course if they went any deeper into the student talent pool. Each year six or seven students who missed the AP cutoff were bold enough to beg to be let in anyway, and were told no.

The widespread assumption was that an AP course was like fine china, only to be brought out for the best company. A teacher at Blair High School in Pasadena, California, with a mix of high- and low-income students, told me in 1990 that his history department did not offer an AP course because "our kids just aren't up to it." The attitude explained the national attention focused on Escalante, a notorious anti-gatekeeper. He was so contemptuous of prerequisites that once, with just a grunt of assent, he let into calculus a boy who lacked the required second year of algebra and had been warned by his counselor against taking Escalante's class. The student did well in the course, scored a 5 on the examination, and made Escalante even more opposed to curricular obstacle courses.

Escalante's one-man campaign against gatekeeping produced converts. Walter Dewar saw *Stand and Deliver* and could not get it out of his mind. He taught mathematics at Newman Smith High School in Carrollton, Texas, twenty-five miles north of Dallas. He paid his own airfare to Los Angeles in 1988 and videotaped Escalante teaching, then found thirty-seven students at Newman Smith willing to try an accelerated program—both Geometry and Advanced Algebra in tenth grade, then Precalculus as juniors and AP Calculus as seniors.

Dewar and a colleague, Elizabeth Garza, prepared a list of every minority student who had scored an 80 or above in Algebra 1. To each of those students they offered a deal. Join the program, they said, and we will help you. We will create a special one-hour after-school class, Monday through Thursday, during your sophomore year to work on homework and SAT preparation. He discovered girls were susceptible to social lures, such as a calculus night at a local pizza parlor where geometry students could enjoy free food, watch *Stand and Deliver,* and listen to Dewar make a pitch for more students in calculus.

In 1996, 169 Newman Smith calculus students took the AP examinations; 128 earned grades of 3 or above. There were seven 5s on the calculus AB and fifteen 5s on the more difficult calculus BC. Half of the top grades were scored by females. Dewar calculated that his school had more than 10 percent of the girls scoring 5 on the BC in the state of Texas, and more than 10 percent of all the African Americans scoring 3 or above on either of the tests in the state.

At Shaker Heights High, AP access widened in reaction to very different circumstances. Shaker Heights had been a well-known elite school since early in the century. After World War II the Cleveland area population shifted, and Shaker Heights changed from predominantly white to half black and half white. Most of the students of African and of European descent were from middle- and upper-class families, although a small portion of the blacks lived in a low-income section of Cleveland that was part of the Shaker Heights school district.

When Jack Rumbaugh became principal, he noticed that many students, particularly from black families, were being allowed to slide through with few challenging courses. One way to stop this, he thought, was to double the number of students in AP. Like Dewar, he tried to stimulate interest in mathematics in the ninth grade, and bumped against the hard outer shell of American teen culture. For many students, black or white, it was not fashionable to appear to love school. African American teenagers who did all their homework and participated in class were particularly vulnerable. Some of their black friends could not resist teasing them for what they called "acting white."

Rumbaugh organized a faculty achievement committee to find ways to exploit peer pressure and hero worship. Just as Dewar had done in Texas, Shaker Heights staff members like Mary Lynne McGovern combed seventh and eighth grade records. They identified those with grade averages of B or above, particularly the African Americans. They checked the courses each child had selected to see if they would lead to calculus. They marked the folders of those taking an easier load and invited them to become what became known as Minority Achievement Committee (MAC) scholars.

Black juniors and seniors with good academic records ran the MAC program. Each picked a likely ninth grader to introduce to the social advantages of hard work and good grades. They reminded the prospects that MAC scholars included attractive members of the opposite sex. There were special outings and meetings. They created rituals for the small, select group, meeting once a month with boys in coats and ties and girls in dresses.

Other students noticed. Some were jealous, an emotion the MAC leaders utilized to increase membership. The seniors and juniors checked the report cards of their ninth and tenth grade protégés. They offered assistance in courses where the younger students were having difficulty. Shaker Heights' AP classes grew in size. The percentage of those passing the AP test dropped slightly, but Rambaugh did not worry. He was glad that more students had been stretched to the limits of their abilities.

At Mamaroneck, where AP courses were less welcoming, Levite spent his junior year in the regular U.S. History course, coasting along at a frustratingly medium speed. The teacher was in her second year at the school and did not push very hard, but Levite impressed her so much she had him teach a section on World War II. He received a 95 for the course. In his senior year he took AP European History, as Roush had suggested, finding it just as demanding as had been promised. His grade was an 88 and he received a 3 on the AP test.

He was admitted to the American University in Washington, where so much of the U.S. history he loved had taken place. He majored in political science, with a double minor in literature and philosophy, and contemplated a career in journalism.

David Abramowicz, a member of the class of 1997 and eventually editor-in-chief of the *Globe,* heard Levite's story. It made no sense to him that students were being denied a chance to take good courses because of a ninety-minute test. In a 1996 editorial on ways to improve Mamaroneck, Abramowicz wrote about gatekeeping.

"It is absurd that some students who want to be in honors and AP classes, and say that they are willing to do the work required for those courses, are still denied entry into those classes," he said. He said it was wrong to bar a student because of an 88 rather than a 90 in a prerequisite course, or because there was not enough room. "A student should not be punished for lack of room. It is the administration's responsibility to find room for a student who wants to expand his mind and take a risk.

"Should an AP teacher lower the level of the class for such a student? No. Should that teacher change his grading system for that student so that the student receives grades that are equal to his classmates? No. But if our school really wants students to achieve their maximum potential, then it shouldn't deny them the opportunity to learn more and work harder."

Some teachers who administered the system confessed to having second thoughts. Roush began to read widely in the area of brain research. He noted growing support for the notion that young intellects were much more capable and complex than most schools gave them credit for. The gatekeeping system, he thought, was supported by widely held and deeply rooted beliefs about the nature of human intelligence and the capacity of different people to learn. But when teachers and administrators questioned those beliefs and began to act differently, he thought, the results could be amazing.

The social studies department rejected several more people for AP American History in 1995. One of them, a tall redhead named Justin Stein, was in Abramowicz's opinion one of the smartest students in the class. He was erratic, to be sure, sometimes pushing deadlines to the last minute or submitting substandard work, but there was no question he had brains. He grudgingly took the regular history course with Ciotti, who made certain he had special projects. By the time the school year had ended, Stein decided it might have been all for the best, because AP Calculus had taxed him severely and two AP courses might have been too much.

Another Mamaroneck student, Kerry Constabile, responded to her rejection in an unusual way. She knew she was a borderline candidate. Her freshman grades were terrible. She cut class in

Global Studies and turned in shoddy work. But by the middle of her sophomore year she had become active in JSA and begun to see the hidden delights of both political science and history. She lived in Larchmont. Her father was a lawyer and her mother a real estate agent. She attended a summer course at Stanford University in which she took the equivalent of AP Politics and Comparative Government. When she returned to Mamaroneck in the fall, she begged for a chance at AP American History. Ciotti said no. Her record was too weak.

Constabile was placed in Donnison's regular history class. She told the teacher she planned to study on her own and take the AP test anyway. She bought one of the commercial guides to AP History, with many sample tests and reviews of the key periods. She found sample questions on the Internet. One of her teachers at Stanford sent her materials. Friends in the AP course gave her copies of all the DBQs they did in class.

Other students shook their heads in wonderment when they found Constabile in the library, doing homework she had assigned herself. By the time the test day arrived, she was confident. She reminded herself not to ramble on the DBQs. At the end of the three hours she felt she had done her best.

Not too many weeks later, she learned that she had passed. Without any help from the teachers and counselors paid to get the best from their students, she had found out for herself how high she could go.

If she had attended Wilson High in Washington, D.C., or Southside in San Antonio, or any of a number of disadvantaged urban schools that had resolved to encourage their most ambitious students, she would have been welcomed into AP History. Unfortunately, she had attended one of the nation's best and most advantaged schools, and it had no room for her.

IMMUNE TO FAILURE

Elite public schools assign their less motivated students to easier courses for many of the same reasons that they keep some motivated students out of their most rigorous classes. The risk of students stumbling academically and losing interest in school is too great, some educators say. But failing to challenge them also has risks—wasting their time and leaving their energies untapped.

Joy Sarlo had the usual uncertainties of a Mamaroneck student with a mediocre record, but she knew she wanted to build an independent life and prove that she could overcome difficult situations herself. Some of the instruction given her at Mamaroneck overlooked that need.

In her sophomore year she had had ambitions to be a veterinarian, but even her dog Fuchsia, a sweet-tempered black mastiff, could have told her that her 73 in Biology would be a handicap. She took Biology again that summer. By repeating, she thought, she could focus her energies. Instead, she encountered a not untypical summer school course, designed to carry indifferent students over a barrier to graduation without much strain. The teacher passed out the textbooks and went over some points, Sarlo said, but much of the course was watching videos—nature films, instructional films, documentaries. She felt as if she had spent her summer in a cave watching lights flicker on the wall. She remembered little of what she had learned, but her grade was a respectable 85.

She liked Paul Martin, her counselor, although both she and her boyfriend Chris Silo thought some counselors paid less attention to less academically gifted students than they did to classmates with ambitions for Cornell or Swarthmore. Her parents remembered the same two-track system when they were students at Mamaroneck. John Sarlo had graduated in 1969. Dawn Sarlo had dropped out before graduation to live in a house in the country with John and his rock band. Their daughter was not interested in scoring a 1400 on the SAT so she could go to Princeton. But she wanted a chance to apply herself and be judged by a teacher who understood her individual abilities and goals. She also occasionally yearned to be challenged, to be given a task that demanded more than she thought she could do.

In some classes she got exactly the kind of assignments and assessments that she desired. In others, despite Mamaroneck's high standards, she found she could slip through with little effort, because the school did not consider the course important, because it wanted to be generous in making a difficult subject palatable, or because the instructor was distracted.

Sarlo took Richard Ciotti's U.S. History and Government class, a required junior-year offering that ended with a Regents examination. Ciotti was a skilled teacher with a talent for engaging disengaged students. Sarlo liked him. She found American history more interesting than other social studies courses. Half of the U.S. History Regents test demanded recall of facts through multiple-choice questions, but Ciotti did not give multiple-choice tests. Like many Mamaroneck teachers, he considered them memory-plumbing devices that had little to do with learning. At the end of the year, he handed out a few old Regents multiple-choice tests for practice, but that was it.

For homework Sarlo read each textbook chapter and answered the questions at the end. Each marking period, Ciotti gave the class an essay test, usually something they could write at home. This was the meat of the course, a way to coax analysis and personal reflection out of students too accustomed to parroting facts.

Sarlo received an 83 in the course. She was happy with the grade, even if she thought she had not done much to earn it. Her report card indicated she missed eighteen days of classes, most of them, she insisted, just tardies. She often failed to leave home early enough to allow for the difficulty in finding a parking space.

She approached the Regents test in June with what was, for her, unusual confidence. These were the best marks she had ever had in a social studies course. She thought she understood what was expected. She sat in the gym with dozens of other students and worked through the test. The essay question went well, but the forty-eight multiple-choice questions were another matter. She spent more time on them than on the essays. They demanded factual knowledge and an ability to determine the reasons why certain events occurred. When her results arrived in the mail that summer, she saw that the multiple-choice had nearly ruined her. Her score was 65. One point lower and she would have failed, and been marked as meeting just the Regents Competency Test (RCT) qualifications for graduation.

Sarlo took a keyboarding course to build her typing skills. The teacher put little emphasis on speed. Tests were simple: Type two letters perfectly by the end of the period. She was almost never timed to see how many words she could type in a minute. Her final grade was an 87, but when she had to type a report for Social Studies at the end of the term, she asked her friend Erin Campbell, a blonde stalwart of the swimming team, to do it for her. The basement where the Sarlos kept their computer was very chilly in winter and Campbell was a better typist than she was.

In Rose Scotch's junior Composition and Literature class, Sarlo encountered a teacher who appreciated her enthusiasm and made demands on it. She had been originally assigned to Scotch's fifth period class, but the class was almost as noisy and disorganized as Mr. T's—a circumstance that Scotch attributed in part to the presence of Sarlo and some of her friends. Scotch spoke to her and they agreed it would be best if she switched to Scotch's quieter third period class. Sarlo knew she was not in English to have fun. Like the most SAT-obsessed of her classmates, she felt her progress in the class would affect her verbal score and her ability to get into the college she wanted.

Scotch was a very slim, brown-haired woman in her fifties. She gave an impression of delicacy mixed with unapologetic passion for the poems and stories she taught. She demanded a great deal of writing, much of it in class. The English department assigned its faculty only four courses a term so there would be time for individual writing conferences with students. Scotch considered this a unique opportunity to critique style and shore up weaknesses in grammar and vocabulary.

Sarlo had five writing conferences during her junior year. She did not enjoy them. Scotch pointed out mistakes in grammar, misspellings, and words that did not mean what Sarlo thought they meant. Scotch had instilled a love for writing in many students. She praised parts of Sarlo's work and was as gentle as she could be in pointing out her weaknesses. Yet Sarlo left each conference convinced that Scotch did not think much of her work.

She knew Scotch was a decent person. She was willing to make allowances for a teacher who cared so much for her subject matter. Nonetheless, Sarlo's sunny personality and physical beauty meant people usually had nothing but pleasant things to say to her. She loathed being told she was not doing well.

Her irritation mounted when Scotch asked her not to participate so enthusiastically in class. Few students were as confident of their social standing or as invulnerable to slights and insults as Sarlo. In class she was one of the only ones willing to risk saying something awkward or wrong. Scotch wanted to entice some of the academic wallflowers into the discussion, which she could not do if the social lioness kept butting in. She felt that many of Sarlo's outbursts were inappropriate and immature. Sarlo said she understood, but it did not make her feel any better about Scotch.

The teacher made her rewrite her assignments, sometimes several times—a routine she used with several students. Sarlo did not always accept this as constructive criticism. Her marks in English, after wandering in the 70s for most of the year, came up in the last term, with a final grade of 80. She had told herself she wanted a challenge to sharpen her skills for the SAT, but that did not mean she had to be happy about it.

Scotch's demands, although gently expressed, seemed particularly excessive to Sarlo when contrasted to what was required in the one semester elective course, Art and Studio Photography, that she took at the same time. The class was taught by Charles Fitch, a tall and handsome photographer and ecologist who had been working in Mamaroneck since 1965. Sarlo knew it would be easy, and that was the point: a breather to leave room for her labors in the academic courses. But she was still surprised by how little she was asked to do.

Fitch did not take attendance, at least not in her case. Her report card would say she had only two absences. The truth was she was absent almost every day and appeared in class only four or five times the entire semester. It was an unwritten rule that juniors and seniors enrolled in certain courses, such as Art and Studio Photography, did not need to attend regularly. Sarlo said Fitch told her all he wanted to see was some evidence that she had worked with the camera. "Just bring me the pictures," he said.

The school course catalog provided a description of the class: "This course is designed for students who wish to explore the personal creative aspects of photography. Students will be encouraged to develop projects based on their interests, including modeling, studio work, nature, sports and product photography. The instructor, a professional photographer, offers an individualized approach based on the student's artistic goals and level of technical understanding. Students will do their own black/white darkroom work. This course is especially recommended if the student is thinking of doing professional photography or is an art major who must prepare a color portfolio of their art." Suggested equipment was a "modern 35mm single-lens reflex camera."

The actual course as experienced by Sarlo was different. She did not own a 35mm camera and was not asked to show one when she enrolled. Fitch had been teaching the course for fifteen years, one of a number of his imaginative offerings at both the high school and the Hommocks. He devoted a great deal of time to students who were interested in the subject. Those who did not apply themselves, he acknowledged, he might overlook in the crowded classroom to which he was consigned. He considered himself an easy marker and was willing to let a student with a good attitude get by without much effort. It was an elective course. He felt the student was the one who had to decide whether to take what he had to give. Otherwise he would be just one more lecturing teacher keeping an eye on his attendance and grade book, to him not a way to encourage creativity.

He showed students who attended the class how to use the school's darkroom, but Sarlo was free to have her pictures developed on her own if she wished. She spent two class periods in the darkroom. She learned the rudiments of developing black-and-white film but she did not learn how to print her work. She did not make a single contact sheet.

Nor did she turn in any pictures for the first marking period. Fitch left the impression that he wanted the students to use that time to familiarize themselves with the equipment. He said he would not require any finished work until later. Toward the end of the second marking period, Sarlo borrowed an old Olympus camera from her boyfriend's mother and went to Manor Park in Larchmont with Erin Campbell, her faithful typist, who volunteered to appear in some of the photographs.

The park included a small beach, gazebos, grass, and the lapping waters of Long Island Sound. Sarlo took some pictures of Campbell and looked for passersby to photograph, asking each for his or her permission. After an hour, she thought she had enough shots to demonstrate her style and technique. Only when she got home and tried to remove the film from the camera did she realize that the roll had not caught on the spool. Not a single frame had been exposed.

Frustrated but not defeated, she returned to Manor Park the next day. She clicked the shutter as fast as she could. The term was ending. She had papers and tests due in other classes. She made twenty-four exposures. She tried to get more people into the frames, but sometimes she settled for trees and grass and beach. She had the film developed at a one-hour photo shop and took the prints to school. It was the last day of regular classes. When she reached the photography room at the usual class time, Fitch was not there. She asked at the main office where he might be. No one knew.

Sarlo brought the pictures home and put them in a drawer in her living room. She wondered how her work could be assessed without the teacher receiving the course's only assignment, but given the way the class had been conducted up to then, she had a feeling she would not be penalized.

When her report card arrived in July she saw, as she suspected, that showing no work had not been an obstacle in judging her progress. Her final grade was an 85, a nice, solid B.

She shrugged. She said she had no deep regrets but still wished she had had a chance to show the teacher the pictures. She felt they might have earned her a higher grade.

SAMURAI ON THE SECOND FLOOR

"**W**hat happens if I explain the whole thing fully and nobody is in the dark or anything?" the student asked.

Sherwood looked pleased. "That would be amazing. I would be very proud of you."

The day was proceeding as it usually did, full of digressions, mischief, and occasional insights. A teaching style as unorthodox as Team 9's inspired creativity, but it had to tolerate bits of nonsense too. If teenagers were going to exchange ideas and seek inspiration, they had to be given more slack than most ninth grade teachers would tolerate.

The idea was to do for every ninth grader what some of Sarlo's teachers had failed to do for her—work on weaknesses, demand complete assignments on time, and at every opportunity press on teenagers the need to think further than the correct answers on the next test. They were encouraged to consider not only what was the right answer, but why it was important and how it could be explained so that it established the importance—or triviality—of the other questions on the test.

"Now," Sherwood said, "I'm going to talk about some deadlines. Your notes and your fact sheet and lesson plan and bibliography stapled together will be handed in to me or Ms. Cronin the day before your presentation."

The class took a short break in the hall as the bell rang, and then returned for another period. She asked them to settle down and work at their desks, alone or in groups. She moved from group to group, helping individuals and occasionally giving advice and reminders. "On Monday we are having what is called a crossover research day. You are going to be meeting other classes that are researching the same topic as you, and you can share sources and ideas."

She read off a list of topics and the place where each would meet: "The Japanese mind, Ms. Cronin's room; Japanese city life, here; Japanese militarism, Ms. Cronin's room; American occupation, here; Japanese art, Mrs. Landrum's room; Japanese technology, Mr. Ahearn's room . . .

"And if you feel you had a lot of benefit from this, we'll do it again. There are three openings in the library today. Who needs to go to the library?" To forestall chaos, Team 9 and the librarian had agreed to limit how many students hit the stacks each period.

A boy raised his hand. "I need to go real bad. Ms. Cronin won't let me out of the room."

Sherwood raised an eyebrow. "I know why Ms. Cronin won't let you out of the room." She surveyed those asking to spend a period in the library on their own. She pointed to Cronin's prisoner and two others. "If I hear anything bad about you," she said, "I will kill you." For the problem child, she had a special admonition: "Tommy, if I hear one thing bad about you I will never trust you again. Okay," she said, recapturing her upbeat mood. "Take out your notes. I'm going to start circling around."

Hands went up. She sent one girl to another teacher's room in search of a magazine. The student returned empty-handed, saying a substitute was in charge. She advised a girl working on Japanese technology to consult with a boy who had a good publication on the subject. She handed out a completed homework assignment, an exercise in poetry analysis.

"Did we get grades?" a girl asked.

"You get a check or, if you used quotes from the poem, you get a check plus," Sherwood said. A buzz of irrelevant conversation caught her attention. "What are you talking about?" she asked the boy who was speaking.

He pointed to a friend beside him. "He wanted to know who Roger Rabbit's wife is."

"You shouldn't be worried about that. How is that relevant?"

A girl interrupted: "Miss Sherwood, I'm having a crisis." Her topic was Japanese flower arrangement. She had just realized, she said, that she had little information and even less of an idea how to present it.

The boy at her side continued his cinematic conversation: "Well, if you show it in slow motion, she's naked or something."

A girl entered the class and approached Sherwood. Her work had been marked incomplete. "What is my grade now?" she asked. "I know I did chapter two. I felt that I handed in all that. I know I didn't do the hour test or the preparation, but I hoped I had all the chapters done."

Sherwood did not have time for a detailed explanation, but all the girl needed to do was a little more work. "Don't worry, an incomplete is not bad," she said.

"But—"

"Your mom will understand. Do you want me to talk to her or your dad?"

The girl nodded.

"Okay, give me the number and I'll call her."

Sherwood returned to the flower arrangement crisis. "So what are your main questions going to be?" she asked.

"I thought I would draw the forest section and do a how-to guide."

"Yeah," Sherwood said. "That would be very cute."

"Why can't I go to the library?"

"Because we have too many now. You would need some supervision."

"Why don't they send another teacher?" a boy suggested.

"Because if I went over there," Sherwood said, "and someone jumped out of the window here, I might go to jail."

She listened, her eyes widening, as one boy described computer software he had acquired that gave him quick access to thirty books on Japanese culture. He asked why the Japanese economy had been substituted for Japanese poetry as a topic. Sherwood told him the Team 9 teachers had persuaded John Perlman, the English department poet, to present a lesson and thought it would be unfair to force a student to compete with that.

The boy said he preferred the Japanese economy anyway. "My mom said when she lived there, they named a street 'Miusa' for 'Made in USA.'"

Sherwood nodded. "I was reading that the better we do, their economy also goes up because of all the things we have invented here."

A girl showed Sherwood a long list of citations on computer paper. "My mother went on-line and this stuff came down," she said.

Sherwood inspected the list. "Keep in mind, on your fact sheet, it is not just how much you know, but how much you can present," she said.

In Esposito's class, fifteen students had broken into small groups to develop their presentations. This was the day for students taking the same topic to exchange ideas and perhaps form alliances. Esposito bounced from group to group. One girl complained that Restaino had banned presentation handouts on anything larger than letter-size paper. "That's too small," she said. "We want to do a time line and stuff."

"I need help," a boy interrupted.

"I'll be right there," Esposito said.

"I want to use a chart from an encyclopedia," a girl said. "Do we have to retype it or can we just put that in?"

Esposito studied the graphic, too drab for his taste. "You could enlarge this," he said. "You could put it in the scanning machine, but it's not as colorful as we would like."

"Nothing too nitpicky," another girl said.

He reminded them that they would be examined on how much they remembered of their fellow students' presentations. "Ms. Borsellino is going to make the test," he said, "but she's going to make it from the fact sheets."

A girl objected. "We won't have time to make up all those questions."

"No," Esposito said. "I think she is talking about questions you might ask at the end of the lesson to see if they really understood what you were talking about."

In a corner, two girls discussed a film. "Was it good? Was Mike there?" one asked. The other also had questions: "Are you going to sleep over at my house? Your mom will never let me."

Across the room a boy struggled with his topic: minorities in Japan, including the Koreans and the Ainu. "How do I handle this?" he asked.

"If you were a minority," Esposito asked, "would you rather live in the United States or live in Japan?"

"So I got to debate that."

"You are not setting up a formal debate. You see these shows on television? They have seven commentators and they argue."

"But you have to have background information before you can argue."

Esposito asked the names of the other two boys doing the same topic. "What if you had all three of you debating in front of the class?" he asked.

"But we're not doing that," the boy said, avoiding eye contact. The three boys were not friends and had not considered a joint presentation.

"Let's assume you could arrange it," Esposito said. "If you do that, people start to lean toward some side or another."

"So would I be able to get some other people in my class to participate?"

"I think we could do that," Esposito said. "Is there a bigger point you wish to make?"

The boy seemed puzzled. "That minorities are treated badly in Japan," he said.

"What bigger point do you wish to make?" Esposito asked. He was trying to stimulate "critical thinking"—a popular theme in education journals. He wanted his students to explore facts, look at their weaknesses, and assess their consequences, rather than just memorize them. Schools like Mamaroneck produced young people with well-exercised memories. Their ability to recall obscure portions of old textbooks served them well, to a point, in medicine and law. Whether they knew how to rethink those memories and find the key to curing AIDS or saving Social Security depended on encountering teachers who knew how to nudge them in a creative direction, rather than telling them the answer.

Since the education establishment, with its usual clumsiness, had embraced critical thinking, Esposito had some encouragement for what he had been doing for years. He knew that lesson plans were not the best way to plant seeds. It had to be done child by child. He was trying hard with this boy and his minority project, but he knew the student would need more coaxing to see the point.

"I don't know," the boy said. "Give us a clue."

Nice try, Esposito thought. It had to be the boy's idea, if at all possible. "I don't want to push you in a direction you don't want to go," he said.

The boy paused for a moment. "I want to relate it to our situation in the U.S. People are killing each other. We think we are the only ones who have this problem, but now we see we aren't."

Esposito grinned. "See, now you are getting beyond that point. Maybe Japan is several years behind us in the treatment of our minorities."

Half the class had left the room, off to consult with groups in other classrooms or to the library. Esposito was too focused on the conversation to notice that two of the remaining girls were augmenting their own discussion by tossing wadded wet paper towels back and forth to each other.

"All this hinges on how interesting and well informed your debate is going to be," Esposito said. "You have to liven it up a bit."

The boy had an idea. "Can we change our point of view just for the debate?"

Esposito saw the adolescent imagination engaged. "Sure," he said. "That could get people interested."

"But it could be racist."

Esposito liked that. The boy was thinking. "How far do you want to go in making a value judgment about how Japan treats its minorities?" the teacher asked. Off in the corner, the two girls had stopped tossing paper wads and were discussing the color of their jeans. Esposito did not hear them.

"You could have a comparative poster that shows different kinds of information," he said. "One line could reveal the percentage of different minorities in Japan, and another the percentage of minorities in the United States."

"So the visual aid will be like a graph," said one boy.

"Maybe we could show it as a crossover," said another boy, "showing what people are not permitted to do."

Cronin was moving students around so that the group discussions would be more productive. Certain people did not work well with certain others. The Team 9 teachers had handed out a list of questions to stimulate the thinking of those preparing the presentations. Some students were beginning to realize they were not as well prepared as they had thought.

The idea was to push young minds in ways they were not accustomed. They would be made uncomfortable by having to put what they had learned not in a form that might impress a teacher, but in a form that would educate their friends. It had to be clear and, to a certain extent, entertaining, or they risked embarrassment, which was to some of them worse than a bad grade. It was a way to break down the unnatural barriers between students, both fast and slow. All of them were being shoved into new territory and told to cooperate in finding a way out.

Five students had arranged their desks in a circle to stimulate discussion. "My notes are all screwed up," one girl said.

"Well," said the girl beside her, "how are you going to do it?"

"I was going to describe the emperor and the *shogun*."

"They were wealthy," a boy said.

"You have a biographical sketch of the Tokugawa," another girl said, "but one of the questions is, 'What steps did he take to perfect his power?' That was one I didn't have a clue."

"He killed, like, monks," a boy said.

"Was his father a lord?"

Another corner had students who, in a moment of carelessness, had chosen The Japanese Mind as a topic. Now they were feeling sorry for themselves. "This is the hardest topic," a boy said.

"*Bushido* and *buku*," the boy next to him said. "Let's see your notes on it. Where did you get this?"

"A book called *Samurai*."

The first boy doubted the work's usefulness. "That was probably, like, how they fought."

The boy with the book persisted. "So this guy, like, Lord Bushido, he heads this land and he has to kill himself, and, like, after he kills himself, his samurai get all mad."

Cronin peered into another group. The teacher had a reputation for being clear and direct: "Are you working on your presentation or your fact sheet?"

A boy held up the fact sheet form. "Do we have to use this?"

"No, absolutely not."

"What about the fact sheet?" a boy asked.

"What the fact sheet can't be," Cronin said, "is a long list of disembodied facts."

"What about militarism?"

She smiled at the boy. "You know more about militarism than anybody in this room, including me."

"So I could do something with boxes?"

"Yeah, I love boxes."

At the Japanese Mind group, a curly-haired boy produced a long list of the books he had read. "How are we going to do it?" another boy complained. "There are no facts."

"Well, we have to define *bushido*," the boy with the list said.

"Did you read *The Spirit of Japan*?"

"I didn't read it. I didn't go to the library."

"We should try to define it, though it's kind of hard."

"So, well, put, like, down the terms."

"That should take up a whole page," said a boy happily. "And then, like . . ."

"Stoicism."

"We could put, like, the forty-seven samurai as an example."

"And failure, how deeply they take it. And how meditation brings *rugu*."

One of the discussants raised an eyebrow at that. "The definition of?"

"It's like destroying the inner self. The example I use is, they
dump freezing water on you three times, and when you can't feel
the water, you have reached *rugu*."

"I read something about *bushido*."

One boy looked frightened. "This is a hard topic," he said.

The other two answered in unison: "It's the *hardest* topic."

Cronin was listening to a group of girls plan presentations on
the Tokugawa period. "Now, you tell me you're being creative,"
she said. "I'm concerned how you are going to funnel that creativity to keep your audience interested."

One girl spoke up. "We're going to show how isolation grew
over time. We take it to the class, segregate the class."

The girl beside her interrupted. "We'll make a list. All you
guys are peasants, and we'll do some role-playing like that."

Cronin reserved comment. "Ladies, do you have some primary
sources, like drawings?"

The girls ignored her, pushing the playacting idea. "We both
could be emperors," one girl said.

"Not the emperor," Cronin said. "He doesn't have much
power. Some *daimyo*, samurai, and the *shogun*."

"Or we could ask questions, and whoever answers the most
questions right, they are the *shogun*."

Cronin warned them about context. "The people following
you are talking about Commodore Perry and the opening of Japan,
so you have to end by showing that Japan was not ready for this."

They discussed this for a moment. Cronin decided to tell them
what she thought about dividing the class into Tokugawa social
categories. "An excellent idea," she said. "But if you are going to
play a game, you can leave nothing to chance. The goal or result
has to be very obvious, like Monopoly. The one with the most
money wins. Make it very easy."

She moved to the Commodore Perry group. "They're going to
set it up for you, and you're going to have to blow them out of the
water."

"We'll have singing and dancing," a boy said.

Cronin frowned. "I don't think the Americans came in singing and dancing."

She returned to the Japanese Mind group, still regretting their choice. "Nobody knows what these words mean," she acknowledged. "But that is easy because since you go early, you can set them up. I think it is excellent to go with definitions."

"We are going to use the story of the forty-seven samurai to illustrate them," a boy said.

She nodded. "The thing is—all this stuff you have here—how to hook it so it makes logical sense. You can't just start throwing it at them. Give them a situation—a contemporary business situation, maybe you could get them to understand. If this was Japan, this is the way they would do it. You need something to bring those twenty-two people into what you are doing." They had not been asked to make such connections before. Some were not going to be able to do it, but after Japan would come Africa and other topics. In time, the Team 9 teachers thought, nearly everyone would get it.

"Well, my dad has a contract with a guy who lives in Japan," the boy said.

"That's an excellent idea," she answered. "You want to get into their heads."

"But how do you use these definitions?"

"You need to work these definitions into this communication. You want to weave those things in."

"Ms. Cronin," a boy asked, "was ours the hardest topic?"

MONEY

PRICES AT THE SUMMIT

Elite schools are often defined by the amount of money they spend and how much home owners will pay in mortgages and taxes to support them. The next few chapters explore this relationship between dollars and learning, which can be determined for any neighborhood with just a school district boundary map and the Sunday classified real estate ads. Take, for instance, the home of Nancy and Richard Whitney. They moved to Bronxville, New York, in 1994, settling into a white Dutch colonial at 83 Summit Avenue to raise their daughters Kathryn and Meghan.

Their next-door neighbors at 87 Summit—another colonial—arrived in 1996. The Whitneys had five bedrooms to their neighbors' four, but the extra room was very small. Everything else about the two houses seemed similar. Both needed some work. Both had Bronxville addresses, with the fashionable zip code 10708. Both were on a pleasant cul-de-sac with little traffic in a hilly section of one of Westchester County's highest-priced neighborhoods.

Yet the Whitneys paid $540,000 for their house, while their neighbors paid $350,000, and everyone on Summit Avenue knew why. A Bronxville address was impressive on an envelope, but it did not assure access to the Bronxville school system. The Whitneys' neighbors were on the wrong side of the school district line, which ran down the middle of the Whitneys' driveway. Parents on the neighbors' side had to send their children to the Tuckahoe schools, which were adequate but nothing like Bronxville. The Whitneys were on the Bronxville school district side. That was why they had bought the house.

Nancy was a friendly and imaginative Wellesley graduate who had grown up in suburban Kansas. Richard was a tall investment banker with a passion for golf. After they married and began raising a family, he signaled the importance of their children's education with a remark about his alma mater, the University of Colorado. "I had a good time," he said, "but none of our kids are going there."

A friend of Richard's at his firm, Donaldson, Lufkin & Jenrette, had once worked in the Harvard admissions office. With their daughters almost school age, the Whitneys were hoping to leave their Manhattan apartment and find a house in Westchester. Which school system would catch Harvard's eye? Bronxville, the man replied.

In the 1990s many educators worried about the overcommercialization of public education. Some districts were selling advertisements on the sides of their school buses. Channel One, the satellite news program, brought television commercials into more than a third of the nation's classrooms. Computer companies and textbook publishers and athletic equipment suppliers vied for school contracts.

But no business was closer to elite public schools than the real estate industry. In several districts local real estate agents underwrote the cost of brochures prepared by the schools describing their scholastic virtues. The agents distributed them to clients looking for a place where their children would be suitably buffed and polished for college.

In Mamaroneck the brochure was a letter-size sheet of thin poster board folded in three, produced by school district public relations director Ann Tannen with real estate agents paying some of the printing costs. It had black letters and red headlines on white paper, the final product sturdy enough to stand upright on a coffee table. The cover read MAMARONECK PUBLIC SCHOOLS 1995/1996, accompanied by a black-and-white photograph of third graders sitting on the floor, excitedly raising their hands. A blonde girl in jeans and a SAVE OUR EARTH T-shirt was in the middle of the picture, with an African American pupil, an Asian American pupil, and three others who might be Hispanic American in the background.

Tannen condensed Mamaroneck High into twenty-three separate items of interest, the only significant error being a 15 percent exaggeration in the number of courses.

- over 200 courses
- 11 honors courses—in English, math, sciences and foreign language
- 3 advanced level courses
- 5 foreign languages; evening program in Russian
- 14 advanced placement college-level courses (297 exams written last year, 23% received the highest grade of 5, 57% a grade of 4 or higher, and 83% a grade of 3 or higher)
- science research program
- integrated humanities team in grade 9
- winner of the Rockefeller Brothers Fund award for "excellence in arts education"
- PACE, a 4-year performing arts program: dance, drama, TV, music
- extensive fine arts program
- award-winning music program
- alternative programs designed to increase motivation for students at every level
- technology, home and career skills, business curriculum
- innovative ESL program
- school-business partnerships: senior year internships
- peer tutoring
- teacher-student mentors: multicultural programs

- television studio: student TV show daily
- College Information Center
- Financial Planning Office
- Youth Employment Service
- comprehensive counseling program
- over 60% of students participated in at least one of 26 inter-scholastic sports last year
- over 30 clubs and organizations

A picture accompanying the listing of the high school's virtues showed four students—two boys, two girls, three white and one black—wearing shorts and T-shirts and walking briskly on the track. On the reverse side, the achievements of the graduating class of 1995 were listed, including SAT scores 86 points above the national mean, 75 percent of the class going to four-year colleges, a sampling of college acceptances including eleven into Penn and five into Yale, and awards for six National Merit finalists, seventeen National French Contest winners, and several triumphs for the barbershop quartet.

Emmy-Lou Sleeper, head of the Burbank/Whittemore real estate agency in Larchmont once run by her mother, gave the brochure to prospective buyers. She had been selling houses for thirty-four years. There was a time when the village's police officers, firefighters, and teachers could find affordable homes in the village. That was no longer possible for most of them. The little wood-frame house Sleeper herself had bought in 1954 for $17,000 still carried one of the lowest prices around, but it was $227,000. The average home in Larchmont was $400,000, with an $8,000 real estate tax bill. Some homes went for more than $3 million.

Three things attracted buyers to the area: Long Island Sound, the thirty-minute train commute to Manhattan, and the schools. People also said they came because of the diversity and tolerance of the community, and Sleeper supposed that was true. But she remembered the exodus of home owners to Darien, Connecticut, and other distant towns in the 1960s, when word spread of an influx of young Jews and Catholics into Larchmont and Mamaroneck.

Sleeper's sons had graduated from Mamaroneck High in 1969, 1971, and 1974 and had gone to Dartmouth, Yale, and Syracuse. She was happy with the school system and was, as a result, displeased by the election fight over the budget in 1993. If the budget had been defeated, the story would have been in *The New York Times*. She cringed whenever there were stories like that in the *Times*. Most of her clients read the newspaper carefully. They were Manhattanites who saved their money and abandoned the city for the suburbs when their children reached school age. They had several choices—Millburn, Great Neck, Jericho, Scarsdale, Bronxville. Anything that suggested any trouble in the Mamaroneck schools made her uncomfortable.

Suzanne C. Moncure, a sales associate with the Houlihan Lawrence real estate agency a few blocks from Sleeper's office, had come to Larchmont in 1986 without thinking about the schools. She was then a vice president at Citibank married to another New York commuter. All she wanted was a nice place convenient to the train station. Once she had children, she began to pay more attention to the education statistics. Moncure gave out the same school brochures that Sleeper did, and offered her own insights as a parent. She had some sympathy for the view that school system fat could be trimmed, but she voted for the budget anyway.

Like all real estate agents, Sleeper and Moncure had to be careful what they said about the schools. Passing out literature on test scores and class sizes was fine. Speaking of subtle differences with equally affluent communities like Scarsdale was acceptable. In the 1960s Sleeper was in the habit of pointing out—based on a study she is no longer able to locate—that although students from Mamaroneck and Scarsdale went off to selective colleges in large numbers, more of the Scarsdale students dropped out. According to the study, she said, they had difficulty adjusting to life away from Scarsdale High's punishing academic demands.

When potential buyers said they were not worried about the public schools because their children would go to private schools, Sleeper took another approach. She said she appreciated the ability of such schools to prepare young people for college, but what of the competition? At Exeter, there would be three or four times

as many people applying to Princeton as would apply from Mamaroneck. At the ultracompetitive prep school, it was harder to
stand out. Some real estate agents in neighboring communities
used a similar argument against Mamaroneck. It would be difficult, they said, for an average child to win enough notice at such an
academically oriented school.

What the real estate agents could not do when describing their
schools was use any terms that might be construed as racial, religious, or ethnic code words. Vague adjectives like "troubled" or
"mixed" or "not up to standard" when describing school districts
might be construed as an attempt to discourage whites from looking at integrated neighborhoods. The federal Fair Housing Act
prohibited such language. The federal code said it was unlawful to
encourage "for profit, any person to sell or rent a dwelling through
assertions that the entry or prospective entry of persons of a particular race, color, religion, sex, familial status, or national origin, or
with handicaps, can or will result in undesirable consequences for
the project, neighborhood, or community, such as lowering of
property values, an increase in criminal or antisocial behavior, or a
decline in the quality of schools."

Real estate agents could give prospective customers materials
that had been prepared by the schools, like the Mamaroneck
brochure. They could suggest buyers visit the schools, a request
that Mamaroneck principals welcomed. At the high school, Paul
Martin, the head counselor, received visiting parents and answered
their questions. He conducted the tours himself or found a willing
teacher, counselor, or articulate student.

Watching young couples come into her office, Sleeper became
convinced that the parents of each decade were more concerned
about the schools than the last. There was, she noted, a measure of
guilt involved. By the 1990s more than half the families with children in the Mamaroneck schools were the product of two-career
couples. There was less time to make up at home any deficiencies
in the classroom.

She realized she was selling houses to such people because of
their pervasive belief in the wonders of education, entwined with
strong beliefs that their children had special gifts that only the best

teachers could nurture and develop. Every mother who came to see her seemed to think her child was special. Whether they were or not, it was the belief that moved them.

At the Houlihan Lawrence agency office in the center of Bronxville village, branch manager Vera Blenderman calculated the financial consequences of buying a Bronxville house that was not in the Bronxville school district. The Cedar Knolls neighborhood, west of the railroad station, had a Bronxville zip code but was part of the Yonkers school system, with lower taxes and underfunded schools. She calculated that the Cedar Knolls people paid 35 percent to 40 percent less for their homes than for a comparable property in the Bronxville school system. Many of those with high school–age children sent them to Riverdale Country Day School, a short commute, or one of the more distant private boarding schools. Residents with only one or two children figured the private school tuition would eventually equal the savings on mortgage and taxes from buying in Yonkers. Those with three or more children were more likely to look for a house in the Bronxville system.

The Whitneys had close friends in Lawrence Park West, another affluent Yonkers neighborhood next to Cedar Knolls. The couple had children the same age as the Whitney girls and a much grander house bought for the same price as the modest Whitney colonial. But as their children approached school age, they worried about what to do, while the Whitneys looked forward to staying in Bronxville.

Bronxville High was among the top twenty-five public schools in the country, as measured by the strength of its college-level courses (see Challenge Index), but it was a success in miniature. Its senior class in 1996 had only eighty-four students, the smallest of the top twenty schools. It shared the same large brick building with the Bronxville middle and elementary schools, providing a tightly knit program that elementary school parents like the Whitneys found reassuring.

Kathryn, their strawberry blonde first grader, could already read. Two of the teachers in the elementary school, they noticed, came from the Dalton School, the exclusive Manhattan private school that would have charged them $20,000 a year in tuition if they had stayed in New York City and survived the admissions process. Instead, they were in the Bronxville schools as long as they wanted for the $11,000 a year they paid in real estate taxes. And if they happened to have a third child or even more, there would be no extra charge.

They were happily engaged in a self-reinforcing, self-fulfilling process. Bronxville's real estate values, like the housing prices in all such neighborhoods, were supported by good schools, which in turn drew affluent residents who could afford to pay high taxes to keep the schools sound in order to reinforce the real estate values. The process seemed likely to keep elite public schools well endowed indefinitely, except for the discomforting fact that most people in such communities did not have children in school, and many of them were not sure they could afford to educate their neighbors' children at such high prices.

MRS. CRAWFORD'S TAXES

The superintendency of the Mamaroneck
School District came to Norman Colb in 1983 easily, as if he had
wandered into a neighborhood party and won the door prize. He
was only thirty-nine, had no doctorate, and had never even been a
principal. But headhunter Ira Krinsky thought Colb, an assistant
superintendent for the schools in Newton, Massachusetts, was perfect for Mamaroneck. Colb was an innovator. He had experience
at upscale high schools such as Brookline, Newton South, and
Newton North. Krinsky telephoned Colb and asked if he was interested.

Colb had not expected the call, but was flattered by it. He
thought superintendents did exceptionally important work, although some social critics see them more as publicity-conscious
troubleshooters, the samurai of America public education. They
are hired to save districts from whatever their school boards consider the latest threats to their reputations. Superintendents do
their best, but on the average they are gone in four years. They
usually leave quietly, confident that some other troubled district
will call. The pay is good—$57,000 in Mamaroneck in 1983, rising
to $140,000 in 1996.

Colb had the confidence of a man who knew he had no chance for the job. He would go through the exercise and learn something for that future day when he had enough of a résumé to be a contender. The committee of citizens and staff assigned to screen the finalists sat in the boardroom while Colb paced in front of them. He said that he had great respect for teachers and made a practice of finding as many ways as he could to communicate that respect. He said he wanted to stimulate students intellectually and take Mamaroneck's academic tradition to an even higher level. After three hours he looked at his watch and, ignorant of the protocol, said he would take one more question. This could have been seen as colossally naive and rude, but the screening committee interpreted it as admirable grit. The school board also liked him and hired him.

For many years it went fine. With the help of Cal Schlick, the district's assistant superintendent for curriculum, Colb launched several innovative programs, particularly at the elementary school level. He stayed late for meetings four nights a week. He monitored the classroom work of probationary teachers. High school scores rose. The number of Advanced Placement tests increased. The recruiters for the nation's hottest colleges continued to stop by at the high school.

In 1990, the beginning of Colb's eighth year as superintendent, an economic recession began. The board's contract with the teachers was rich in benefits, the salaries among the highest in the country. Some critics began to say the district had to trim the fat. Why was Scarsdale able to educate the same number of children for $5 million a year less? The district had two assistant superintendents in charge of labor management, a man and a woman who were polite, genial, and knew all the teachers. They both retired at the same time. The board replaced them with a Long Island attorney who promised to negotiate a better deal in no time at all.

Instead, war ensued. The attorney's bargaining style seemed intentionally combative. The talks slowed. Eventually an agreement was signed, but little money was saved, teachers were alienated, and the district's political standing declined. At that point, coincidentally, the Westchester Taxpayers Alliance decided to make the superintendent public enemy number one.

The taxpayers' group had grown slowly in the 1980s as the property value increases of the 1970s continued and real estate taxes went up with them. The group persuaded a few school boards to rework their budgets, but with Wall Street booming, wealthy villages like Scarsdale and Chappaqua did not fret about another 3 percent tax rise.

The Mamaroneck district, with four elementary schools, one middle school, and one high school, was different. The village of Larchmont and town of Mamaroneck were a smaller version of Scarsdale, with big houses owned by doctors and financial analysts willing to pay high taxes for good schools. The village of Mamaroneck, a different entity from the town of Mamaroneck, had the wealthy Orienta Point neighborhood, but it also had the Flats, where Sarlo and Telesford lived. It had many residents with modest incomes—police officers, secretaries, nurses, contractors, shop owners. All three municipalities had significant numbers of retired people on fixed incomes.

Edward T. Clarke, tall and good-humored, had managed the Bank of New York branch in Larchmont before his retirement. He bought his ranch house in the Larchmont hills in 1959 for $27,000. By 1995 the mortgage was paid off and it was worth more than $400,000, but he was not going to sell it. His daughters still lived in the area. His wife did not want to leave a community that had been their home for forty years. His annual real estate tax bill was $8,700. He could afford it, but he knew many people who had not been able to plan so well. He worried about Betty Crawford, the eighty-three-year-old widow who lived up the street. Her annual income was $12,000, mostly Social Security. Her mortgage also was paid off, but her annual real estate tax bill was $9,000, leaving her less than $60 a week to live. Bit by bit, she had nibbled away nearly all her life savings and would have to sell her house.

Leaving the area did not bother all of Clarke's neighbors. The average Larchmont home owner stayed only seven years. As a banker Clarke had seen parents with school-age children mortgage themselves to the edge of bankruptcy to send their children to Mamaroneck schools, with the additional $10,000 tax bill for a

$500,000 house. Once their progeny had their diplomas and college acceptance letters in hand, they sold their house to another family with Ivy League ambitions and sought more affordable shelter in Pelham or Pound Ridge or Armonk, or maybe even Florida if their working days were over. This pumped up the prices of homes and raised the level of taxes that Clarke and his wife and Betty Crawford had to pay year in, year out, without any children in the schools.

It did not seem to them that their money was always well spent. They were paying for Colb's district car and an insurance policy on his life. The school budget showed expenses for telephones and food at administrative headquarters that seemed high.

Evenings at the Larchmont Federal Saving and Loan Association on the Post Road, Clarke met with Eugene Levey, an accountant, and other activists in the Larchmont/Mamaroneck Taxpayers' Alliance, the local branch of the Westchester Taxpayers Alliance. They nominated two candidates for the school board and asked that voters reject the school budget.

As in other wealthy Westchester communities, the Mamaroneck school board was made up of volunteer good-government advocates who abhorred electioneering. Each year a school board nominating committee interviewed anyone interested and decided who would go on the ballot. Usually the nominated candidates were connected in some way with the current board members and were elected with no challenge.

The school budget nearly always passed without incident, the last defeat occurring in 1969. In 1993 the board had raised taxes 3.45 percent, following a 4.62 percent increase in 1992. The board put on the ballot a $51,767,000 budget to support thirty-seven hundred students, or $13,991.08 per child. The Taxpayers Alliance asked the board to cut this by 5 percent. Colb's free car, they pointed out, included gasoline, maintenance, and insurance. His $300,000 life insurance policy had an annual premium of $16,000. The alliance thought this was exorbitant. School district office workers were ordering food from local restaurants "like they were on some sort of expense account," Clarke said. The district's telephone bill was $180,000, $1,000 every school day. The "telephone expenses" entry in the budget included, for reasons that mystified the taxpayers alliance, lighting and oil costs.

Clarke's three daughters had gone through the school system, so he appreciated its quality. But the more exotic feathers in the system's plumage struck him as wasteful. The alliance's survey of class size had found twenty of the high school's one hundred seventy-five courses attracted ten students or fewer. It said some courses had only two or three students. Many seemed to be little more than hobby classes: Cooking, Child Psychology, Jewelry Making.

The school board shrugged off the alliance critique. It was accustomed to the occasional complaints, but the members thought most of their constituents would tie them to the Metro North commuter tracks if they ever let money get in the way of the schools' reputations. That was what brought them to the district and what would guarantee good prices for their homes when they left. They thought many retirees had forgotten that their own children had benefited from a Mamaroneck education and that they had built up valuable equity in their houses because of the good schools.

The alliance's corps of energetic members printed up seven thousand antibudget leaflets and placed them under windshield wipers at supermarket parking lots. They went door-to-door in neighborhoods where they knew there would be a high percentage of people like themselves. The main local newspaper, published by the Gannett chain, did not find the alliance's campaign very newsworthy. But a free local weekly, the *Sound View News,* filled its front page with caustic editorials written by an alliance member, who flayed Colb for his car and other perquisites.

Colb responded by organizing two dozen coffee klatches to counter the alliance's arguments. When a home owner asked why the school system could not eliminate Chinese and Italian language courses and save $150,000 in teacher salaries, Colb welcomed the chance to do his own arithmetic. "It's a good question," he said. "You'd save maybe thirty dollars on your annual taxes." But the news that language classes had been cut would spread to school officials and real estate agents in neighboring towns who would use the information to lure home buyers who might otherwise have

chosen Larchmont or Mamaroneck. "So let's say you lose one percent on the value of your house," Colb said. "So you've saved
thirty dollars, but you've lost four thousand dollars."

"I can understand paying taxes when I put my kids through
this district, and we had a lot more kids to educate then," asked an
older man. "But why should I pay now?"

"Well," Colb said, "you pay now because that's what it means
to be a member of civilized society. The single most important
thing is to pass on this legacy to the next generation. If you don't
understand this responsibility, I can't convince you of it."

To questions about his salary benefit, Colb adopted a bemused
tone. "I don't know if you know this, but I've been out one hundred forty nights a year every year for ten years. That's a lot of
nights. I get to the office about 7:30 A.M. and leave at 5 P.M. My
evening commitments typically begin at 7:30 P.M. and last until
10:30 at night. I'm raising two kids. These are their formative
years. I love this job and I don't like the sour-grapes sound of this,
but quite frankly I think superintendents are phenomenally under-
paid."

The day of the May 1993 election, voter turnout soared to
nearly five thousand, double the usual number. The budget trailed
badly in the portions of the districts with modest family incomes,
those served by the Mamaroneck Avenue and Central elementary
schools. The wealthier parts of Larchmont and Mamaroneck that
fed into the Murray Avenue and Chatsworth Avenue schools voted
mostly yes. The budget passed by thirty-eight votes.

Colb was relieved. The budget was safe, and the two alliance
school board candidates had lost. He, however, had had enough.
He knew from experience that the alliance would be encouraged
by its near victory. When conservatives dominated the school
board in Newton in the late 1970s, one new board member had
sent him a letter: "You will find I can be a very good friend and a
very difficult enemy. To assure the former, I would like the names
of any communist sympathizers and socialists on the staff." The alliance was nothing like that, but it had left the same bad taste in his
mouth, and he knew there would be pressure for more cost cutting. Colb had begun to look for a new job in 1992 when the teach-

ers union negotiations created problems he did not think he could resolve. He accepted an offer to be headmaster at the Menlo School, a private school in Atherton, California, on the San Francisco peninsula, and left in the summer of 1993, the closeness of the vote on the budget confirming his sense that the district needed new leadership.

His replacement was Mary Anne Mays, an administrator who had spent most of her career in Long Beach, California. She had well-honed instincts for dealing with taxpayers. She had seen what Proposition 13 had done to school funding in California and knew it was foolish to ignore antitax fervor. She cut back on food and telephone costs at the school headquarters. She expanded a community advisory budget committee of teachers, parents and students by appointing dissident voices, including Ed Clarke.

The committee included Dan Hopkins and a politically attuned junior, Matt Wexler. The most influential parent was Jim Wilbur, the financial analyst at Smith Barney who had combed district records before his family moved to Larchmont and whose daughter had been in the troubled honors algebra class.

Wilbur had politically unfeasible ideas for relieving the pressure on real estate taxes. The district could sell the creaky high school building to some cash-rich commercial interest—Wal-Mart was the first name that occurred to him—and use the money to build a new structure. A rebuilt school could have new fiber optics, computers at every desk, and no more long gallops from Post to Palmer. Why not put the new school right on top of the new Wal-Mart?

After enjoying this fantasy for a while, Wilbur put it aside. He knew that school districts doing as well as Mamaroneck would never risk such experiments. The most interesting laboratories of new courses, structures, and leadership were communities in trouble, like East Harlem or East Los Angeles. Wilbur helped his committee find small savings here and there. He had little sympathy for the taxpayer alliance. What he wanted to tell Clarke was: When you tell me I can quit paying for your Social Security, I will tell you to quit paying to educate my kids. But he kept a polite silence.

Clarke saw that Mays had co-opted him. Eleven of the committee's twenty-four members were or had been school district employees. Only two did not have some connection to the schools as a parent, student, or staffer. He might be able to use the committee to collect more information, but its recommendations would not bear his stamp. He would have to depend on other forces to win the next budget vote.

Fifteen of the forty local school budgets in Westchester County were defeated in 1993, and a few others had close calls like Mamaroneck's. The percentage of residents with school-age children had declined from the baby boom years of the 1960s and early 1970s, although enrollments were beginning to rise again. Mamaroneck officials assumed that they could fight the alliance indefinitely with the threat of falling property values. But the other Westchester votes and some national research suggested that to many voters affordable tax rates could be as important as good schools.

An investigation by Karen Jenkins Holt, a staff writer for Gannett Suburban Newspapers in Westchester, discovered that two or even three successive budget defeats did not damage a school district's reputation irreparably, at least not in the eyes of real estate agents and their customers. It took years, Holt concluded, before the message went out that a school system was not a good place for children with ambitious parents. Even then, she said, "districts with reputations for conflict about spending may still find favor with home buyers whose prime concern is taxes."

Real estate agents told her they never had a client ask about a school budget vote, but buyers were very careful to ask about the annual tax bill. Questions about school quality came up, but few parents did as much research as the Wilburs had, and the information they had was usually anecdotal and dated. A friend whose children had once been in the district would tell them the high school honors courses were great. A boss would say his cousin thought the elementary schools were light on multiplication. It took some time to change such impressions, as ill formed as they often were.

The taxpayers' alliance had heard some of this, and took it as support for the notion that Mamaroneck property values could survive a school budget cut. In an open letter to Mays, Clarke attacked teacher salaries.

> The time has come to renegotiate the contracts. The median teacher salary at this time in our School District is $71,437, plus 31% for benefits ($22,145) for a total compensation of $93,582. This year 36% of all teachers earn salaries in excess of $75,000 annually (highest in New York State). Next year more than 57% of all teachers will earn salaries in excess of $75,000 annually. One of our teacher's salary is $87,000 plus 31% for benefits. M.U.F.S.D. has the highest median teachers' salaries in the state of N.Y. . . . The Budget Committee must force the Board of Education now to end this extravagant spending. Coupled with the liberal fringe benefits, this elite group will swim in the pool of luxury while many of us will drown in the cesspool of intolerable taxation.
>
> The current contract gives the teachers a raise of 4.75% to a maximum of 5.75%. The students have no idea of the salary and benefits of the staff, nor do they care. Changing the teachers' salary structure will not affect the students' education.

Classes should be combined, he said, to bring class size up to "the 20–30 range." He suggested cutting the $411,417.56 in annual consulting fees. Students attending the school system illegally by giving false addresses should be rooted out. Administrative expenses should be trimmed.

His argument was repeated at school board meetings across the country as taxpayers asked why school expenses had risen in the 1980s while enrollments fell. "In 1973 we were educating 6,284 students," Clarke wrote. "In 1993 we had 3,718 students. During the past 20 years the school tax rate has grown from $70.63 to $283.60 per thousand-dollar assessment. Tax rates are up 300% while student population dropped 41%. Can the School Board do better? They must do better."

Officials of the Mamaroneck Teachers Association read the letter and understood its implications. A week later Lorna Minor, the association president, and other key union leaders met with Mays and arranged a political retreat. With just one year remaining on their contract, the teachers agreed to a slight reduction in their pay increase in exchange for a guarantee that its health and insurance benefits would be locked in for three more years.

The alliance was not impressed. In a flier illustrated with an unflattering picture of Mays, the group said this "transplanted educator" had struck "a lethal financial blow" to taxpayers. "This 'sweetheart deal' was approved by your School Board . . . without any public discussion," it said.

Mays's and the teachers' political instincts were at least as good as the alliance's. The $52.8 million budget she proposed included a 3.21 percent tax rate increase, the smallest in two decades. Some teachers spread the word that the taxpayers' group included sympathizers with the conservative Christian Coalition, a national group seeking to win control of school boards in several states. It was a damaging charge in a community with so many Jews and liberal Democrats. Alliance leaders denied it, but they went into the next budget election with less confidence than they had had before.

Voters poured into the polls, stimulated by the budget controversy and the previous year's close vote. At the Central School polling place, an alliance stronghold, John Perciasepe said he voted against the budget despite having two children in the district schools. "We are paying too much for what we get," he said. Cynthia Lewis, with one schoolchild, voted yes. "Some people are voting for the sake of voting no and don't care about the issues going on," she said. Stanley Drachman might have been considered a guaranteed no vote, since he was retired with no children in the schools, but he voted yes. He said he did not like what he had heard about the alliance's links to the Christian Coalition.

The budget passed by 787 votes, a 58 percent approval rate. The designated board candidates, none of them alliance allies, were easily elected or reelected. The alliance lost momentum, with Mays closing off other budget excesses and making symbolic gestures, such as turning down the designated superintendent's parking spot. For many mornings thereafter she could be seen driving forlornly through the Post lot in search of a space.

Most of the budget defeats in Westchester County struck districts with less affluent residents and less celebrated schools than Mamaroneck. Scarsdale, Greeley, Bronxville, and other highly rated schools inspired brand loyalty. They were as marketable as Marlboros in Poland or Coca-Cola in China.

They also remained open to assault from taxpayer groups. Their classes were small. Their schedules were full of courses that seemed exotic and expensive. Their teachers, at least in Westchester County, earned salaries far above the national norm. But parents willing to meet two hours every week to seek the dismissal of a mathematics teacher were not going to shrink from raising their tax bill $100 each year to keep up standards. They had more than enough energy and political sophistication to block most taxpayer assaults, no matter how much they sympathized with Betty Crawford and her $9,000 tax bill.

SEARCH FOR EQUALITY

Cooled by Pacific Ocean breezes, tucked into a cozy hill above a pine-scented university town, La Jolla (pronounced "la hoya") High School seemed to have achieved all that an American public school could hope for. It produced all three of California's Westinghouse Science Talent Search finalists in 1995. It sent more than 93 percent of its graduates to college. It had about half of all the National Merit semifinalists in the San Diego Unified School District, despite having only 5 percent of the district's high school students. It ranked just below Bronxville in the strength of its AP program. Its AP pass rate of 86 percent compared to 28 percent for the San Diego district. Even its football team was winning.

Yet public spending per pupil at La Jolla was only $3,700, while San Diego schools in poorer neighborhoods were getting as much as $6,200. This was very unusual. In the United States many affluent schools got as much, and in some cases more, in state aid than their less wealthy neighbors. But by the late 1990s that system seemed to be changing. In dozens of states, including California, legislators and lawyers were trying to reverse the balance and reduce the amount of state money going to schools in affluent neighborhoods.

It was sometimes called the "Robin Hood movement"—an effort by urban and rural parents' groups and lawyers, with the assistance of state legislators, to take from the academically rich and give to the poor. It was a measure of California's commitment to equalizing educational opportunity that this shifting of resources had gone so far that a school like La Jolla could be operating at such a financial disadvantage.

When Concord, Massachusetts, established one of the first American public schools, a town committee said "the children of all classes, rich and poor, should partake as equally as possible in the privileges" of the enterprise. That was in 1831. The effort to advance similar principles in the 1990s was not so welcome. Elite public schools began setting up private foundations to make up the difference between what state governments gave them and what they thought their children deserved.

To support its hilly campus of one-story stucco buildings, La Jolla High had not just one foundation, but three: the La Jolla High School Foundation, which sought money for the school and its classes, the La Jolla High School Scholarship Foundation, which helped graduates go to college, and the Parker Auditorium Foundation, which supported the school's 400-seat theater. A large bulletin board in the school office lobby listed dozens of foundation givers, designated as "Contributors," "Friends," "Members," "Sponsors," "Trustees," "Patrons," "Donors," or "Benefactors," depending on the size of their gifts. The two academic foundations together raised $200,000 a year, about $150 per student. They sought ways to acquire more private money because the threat to their public funds was far from over.

In the 1990s, with a series of lawsuits and the support of articulate educators like Jonathan Kozol, author of the best-selling book *Savage Inequalities,* the Robin Hood movement quickened and deepened. Efforts to equalize school spending were being litigated in more than a dozen states. In many other states, legislators were taking action. The movement had no charismatic leader, except for the soft-spoken and untelegenic Kozol. It had no discernible national organization. But it had found ways to dig at wealthy districts' money, including some so subtle that it was not immediately clear what they were.

When New Jersey Education Commissioner Leo Klagholz imposed a new management efficiency program on schools, it was advertised as part of Republican Governor Christine Todd Whitman's program to streamline government. "It is well known that we spend more per pupil than any other state," she said in her 1995 budget address. "But it is embarrassing that we rank forty-ninth in the percentage that reaches the classroom." The program was designed to reduce state aid to districts where administrative costs were more than 30 percent above the state average. Such language evoked images of bloated urban districts staffed with political appointees, but the bill was actually designed to reduce funds to the wealthiest schools. The most inefficient schools, at least as measured by Klagholz, were in the most affluent districts. The commissioner included in his definition of administrative costs the extra guidance counselors and librarians that the suburban schools enjoyed. The hardest hit district was Livingston Township near Newark, home of high-performing Livingston High, with a projected loss of $1.2 million.

Some affluent parents in cash-poor urban school districts such as New York City and Washington, D.C., began fund-raising for their local elementary schools several decades ago. The movement received a boost in 1978 in California when Proposition 13 passed. The ballot measure reduced the level of local property taxes and gave the state far more power than it had had before to shift resources to poorer districts. The equalization movement forced another spurt of foundation making, this time with the wealthiest districts the most active participants. About two thousand secondary schools created foundations.

No way has yet been found to measure accurately how money affects learning. Two studies looking at the same data—and using statistical methods that gloss over human factors like motivation and politics—came to different conclusions. A 1994 Brookings Institution report, *Making Schools Work: Improving Performance and Controlling Costs,* said that more money made no difference, at least when spent in the usual way. An article in the April 1994 issue of the journal *Educational Researcher* said higher spending did produce higher achievement, depending on how it was spent.

The Brookings report, led by Eric Hanushek, a professor of economics and political science at the University of Rochester, used an academic device called "vote counting" in which all the studies of spending and achievement were thrown onto the table and examined for the strength of the correlation between how much was spent and how much was learned. Only about 20 percent of several dozen studies showed a strong positive effect. Vote counters, acknowledging the limitations of any study in reflecting reality, concluded that for there to be an actual connection, it would have to show up much more frequently.

The *Educational Researcher* report, by Larry Hedges, Richard Laine, and Rob Greenwald, took the same studies but assumed each project measured adequately the programs addressed. They measured how much certain reported effects of new spending, such as standardized test scores, went up in each case. They ignored the broader correlations that had left the Brookings researchers on the fence. They concluded that when money was spent to augment teacher training or experience there was a measurable increase in student achievement. Money spent to reduce class size or improve administrative staffing or facilities had less of an effect.

Were the two reports contradicting each other? An article in *Teacher Magazine* analyzing the two studies concluded they were not. It cited Richard Murnane, an economist and professor at the Harvard Graduate School of Education, who said the two reports were describing different parts of the same elephant. The Brookings study meant the majority of school districts did not use money in ways that made a big difference in learning. The *Educational Researcher* article meant a minority of districts used money effectively enough to compensate for the failures of the majority of schools.

High-performing districts like La Jolla found their test scores did not decline with less state money. Student achievement still depended in part on family background, and such districts had a natural advantage. But their inherent blessings did not dampen the urge to fight off the budget reformers. The demand for private foundation support grew so quickly that Dan McCormick, founder of the Williamston, Michigan–based School Educational

Foundation Consultants, created a business out of it. By 1995, he said, he had three hundred public schools as clients.

Local foundations could not raise anything near the multimillion-dollar budgets of their school districts, but 95 percent of that money was dedicated to salaries and maintenance, leaving only a thin margin for school improvements and experiments. In this area, an extra $100,000 a year could make a big difference.

There was little reaction from urban schools to the suburban fund-raising. Most of the foundations received little publicity, but those urban fund-raisers who heard of them were concerned. Amanda Broun, director of the Center for Policy and Program at the Public Education Fund Network in Washington, D.C., ran programs backed by major foundations that encouraged reform in decrepit urban schools. From her own daily search for funds, she knew how limited was the supply of private dollars for education. If the suburban foundations, with their potent business connections, began to tap into those sources, she feared there might not be enough money left for the poor schools she served.

The suburban school foundations, she said, offered one more way to let the taxpaying public off the hook. Homeowners might think: If a foundation found a way to pay for an extra art teacher, why did they have to tax themselves to pay for that teacher?

Such concerns made no sense to McCormick. He saw no sign of any drop in taxpayer support for schools because of the creation of local foundations. Foundation advocates said they did not tap national sources of funds. It was all local and ad hoc, as homey as a bake sale. The Newton Schools Foundation in Massachusetts held spelling bees for adults, with local business executives competing with local doctors and Newton College professors to correctly spell *cemetery* and *meretricious*. Bellaire High outside Houston engraved a brick in the school courtyard with the name of each $8 contributor. Hillsdale High School in San Mateo, California, bought a set of folding chairs for graduation with $20 contributions from graduates like me whose names were affixed to the chairs.

As the suburban schools became more resourceful, the equalization movement began to stumble. A 1996 analysis by *Education*

Week showed state supreme court rulings split evenly, eleven for the movement, eleven for the state governments. Lower court rulings were almost as close, six for the states and five for the plaintiffs. State lawmakers began to say openly, with some support from the courts, that the Robin Hood movement was too expensive in an era of sharply reduced federal support for education. Few state legislatures were willing to eliminate local property taxes—the core of the inequity—as the basis for school funds. Instead they imposed complicated methods for raising extra money and ladling it out to underfunded districts.

Texas required its wealthiest districts to choose from five options for shedding a portion of their property tax revenue so that it could go to poorer districts. But the formula was so complex and so divorced from social reality that some rural districts with many poor students were required to give money to big city districts like Houston, where some of the funds found their way to Bellaire High, a high-achieving school in a largely affluent neighborhood. Some lawyers and judges sympathetic to the equalization movement accused courts of keeping standards so low that the poorer districts could not receive much help. In her dissent against a 5–4 ruling of the Texas Supreme Court upholding the state's funding formula, Justice Rose Spector said the state had changed the rules, settling for a lower minimum standard so that it would not have to shift so much money from richer districts or raise state taxes. Colorado and Texas legislators tried to change their taxing systems in 1997 to help poorer schools, but the bills in question also gave tax relief to suburban home owners who had little to complain about.

The U.S. General Accounting Office reported in 1997 that despite the effort to equalize spending, wealthy districts in thirty-seven states outspent poor districts on average. In the 1991–92 school year (the most recent period for which the agency had comparable data) high-income school systems spent 24 percent more per student than low-income systems.

"There is a deep-seated reverence for fair play in the United States," Kozol wrote in *Savage Inequalities*. "In many areas of life we see the consequences in a genuine distaste for loaded dice; but this is not the case in education, health care, or inheritance of wealth. In these essential areas we want the game to be unfair and we have made it so; and it will likely so remain."

Kozol's pessimism stemmed from his despair at what he considered America's ultimate failure: The richest country in the world had found no way to free poor people from squalid urban ghettos and allow them to move into low-cost housing in the suburbs, with access to better jobs and better schools. There were attempts to move ghetto residents out, but nothing happened on any significant scale. Large numbers of inner-city Americans escaped through their own efforts, buying small homes in Queens, New York, or Whittier, California, or New Carrollton, Maryland, or other modest suburbs in a pattern as old as the automobile assembly line. But the ghettos remained, their populations less black and more Hispanic, still plagued by terrible housing and bad schools.

Most suburban communities resisted attempts to construct low-cost housing within their borders for the same reasons they promoted high-achieving schools: desire for success for their children, fear of lowered property values, preference for neighbors like themselves, as well as ethnic prejudice, greed, and selfishness.

There is no conceivable way, in a democracy committed to strong local government, to overcome those biases to the extent that social reformers like Kozol wish. But American schools probably deserve more credit than they have received for addressing inequality of spending on children with special learning problems. In the last twenty years the federal and state governments have made significant efforts to increase spending on learning disabled, physically disabled, non-English-speaking, and even academically unmotivated children. Those new dollars have had much to do with the disparity of spending on academic achievement in rich and poor schools.

Richard Rothstein and Karen Hawley Miles, director and codirector of the Economic Policy Institute in Washington, D.C., spent months breaking the obtuse codes in which school budgets are written. In order to track down the source of the spending differences, in a remarkable feat of bureaucratic excavation, they dug beneath the expenditures reported by what school bureaucrats call "function," such as instruction or support services, and "object," such as salaries and supplies, and reworked the numbers so they could see how much was spent on actual programs.

They discovered that from 1967 to 1991 money poured into programs for students with special needs. The nine districts they studied increased per-pupil spending by an average of 73 percent, but only a fourth of that increase went to support regular education. Regular classroom spending dropped from 80 to 59 percent of all spending during the twenty-four years studied. About 60 percent of the new money went to special and compensatory education for students with disabilities or disadvantaged backgrounds, bilingual education for recent immigrants, desegregation for racial minorities, and programs to keep students who were in academic trouble from dropping out of school. Special education rose from 4 percent to 17 percent of all spending.

Programs to deter dropouts did not exist in any significant way in 1967 for the districts studied, Rothstein and Miles said. Such efforts accounted for 8 percent of the new spending in the following twenty-four years. Money was found for pregnant and parenting teenagers, alternative schools for students who worked or cared for siblings during school hours, and students suspended for disciplinary reasons. The only bilingual program the authors could find in 1967 was in the Fall River, Massachusetts, school system, helping recent Portuguese immigrants. By 1991 bilingual and other forms of compensatory education had taken 7 percent of the new money. Eight percent of the new money went to expand school lunch programs, as required by federal law.

The study shed light on what the shift of funds had done to the disparity between urban and suburban spending. The city districts, having a higher percentage of students needing special help, were forced to divert more money away from regular students than the suburban districts. The largest urban district in the sample was Los Angeles, the second-largest school district in the country and one of the most troubled. Regular education there fell from 87 percent of spending in 1967 to 51 percent in 1991, nearly twice the average share decline for the other eight districts in the sample.

Given the burdens urban systems have assumed, it is fair to ask if ways could be found for suburban districts, particularly those with fewer disabled children, to assume some of the urban load. But it is also important to understand that the disparity arose in large part because of demands placed on urban schools by well-meaning legislators, not by any conspiracy to spend more money on the suburbs. Elite schools have an opportunity to ease the disparity if they can demonstrate an interest in poor, less motivated students and a willingness to reach out to them.

REACHING OUT

OPEN BORDERS

Efforts to extend the benefits of high-achieving schools to less-favored neighborhoods are uncommon but happen often enough to suggest what might occur if more school districts reached beyond their borders. Although elite schools are reluctant to experiment, those that take risks have had some success if for no other reason than they have the resources to survive the bumpy early years of any new program.

Elite schools have developed programs such as AP that have worked elsewhere when teachers have believed in them. As the next few chapters demonstrate, well-endowed schools have created nurturing student enclaves, shown the worth of keeping imaginative teachers, rethought the use of time, demonstrated the power of outside tutoring, and even hinted at ways to alter radically their prize- and test-obsessed cultures and still promote learning. In a few cases, elite schools have even contradicted the instincts that gave them birth and reached out to children far outside their boundaries, such as Juana Garcia of south San Diego.

One night when Garcia was thirteen years old, she and her family walked across the border from Mexico. They found their way to a tiny wood-frame house, pink with brown shutters, at the back of a driveway on K Street. It was just big enough for Garcia, short and round-faced with wavy dark hair, and her mother and brothers. The block was full of small stucco houses of various sizes. The family had little money. Garcia savored small pleasures, like leaving the Christmas lights strung around the front window all year long.

Her school, Memorial Junior High, was a block away. It seemed fine. There were some fights, but the work was not difficult and the location was convenient. Then she heard that some children in the neighborhood were attending Muirlands Middle School and La Jolla High School, thirteen miles north on Interstate 5, in an affluent community near the University of California, San Diego. This was the Voluntary Ethnic Enrollment Program (VEEP), a busing plan devised under a court desegregation order to expose poor children from predominantly Hispanic neighborhoods to the demands of suburban public schools.

Garcia persuaded her mother to sign the VEEP application form, although the girl was the first to admit the change was not entirely pleasant. She boarded the bus each day at 6:30 A.M., exchanging what would have been a one-minute walk to Memorial, and later a five-minute walk to San Diego High, for a twenty-five-minute trip in a bus full of sleepy, irritable teenagers.

She had to work harder. At La Jolla High she could no longer glance at the textbook, smile at the teacher, and be guaranteed an A. She had to develop a work routine. Going home each day, she got off the bus at 3:00 P.M. and studied until 9:00 P.M. or 10:00 P.M., with one break for a soft drink and another for dinner.

After a few weeks, she became comfortable with the rhythms of homework and examinations. She earned As and Bs at La Jolla, and began thinking about going to the University of California, Santa Cruz, or UC Riverside, or perhaps San Diego State University. She thought she might become a pediatrician.

Every high-achieving high school in the United States has parents and teachers who wish their student populations were more varied in income and ethnicity. Most elite schools draw students from neighborhoods that are predominantly affluent and white, in some cases with substantial numbers of Asian Americans. African

American and Hispanic families with high incomes can move into such neighborhoods, if they can stand the police scrutiny and other discomforts of being the only minority home owners for blocks. But efforts to introduce low-income housing into affluent suburban neighborhoods have been largely unsuccessful, making any significant change in the ethnic and class background of the student population unlikely.

Some schools have tried in small ways to rectify this. Lexington High School in the western suburbs of Boston has one hundred African American students from urban neighborhoods who come to school by bus each day. It is one of the suburban schools participating in the METCO (Metropolitan Council for Educational Opportunity) program, similar to but smaller than San Diego's VEEP program. Many METCO participants, like the VEEP children, have been riding buses to schools in the suburbs since they were in elementary school.

Eight affluent public high schools in Connecticut, seven in Massachusetts, four in Pennsylvania, two each in New York and Minnesota, and one in Wisconsin have enrolled students from poor urban neighborhoods as part of the program A Better Chance. A family in each community has provided room and board for what is usually one student per school, with the communities paying the average annual cost of about $55,000. At Edina High in Edina, Minnesota, and Strath Haven High in Swarthmore, Pennsylvania, five or six urban students attend and live together in houses the communities have provided for them.

Scarsdale's Student Transfer Education Plan (STEP) has for several decades sponsored an African American student, usually from the rural south, to live with a local family and attend the high school. Some high-achieving schools have special magnet programs, such as Bellaire's foreign language academy in Houston, that draw some minorities from outside the district. In Bellaire's case, an additional fifty minority students come in as part of a citywide effort to balance the portions of ethnic groups at each school. Suncoast Community High in Riviera Beach, Florida, a predominantly African American community, has created a strong academic environment with a combination of science and International Baccalaureate (IB) programs. Thirty-eight percent of the students are black and 7 percent Hispanic, one of the highest minority percentages in the country for a magnet school with such rigorous academic demands. Any student in the area with a 2.0 average in middle school can apply for the school's interdisciplinary program. Those applying for the science or IB programs must have a 3.0 average. Stanton College Preparatory School in Jacksonville, Fla., a multiracial public school that sounds like a private school, has used its IB program to inspire an extraordinary amount of AP test-taking, an average of four tests for every student.

Many educators think there is room for more such efforts. Kozol's *Savage Inequalities* dramatized the roomy comfort of suburban schools compared to their crowded urban counterparts, which lack sufficient supplies, enough good teachers, or even functioning plumbing. High-achieving schools with relatively diverse student populations, such as Mamaroneck, show that efforts to inspire unmotivated children by bringing them into motivated schools can be clumsy and erratic but have some impact.

La Jolla's VEEP students prove that even a method as disruptive as busing can have surprising results, although it is unlikely it would have worked as well as it did without J. M. Tarvin. He was raised in a Kansas farm town and fell in love with San Diego while serving in the navy. He went to work as a school administrator and acquired a reputation as a troubleshooter. He became La Jolla principal in 1985 and quickly turned the VEEP program into a crusade. By 1996, when Tarvin retired, VEEP accounted for 32 percent of La Jolla's enrollment of about fifteen hundred students. It had increased the school's portion of Hispanic students to 26 percent. Some San Diego school district officials argued that the bused students would be better off lending their energy and ambition to their neighborhood schools, but Tarvin—a large man with a thatch of gray hair and a very direct manner—challenged the thesis.

At La Jolla, the VEEP students were coaxed into difficult courses and challenged to compete with their suburban classmates. As a result, Tarvin said, their SAT scores were 350 points above the districtwide average. Teachers at both the high school of unusual devotion to education, and they would be expected to do well. Tarvin would not hear of it. La Jolla, he said, motivated the VEEP students in unique ways. Other schools had Advanced Placement programs, he said, but some did not teach the courses very well and some let their students avoid taking the AP test. He said he knew of a San Diego school that in 1994 gave one hundred twenty-five passing grades in AP American History, but only gave twenty-five tests. Of those, only five passed.

In her senior year, Garcia took Advanced Trigonometry, Computer Science, English Literature, Economics, Driver Education, and Advanced Placement Spanish. She had a 3.0 average. Which course was the toughest for a girl from Mexico? "Spanish," she said, with a grin. "I'm having trouble getting that grammar thing."

Few schools have ever gotten so much out of so little money. La Jolla limped by on per-pupil expenditures of $3,700, with its best-paid teachers making only $50,000. Despite those seemingly limited resources, the school gave more AP tests and won more science awards than New York schools that spent $10,000 per student and paid their most experienced teachers more than $80,000.

For the program to succeed, La Jolla's teachers had to overlook not only their meager salaries but their overstuffed classes. English Department Cochair Maria Lipton had one section of AP English with forty-one students, twice the normal size for such a course in Westchester County. Nonetheless, 82 percent of her students passed the AP examination.

Tarvin made up for his feeble budget by pulling La Jolla parents and businesses into school activities and encouraging several moneymaking schemes, including the three school foundations. He helped seniors organize an antiques show that earned $40,000. He arranged to lease out the school auditorium for professional shows. His frequent skirmishes with officials at the school district headquarters and his insistence on high academic standards might have gotten him reassigned more than once were it not for the fact that, like most big-city school systems, his enemies downtown also had problems. To parents asking if he could survive as principal, Tarvin would nod and thank the good Lord that the average tenure of an urban superintendent was only 3.7 years.

He held potluck dinners in south San Diego to recruit more families to the VEEP program and explain how La Jolla was producing talented graduates who won lucrative scholarships, many supplied by the school's foundation. For many VEEP parents, the busing system not only raised their children's academic level but eased their child-care worries. "My wife and I, we both work," said Arturo Guzman, a day laborer whose daughter Maria was in the VEEP program. "The bus takes a little longer, so I have more time to take a job."

There was some social cost to taking the bus. Some of Garcia's neighborhood friends made fun of her. "Hey, Juana, only the Richie Riches go to that school," one said.

"No, I'm not rich," Garcia said. "I just don't want to go to San Diego High School."

She offered her impression of what her life would have been like at San Diego High. There would have been less homework, fewer tests, and less of a future. "They don't care about the students there," she said, sounding like Tarvin. "They just pass them on to the next grade." She had as much right to her ambitions as the daughter of a navy admiral or the son of a UC San Diego chemistry professor, and she was going to exploit the energies of La Jolla High for all they were worth.

2 4

COCOONS

In the middle of the 1970s a few Mamaroneck educators began to consider ways to help their most troubled students. The school was at the height of its population boom—two thousand teenagers throbbing with high spirits and ambition. The football team was winning championships. Dozens of seniors were getting into Amherst, Brown, and Cornell.

What bothered the faculty were students getting lost. It was not easy to deal with academic problems anywhere. At Mamaroneck, like other schools with its ambitions, a bad report card felt like a dunce cap permanently attached to one's skull. For those willing and able to achieve, absorption in one's homework defined the Mamaroneck experience, and some students were not part of it.

The school had tried to help less academically oriented or less conventional youngsters—perhaps as much as a quarter of the student body—by creating small experimental programs within the larger school. Many high-achieving schools had made such efforts. The result, they hoped, would be warm, soft cocoons safely tucked into corners of the campus, offering students something more than the unfocused diversion of a course like Graphics 2/3. The programs drew teachers who thought the affluence and intelligence that characterized the school could justify itself only if it helped everyone learn. They wanted to connect students to the real world and real people in a way that would make academic life both more demanding and less frustrating.

In the late 1960s Mamaroneck began what was called the School Within a School (SWAS). It offered about ninety students a loose, interdisciplinary approach to Mathematics, Science, Social Studies, and English. Among its founding teachers was Don Phillips, the social studies department's tall mischief maker. He grew up in New Rochelle, where his father had been the school superintendent. His height and intellect made him awkward and uncomfortable in social settings. A fervent reader, he hated most rules and discipline, and loved the freedom at SWAS. If the social studies course he was teaching needed more time, he held extra classes in the late afternoon or evening. The students attended court sessions, newspaper editorial conferences, and fashion shows. SWAS attracted students with an interest in the humanities and a disdain for convention. Phillips insisted that everyone call him Don. Many students would tell Phillips years later that SWAS was the best educational experience of their lives.

There were, however, other students struggling in the 1970s who had little to gain from the happy unruliness of a Phillips class. Their parents often had lower incomes and no college degrees. While Larchmont kids thought strict classroom discipline was cheesy and old-fashioned, these children craved it, at least when it came from people who cared about them and did not have the disadvantage of being their parents.

For such students the school board and the district's chief innovator, Assistant Superintendent Cal Schlick, created a program called APPLE (A Place People Learn Excellence) in 1977. The idea was to create a small family in the far northwest corner of the Post building's first floor. No more than twenty students from each of the ninth, tenth, eleventh, and twelfth grade classes would be admitted. For their four years of high school—with some exceptions for special electives—each APPLE student would have just one teacher for mathematics, one for science, one for English, and one for social studies.

Five teachers were responsible for what the seventy or eighty APPLE students would learn in high school. This was a challenge for any instructor. They had to prepare four different lessons each day (one for each age group) and make special efforts to monitor the individual progress of each student. Instructors could not throw up their hands each June and pass their worst students on to the next grade level, telling themselves they had done their best. They *were* the next grade level. Over the years, the APPLE files filled with letters from happy parents and successful graduates, and commendations for projects such as the sixty-two-minute video documentary on the federal deficit produced by the APPLE class of 1990.

The advantages of developing long, well-disciplined teacher-student relationships seemed obvious to the APPLE teachers, although American schools were slow to adopt the idea. Daniel L. Burke, writing in the January 1996 *Phi Delta Kappan,* described similar experiments in Ohio, Massachusetts, and Minnesota that produced startling increases in teacher satisfaction and student confidence. Yet, he admitted, he detected no rush of imitators.

Creating curricular cocoons buttressed the arguments of educators who thought students did better in ability groups. Their success contradicted the arguments of Oakes and other enemies of tracking that less-motivated students always suffered when segregated from more motivated students. But efforts as intense as APPLE were so rare, even in well-financed schools like Mamaroneck, that they rarely entered into the argument between trackers and anti-trackers.

The APPLE leader in the 1990s, Mike Sudano, was a short, muscular bundle of optimism with the happy patter of a summer camp director. He fashioned APPLE into a family with inside jokes and traditions. Many of his students had trouble in their own families. They needed a sense of order and belonging to draw them to the lessons he wanted them to absorb.

They had to want it, he insisted, or they would not be admitted. One applicant, Omari J. High, a tall, broad-shouldered boy with a wispy suggestion of a mustache, appeared before the APPLE teachers in December 1994. He had seen more trouble in his life than most Mamaroneck students. He had spent his freshman year at APPLE and done well before moving to White Plains to stay with an aunt after his mother died. At White Plains High, he did not find anything like APPLE's protective environment. His grades and attendance record deteriorated. He flunked mathematics and English, received a D-minus in Global Studies, Cs in Biology and Physical Education, and a B in Spanish.

His father blamed his son's academic troubles on the fallout from his wife's death. The APPLE year had gone so well that he wanted the boy to move back with him so that he could enroll again at Mamaroneck and rejoin APPLE. He accompanied his son to the interview, but when he tried to answer questions for the boy, Sudano interrupted him. The teachers insisted the younger High do the talking.

There was suspicion in the room that one of the reasons for the boy's return to Mamaroneck was his limited chance to play football for the big, multitalented White Plains squad and his much better athletic prospects at Mamaroneck. Harry Peterson, the APPLE Health Studies teacher, was also the football coach. Mamaroneck had maintained a winning record and often made the playoffs. But it was in a small school division where good players were at a premium. That same year neighboring Scarsdale was so short of boys willing to hurl themselves at helmeted ballcarriers that the school announced it would not field a varsity team.

The APPLE program had several good athletes, and the staff went to great lengths to convince them that their first priority was school, not sports. Sudano and APPLE social studies teacher Gerry Trezza had been successful football coaches at Mamaroneck, and Frank Pia, the tall and balding English teacher, had played in college. They hoped their background lent authority to their view that games came after homework.

"First of all, welcome back," Sudano said to High. He smiled at the boy twisting in his chair. "The good news is it's nice to have you back. Your seat is still warm. It was a great marriage for one year."

The boy and his father had told Sudano they thought he ought to repeat the sophomore year, since his studies at White Plains had gone so badly. Sudano agreed. "But the bad news is that our sophomore class is now at seventeen kids, and we don't like to go past sixteen. So we're going to expect a little more maturity from you. We're going to ask a few questions, short and sweet." High shifted again in his seat.

Pia, a certified school psychologist who had been with APPLE from the beginning, asked the first question. "What do you think my concerns about you are as an English teacher?"

The boy thought for a moment. "It was the homework . . . and the reading."

"Why do you think I asked you that question?"

"'Cause you wanted me to remember what I did."

Pia smiled. "What are your strengths?"

"My work in class was good."

"So we have to concentrate on the homework. How much homework do you have to do for each class?"

"Thirty minutes."

Pia nodded. "So how much each night?"

"Two and a half hours a night." This was far above the American average. The APPLE staff had learned that unless they imposed a heavy load, their students would never have a chance to see the rewards of sustained effort.

Peterson picked up a copy of the boy's White Plains transcript. "Global Studies, missed five days, D-minus. How do you explain that?"

The boy's father spoke up. "Harry, let me put you in the picture. The living arrangements were really bad, and he was so tired."

Peterson looked at the boy, not the father. "Did you cut classes at White Plains?"

"Yeah, I—"

"How much homework did you do this year, honestly?"

"Well, I did some homework in study hall."

"But you could have done a little bit at home?"

"Yeah, I could. But the work was hard for me."

"How so?"

"Well, I wasn't used to walking all around the school and seeing all these students."

It was a clever if blatant compliment to APPLE's controlled environment. Peterson did not seem impressed. "What was your favorite class?"

"Spanish. I could do it."

Trezza spoke next. "So why do you want to come back to APPLE?"

"'Cause I know if I don't do the work, you'll call my father."

Charles High interrupted again, explaining his attempt to keep track of his son at White Plains. "His counselors got a little tired of me when I was going to meet all the teachers. But this is a wonderful program."

Tom Gifford, the science teacher, took a turn. "You seem to be a pretty strong science student. What were you working on?"

"Mostly we were doing cells."

"We have lots of labs," Gifford said. "Are you a pretty good drawer?"

"Yeah, I can do. I passed the science RCT [Regents Competency Test]."

"Basically this is a good kid," the father said. "I am surprisingly not as concerned about football as he is. Harry, I want you to know that."

"He'll do fine," Peterson said.

The father could not stop talking. He had invested most of his small ration of optimism in the meeting, and he had to make his case. "We have to get this guy going with the math. I hope he has matured a lot. He won't be doing the things he did last year. I told him if he doesn't do the right thing in school, he won't be doing."

Sudano peered at the boy, slumped slightly in his chair and studying his hands. "So, for all that you have heard, do you want to come back in the family?"

"Yeah," he said. His tone was soft and hopeful.

"Okay, you come see Harry tomorrow."

Peterson smiled. "Yeah, you're going to see me a lot these next two years." He looked at High. "You know what it's like out there, so don't forget."

"So what are you going to bring with you?" Pia asked.

"I don't know," High said. "I don't know what you require."

"You have that loose-leaf notebook?"

"Yeah, still got it."

"Bring that."

Father and son left. The APPLE group conferred. "He has some problems with decoding [getting the letters right] and reading," Pia said.

The others agreed. The more time their students spent with the words and the books, the better they performed. One student had complained to Trezza just that morning that the previous night's assignment had taken forever. The teacher replied, "So?"

At the beginning of the semester they had students read aloud in class to make sure the reading was done and to spot individual problems. By the end of the second week, when students began to realize they were absorbing the material, it became easier to persuade them to do more work on their own at home.

Peterson offered a last word on the motivation of Omari High. "He is respectful, but he can get loud," he said. "But wait to call the father, just for the big stuff."

In the Palmer building at the other end of the campus, as far from APPLE as was physically possible at Mamaroneck, was the school's other cocoon, PACE, the Performing Arts Curriculum Experience of Mamaroneck High School, first established in 1975.

In a New York metropolitan culture suffused with Broadway legends, PACE had a reputation as a part-time version of New York's High School of the Performing Arts. There was nothing quite like it at any other Westchester school. Its actor alumni included Kevin Dillon (younger brother of Matt, who began his film career while still at the Hommocks and did not have time for PACE); Danny Futterman, who played Robin Williams's son in *The Birdcage;* Michael O'Keefe of *Roseanne* and *Life's Work; As the World Turns* cast member Bronson Picket; Elizabeth Berridge of *The John Larroquette Show;* Tammy Minoff of the film *Only*

You; and dancer William Wagner of the Mark Morris Group. Several parents from Rye Neck and New Rochelle paid tuition to send their children to Mamaroneck because of PACE.

As much as they applauded their students' successes, the principal PACE teachers, John Fredricksen and Martie Barylick, did everything they could to squash the notion that they were running a cutthroat theater arts hothouse of the sort made famous by the film *Fame.* The idea had been to create an arts program that was the opposite of preprofessional. The teachers discouraged their students from thinking of the theater as a career. They rarely mentioned the famous alumni. Fredricksen and Barylick thought performing arts helped create thinking, problem-solving, well-rounded, expressive young adults, and did everything they could to cleanse PACE of the backstage trauma they knew would arise from any star system.

No previous performing experience was required to join PACE. In many ways it was very different from APPLE. It was just one class a day, with before- and after-school activities. Students decided for themselves whether or not they would participate. They did not think that their program was anything like APPLE. But it demanded the same emotional commitment and inspired some of the same feelings. The PACE student agreed to become part of the family, willing to put in long hours and deal with the same small core of teachers and students year after year. PACE students often ate their lunches together on the couches in the PACE classroom and sometimes napped there during free periods.

It was art for young people willing to engage in creative silliness and stretch far beyond what they thought were their limits. While other high schools focused on dancing technique, PACE tried to turn each student into a choreographer. The theater students were encouraged not only to act but to write and direct plays. All students were required to take dance, theater, and music for three years, no matter how inadequate they thought they were in some of those categories. Third-year students were required to assess their strengths and weaknesses and then perform in the area they felt least confident.

There was no shortage of opportunities to show what one

could and could not do. PACE productions were usually huge, with double casting and other measures to ensure that most of those auditioning got a part. There were eight one-night shows each year in which everyone got equal time onstage. The school had two theaters, one with two hundred fifty seats and one with one thousand, plus an assortment of rehearsal rooms. Besides PACE, there was also a splendid program for orchestra, band, and chorus. The school had its own television studio, which broadcast daily announcements—the lighthearted *MHS Info*—as well as special programs for a local cable channel.

The PACE introductory sheet, with characteristic enthusiasm, promised that participants "have simply DONE so many projects (from rigging a light, to writing a press release, to conducting a dance audition, to video editing, to directing a one-act play, to singing in a barbershop quartet) that their behavior really is informed by a consciousness of all the elements of these art forms. We send them out into the world of college with the confidence that they will enrich the life of the arts wherever they go!"

Debbie Schoeneman of the class of 1995 attributed much of her mental health to PACE and the nurturing manner of Fredricksen in theater and Barylick in dance. Sometimes they acted like parents, sometimes like best friends, but there was no question of their concern for everyone who spent time in their little world.

Both they and the APPLE teachers were prepared for the emotional outbreaks and distractions familiar to all substitute parents. The APPLE students sometimes seethed with resentment over the oppressive need to absorb subject matter and conform to classroom decorum. They feared failure. Many of them struggled to adjust to the fact that their teachers knew better than to give them much maneuvering room.

PACE classes drew a different kind of student but also had juvenile outbursts. Most PACE students could handle class work and some, like Marshall Lewy, Catherine Bell, Schoeneman, Meera Rao, Adam Arian, Rachel Lissy, and Megan Rooney, were among the most accomplished students in the school. Fredericksen and Barylick found that dampening the competitive instincts of such a group required radical action, including discontinuing what most schools consider the crowning glory of any performing arts program, the annual musical.

The All-School Musical, as it was called at Mamaroneck, was never formally a PACE production, but Fredricksen directed it along with Lunetta Knowlton, the school's skilled choral teacher, and all of PACE's most eager participants wanted to be in it. The producers watched with mounting dismay as each year's casting brought hurt looks from students who were passed over and peevish telephone calls from parents. After the 1994 effort, they divided the event into two: one a musical featuring the entire senior class, to raise funds for graduation activities; the other a Musical Collage of assorted songs and scenes in which everyone who wanted a part got one.

The idea of closeness and continuity survived. Isolated programs with their own standards and traditions could serve some individuals better than days spent in the competitive tumult of classroom exercises, library research, rapid-fire lectures, and mind-draining tests. It took money and time to protect such enclaves, but Mamaroneck had money, and in these cases nearly everyone thought it was well spent.

2 5

FOCUSING

In the special education room on the Palmer building's second floor, Samuel Telesford manipulated a Microsoft Windows program on an Infiniti computer. Dressed in green jacket, baggy jeans, and a faded blue baseball cap, he clicked his mouse on the file "Paintbrush (untitled)." He fiddled with a design he had stored on the disc. The screen went blank for a few seconds. "Oh, man," he said.

It was 9:35 A.M. Sandra Weinman, the special education teacher, was on the telephone a few feet away. "Helen? I have a student who is doing a report on minorities in Japan. And he is having some trouble gathering the information. His name is Reynaldo." She listened for a few seconds. "I'm sending him down right away."

Telesford also had a Japan report due in Team 9, but for the moment he preferred to compose a birthday card for Bruce Hoffman, the Mamaroneck pen manufacturer he worked for some afternoons. This did not bother Weinman. Anything that led her students to work with computers and the complexities of English composition was fine with her.

If the mixing of students of different abilities was to work the way Team 9 wanted, the students who had the most difficulty adjusting to classroom routine had to be shown they could work on their own. Most of them did not need the daylong supervision that APPLE provided. They would prosper, the Team 9 staff thought, if provided an environment where they could reflect on their lessons and find help when needed.

A day with Telesford showed how much individual attention this approach demanded. Schools without Mamaroneck's financial resources could learn from his progress under Weinman and another special education teacher, Brenda Heffernan, but even with the steep national increase in special education funding over the last decade, few schools could give each student as much care as Telesford was getting.

Weinman's room was small, about half the size of an average classroom, but neat and comfortable. It had a clean gray carpet, cozier than the tiled floors of the regular classrooms. Green chalkboards covered two walls. Three computers rested on a long table.

Weinman, a lean woman with long dark hair, hung up the telephone and spoke to Telesford: "You want to print it?"

He wrinkled his nose and clenched his thick-fingered hands. "I want to make it bigger."

"Okay, you go to View. Now you go to File and then to Print."

He began to click on the words at the top of the screen. "Oh, that's right. It attaches to Letter."

Nothing happened. "Why is that not working?" Weinman said. "Oh, here. We go to Exit and then to Program Manager. Remember how we did it before? Now we want to change the format. You want it italic? You want it bold? And what size do you want it to be, the letters?"

"I'll play with the letters."

"Okay, have fun."

"How do I get it to come out like a card?"

She pointed to a computer-made greeting card taped to the wall. "You have to center it, and then we have to cut it out."

Telesford centered the words he had written. He began to add to his message in bold italics, his right index finger hitting the keys one at a time and getting one letter wrong.

To Mr. Bruce:
I hope that this girt because

The telephone rang. "Okay," she said. "I'm going to let you play with it. I have work down here."

The telephone conversation was brief. She approached the other student in the room, a muscular boy with a pronounced New York accent. "Do you know what you have to do with this lesson?"

"Talk about sports in Japan."

"So you have to figure out how to get your students engaged, how to get them involved in the topic. Do you feel comfortable?" It was a question she asked several times a day. It had proven the best way to probe the feelings that troubled them, much better than asking, "Do you feel stupid? Do you feel lost?"

"No," the boy said. He was not comfortable.

"What is the object of the lesson?"

He thought for a moment. "So people will know that Japan is involved in sports like we are."

Telesford crumbled a piece of paper. She turned toward him. "Problem?"

"No, I know what I'm doing."

He had switched to all capitals:

I HOPE THAT YOU LIKE
THIS GIFT, BECAUSE
I ALWAIS SEEN YOU
DRINKIG SODA, BUT
YOU NEVER HADE
A CUP.

"Should I use 'but' or 'and' after 'you never had a cup'?"

"That's fine. You want this all capitals?"

"I'm going to write it and cut it."

"Read what you said. 'I always seen'? Or 'see'?"

"Oh, 'see.' "

"And before you do anything, do your Spell Check." She pointed to the words on the Windows menu. American schools have adopted a Shakespearean disdain for good spelling. It is the thought that counts, not the arrangement of the letters. The computers would enforce some uniformity, if the students remembered to click the proper icon.

He tapped the mouse with his finger, but nothing happened. "No, Sammy, you're doing it too quickly," she said. She moved the mouse slightly and clicked again. A box suggesting options appeared.

"Say yes," she said. The spelling was fixed.

A third boy in a winter coat appeared at the door.

"What's happening?" Telesford asked, quickly assuming his familiar role of social arbiter.

"I'm bored," the newcomer said.

"You know what we could do," Weinman said. "You could make an appointment for us at the language lab."

The late arrival peered at Telesford's computer screen as he passed. "You spelled 'birthday' wrong," the boy said.

"Oh?" Telesford looked again. He had written "HAPPY BIRDAY." When he clicked the Spell Check function, it gave him varieties of *bird* and *birdies*.

Weinman spoke to the student sifting note cards. "You have to show ways how Japanese baseball is different, not similar. And you're also going to be talking about what?"

"I am going to show a clip of a Japanese baseball game."

She smiled. "And then you can show a clip of an American game and show how they differ."

Telesford worked the computer keys. He had switched back to lower case.

    to mr. bruce
    frpm sam

He saw his mistake. "Oh, man. I did it again. I'm getting tired. Oh, man." He retyped the two lines and printed them.

Two more boys entered the room. Weinman looked thunderstruck; she had not expected them. "Oh, no. You're kidding," she said.

"It's Thursday," one said.

"I can't believe it." She turned to the baseball student. "We need to work. When can we make it?"

"I have Social Studies second period tomorrow."

Several more students had entered the room. Two were leaning over Telesford, watching him work. "You're stepping on my foot, man," he said.

Weinman turned to Telesford. "Let's see how you're doing. That's *nice!*" Many of the students were chatting and joking. "We're going to PACE," Weinman announced. "We're going to dance."

Before leaving, she said to Telesford, "Why don't you work on your report, too. And you won't turn off the computer, will you? You know what happens when you do." A glitch too complex for quick repair wiped out several functions whenever the power was shut off.

As the room emptied, Telesford cut the printed words out of the paper and applied paste. A screensaver slogan marched across the computer in large capital letters: WELCOME TO JAPAN DOZO. WELCOME TO JAPAN DOZO. WELCOME TO JAPAN DOZO.

He pasted the strips of words to a folded paper in the shape of a greeting card. He fixed one strip to the wrong spot, then corrected his error. He waited for another special ed teacher to arrive and help him with his Japan report. The woman did not appear.

He had worked on the birthday card during his third period English class. At the beginning of the semester, third period had been his electricity class. He was good at the subject. He was getting a B, but Weinman and his counselor recommended he drop it so that he had an extra period to work on English and Social Studies. If he was going to receive a regular diploma, he needed to sharpen his language skills.

At 11:22 A.M., after eating a sandwich from a paper bag, Telesford joined a pickup basketball game in the gym. The well-lit facility was halfway between Palmer and Post, just off the enclosed walkway connecting the two. Teleford took off his coat, revealing a T-shirt that said EASTERN CONFERENCE CHAMPIONSHIP KNICKS 94. His muscular torso seemed to burst out of the fabric. In the game he did not run much but acted as enforcer, shoving one boy who had fouled a teammate.

At 11:46 A.M., just before fifth period, Telesford dropped all his books in A206, Heffernan's room in the Post building. Without a single book or piece of paper, he walked down the hall to his health class. On the board the teacher had written the class rules:

Right to Pass
No Killer Statements (No Put Downs)
Speak for Yourself, Use "I" Statements
LISTEN. During Discussion only one person speaks at a time
Confidentiality. Do Not Gossip.

"Anne DeWare will be here shortly," said the teacher, Bobbi Siegelbaum. She was very slender and animated. The classroom rattled with the conversation of twenty-five teenagers. "I don't want to see a lollipop," Siegelbaum said. "Would you please all settle down? We're going to do a lesson today. Stop eating candy. Stop eating, *period.*"

The hubbub subsided slightly. "We're going to do a lesson on COAs. Do you know what COAs are? Children of Alcoholics." She waited for more attention. "Does anyone here have a question about the debate we're going to have on Tuesday on the legalization of drugs? Any questions? The sheets I gave you, you may be able to use for *not* legalizing drugs, but remember you're going to be developing six arguments, three for legalizing drugs and three against legalizing drugs. You need to make your statements and then a paragraph supporting your statements. I will assign you, and then later you will go to the side of the class you feel most comfortable with and continue the debate there. Your paragraphs about your project, telling what you are doing, are due Monday also."

DeWare, the school's drug and alcohol counselor, arrived. She was soft-spoken and short, with graying hair. "I come from an alcoholic family, and that is probably how I got interested in the topic," she said.

She described the fears of a child with an alcoholic mother, Larchmont version. "Is she going to be yelling at me? Is there going to be any food in my house? Am I going to get to my dance lesson? So what people do in these families is that they take a role that protects them against the hurt of such families so they can survive. I am going to lecture you for five minutes. If you have any questions or comments, raise your hands."

She asked the class: "What does it mean to enable?" Wresting a response from a cold adolescent audience was always difficult, particularly in a mixed class. The slower students feared being wrong; the quicker ones feared seeming pushy. After a few seconds of silence, one boy spoke up: "Allowing."

She nodded. "If you let someone look at your homework or your work on a test, that is enabling someone to cheat."

She described four roles that children assumed in the family of an alcoholic. Some became overachieving heroes, some misbehaving scapegoats, some quiet lost children, and some wisecracking mascots. Telesford had been fidgeting, but now he listened. "Again, these are very stereotyped," she said. "You may say, I know a terrific kid and he's not from an alcoholic family and that is very true. In my family, however, I became the hero and I became a real workaholic and a perfectionist."

Telesford went to the restroom. He did not need permission. When he returned he joined a group that produced a quick oral report on the reactions of the hero child to an alcoholic family. Similar reports, each clear and well reasoned, were given on the three other types of child. The students listened quietly to the presentations until the class ended.

During Telesford's trip across the walkway to his art class in the Palmer building, he made several stops. He chatted in Spanish with two girls whose parents were from Guatemala. He hugged John Perlman, the bearded poet of the English faculty, and asked about Perlman's basketball prowess. He inspected the food in the Cooking classroom and hugged that teacher, too.

In art, a student teacher from Manhattanville College, a blonde woman in her thirties making a career change, discussed the sculptor Henry Moore. She said an evaluator would be there next week to watch her present another lesson to this same class. This interested Telesford. "Do we get paid?"

"No, you do not," the teacher said, smiling. "Did you like the masks we did, Samuel?"

"No," Telesford said.

"Yes, you did. I know you did."

One student recognized a Moore piece that was displayed in front of the PepsiCo corporate headquarters in Purchase, five miles away. Telesford was unimpressed by the Moore drawings she displayed. "Yo," he said. "I don't get it. Someone closed their eyes and just started drawing. I just see things."

"What kind of things?" the student teacher asked.

"It's a bone."

"What kind of bone?"

"It could be a tooth."

She looked doubtful but said, "That's interesting."

"It looks like somebody got burned," he said.

She showed them how to produce a cut-rate sculpture using plaster, sealant, and pantyhose.

Telesford pointed to the hose. "You bought those?"

In a stage whisper, a girl said, "I know you like to put them on."

He smiled, then went to the sink and prepared a palette of bright red paint. He put it beside his masterpiece, a devil's mask in stark reds and blacks. The student teacher picked up the mask and began to attach it to a black cardboard rectangle with a hot-glue gun.

"You're gonna mess it up!" Telesford cried.

"No, I'm not," she said.

Telesford walked back to A206, Heffernan's room. It was his refuge on the Post side, as Weinman's room, D228, was on the Palmer side. In A206 he dealt with homework.

Some of the special education students worked in groups; some, like Telesford, by themselves. Heffernan, a bubbly woman with pleasant persistence, assumed the role of the helpful parent. She prodded, encouraged, coaxed, asked leading questions, and double-checked assignments.

She discussed with Telesford the fact sheet he had to prepare on the Japanese-American internment camps. She stood over him in a small study room attached to the classroom as he spread out his books and papers on a table. "You know what I would do?" Heffernan said. "I would take out those two pages from the loose-leaf."

She looked at his work. " 'They are the best,' " she read. " 'They have the best culture and everything.' Why is that a connection to the internment camps?"

"Because they thought they were spies," Telesford said. He wrote his ideas down on a wide-lined sheet of paper.

"I wouldn't be too creative at this point," she said.

"What do I need to do?"

"Just do a couple of sentences on each point in the fact sheet."

"So, I'm going to do A, and then I will do B, and then I will do C."

She stepped back into the larger room to talk to other students while Telesford continued to write. Five minutes later she returned. He read to her a passage from one of his background sheets: "The Japanese came in 1849 for the gold rush and to avoid the military draft in Japan."

She began to dictate: "When they arrived in the United States in the 1900s, they were poor and desperate to work." He wrote this down on the piece of paper.

"What is your next thought?" she asked. "What did they do?"

"I am going to put, 'The U.S.A. was offering good jobs for low pay. The U.S. was offering more jobs for them.' "

"Okay, let me break in and help you focus. What did they do that got people angry with them?"

"They were willing to work for little money." He thought for a moment. "They were willing to work for *less* money. . . . They had anger and resentment underneath."

"Perfect," Heffernan said. "Perfect."

She added, "You're doing this as a teacher in the class, so you don't need to explain and explain and explain. Then you show them the picture. What does this sign say? Get them to participate. It said, JAPS GO HOME."

She watched while he wrote this down. "What else do you think is interesting?" she asked.

"They were put in horse stables."

"You know who is extremely important?" she asked. "Who ordered this?"

"President Roosevelt."

"What are you going to show to illustrate it?"

She was changing the subject. It confused him. Then he caught her meaning. "The thing, the document, it says you have to take just your clothes."

"Okay, you got it," she said. "I don't want to waste time with you getting into a lot of detail." She saw a loose end. "It says here claimants. What are claimants?" she asked.

"People who make claims."

"Excellent! Excellent!"

"But what about the summary?" Borsellino had said he needed one.

"Forget about the summary," Heffernan said. "She just wants a fact sheet." She had to keep her students from wasting time on busy work, particularly if it was clear to her they were misinterpreting the assignment.

"And that's all I would do, Samuel. Just the three quotes."

She left the room. He kept writing. He looked through his notes. He read very softly to himself the phrases he had underlined, and then wrote more.

TOO SMART TO TEACH

Hiring teachers is so difficult an enterprise, so often botched at both high-achieving and low-achieving schools, that there may be little one can teach the other. Common sense suggests that elite schools have an advantage in this, as in other things. But some of the best teachers want only to help children, and since less-endowed schools often have more children in need, the best schools cannot always capture the imaginations of the most motivated educators.

Those who do teach at elite schools encounter the irritations and mindlessness common to all large institutions. To survive with their values intact they need independence, self-confidence, and the recognition that even elite schools do not always deserve the praise to which they have become accustomed.

The third year of Fred Levine's career at Mamaroneck ended in the worst possible way: The principal told him he was being dismissed. He taught Physics and occasionally Earth Science. He had confidence, perhaps too much. His self-sure attitude put him near the bottom of any faculty popularity contest, but one of his strengths was that he did not care very much about that. Unfortunately, that made him particularly vulnerable to the tenure system.

Many parents and some administrators resent the notion of guaranteed employment for tenured teachers. The system makes it very difficult to rectify mistakes. When a faculty member becomes ill or quits, a new teacher has to be brought in quickly without much time to check his or her résumé. Good schools are not immune to bad teachers, and are in some ways more susceptible to declines in faculty performance than less ambitious institutions. Their high standards and impatient parents can lead to faculty frustration and burnout. Their relatively high salaries make it less likely that a weak but tenured teacher can be persuaded to seek work elsewhere.

Principals are supposed to monitor all probationary teachers' progress, sitting in their classes and noting their failings. When the three-year probationary period is up, the principal is obliged to make a recommendation to the superintendent, and the superintendent in turn to the school board. The reviews are sometimes perfunctory, based on whether parents have complained, how well the probationary teacher's students have performed on the Regents, and the teacher's demeanor at meetings and in the faculty lounge.

There is keen interest in parental comments, but they have little practical influence on the hiring decisions. Many teenagers do not talk to their parents about what is happening in school, and parents have few other sources of information on which to make judgments. Some less-than-stellar faculty members survive the probationary period by being pleasant. Some have influential patrons in the superintendent's office or on the school board. Some were strong teachers when they earned tenure, but their skills eroded with age, bad health, and the distractions of personal life. Imaginative teachers with combative personalities, like Levine, are less likely to win approval, and even when they are hired, they often have trouble gaining the confidence of administrators, which only makes them more combative.

Levine grew up in Brooklyn, the son of a housewife and a shopkeeper. He studied physics at Brooklyn College and stayed to teach, but in 1969 was lured away to CBS Laboratories in Stamford, Connecticut, to do sonar and laser research. When the company stumbled financially, he found a job as a researcher and then as a sales executive for a company that organized interstate moves. He was good at sales and found the work invigorating, but his wife loathed his travel schedule and sent in his résumé when she saw a notice of an opening at Mamaroneck High. The department chair liked Levine, a fellow Brooklyn College graduate. He was hired after a five-minute chat with the principal.

Parents who send their children to high-achieving schools envision panels of Ph.D.'s meeting with each teaching candidate, vetting their résumés, subjecting them to long discourses on Dewey and Piaget and Gardner, and repeating the process with dozens of applicants until the right one is found. The real process is often messier and hastier. Many teachers are hired on the run, with little review of their backgrounds and only a department head's instincts as a guide. A few graduates of well-known, selective universities, of the sort parents want their children to attend, are hired, but the vast majority of teachers at schools like Mamaroneck have received their degreees from more modest institutions.

Many Mamaroneck teachers have either taught at or been taught at Catholic schools. Parochial schools have their difficulties but retain some of the traditions of teaching as a calling, not just a job. Teachers with parochial school experience often have firm views about discipline. They are as interested in students' emotional health and in parental satisfaction and in their own salaries as other teachers are, but they also often have a commitment to the transmission of civilized thought and a sense of wonder at God's creations.

Some Mamaroneck teachers arrived with splendid credentials and unusual skills. Mike Roush began work as a teaching intern at the school while finishing his master's degree work at Columbia Teachers College. Cliff Gill had a master's from Columbia and long experience in camp counseling where he had learned how to motivate teenagers. Linda Sherwood had not only been a student and a student teacher at Mamaroneck, and a recipient of a Columbia master's, but had successfully handled five classes of forty students each at Cardinal Spellman High School in the Bronx. A district official had gone all the way to Bowling Green, Ohio, to find Lorna Minor, the AP history teacher. She had a master's degree and an infectious enthusiasm for her subject.

When Jon Murray was hired for the art department in 1978, he was one of seventy people interviewed, but his hiring demonstrated how haphazard the process could be. He came too late to make the final interview list. A friend on the faculty slipped him in. The acquisition of Restaino was even hastier—an interview that took less than two hours and a telephone call offering him the job an hour after that. Ahearn did not want to come to the high school and was hired only because he had, in a moment of characteristic forthrightness, offended the Hommocks principal and had to be moved somewhere else. Borsellino was so upset at the way Mamaroneck handled her first, unsuccessful application that she almost decided not to reapply. The school hiring official forgot to call her back and also lost the observation reports from her last job.

Levine had no formal teacher training. His master's degree was in oceanography. But he had taught successfully in college. As a person of unshakable self-esteem, he thought the school was fortunate to get him.

His first year he taught a college-level physics course, plus Oceanography and two Regents physics courses. He believed he was getting good evaluation ratings from the two assistant principals. Some parents said he graded too harshly, but Levine's colleagues told him his integrated science courses were supposed to be pitched at a high level. By the end of his third year, he felt comfortable and wanted to stay, just the moment that the principal, Joseph Downey, told him he should start looking for another job. He said Levine's desk was messy. His window shades were uneven. He called the students by their last names. His teaching style, demanding and intense, would not work at Mamaroneck.

Levine could not remember ever feeling so angry. He studied the teachers' contract. A small clause in the section on tenure said new teachers had to be told their weaknesses and helped to improve. Had they done that for him? The performance reviews from the assistant principals had been positive. They had included no suggestions for any kind of assistance.

Levine told the teachers' association president he wanted to challenge Downey's decision. The union leader suggested he reconsider. If other school districts learned he had fought a tenure decision, they would not hire him. He would be considered a potential troublemaker, a lawsuit waiting to happen. If he accepted Downey's letter of recommendation, he could start over elsewhere.

Levine was astonished. This was the organization that was supposed to save his job? His meeting with the union's attorney was another disappointment. Two teachers with tenure troubles in other districts were also there. After what Levine considered a perfunctory analysis of each case, the lawyer recommended they all surrender. Perhaps it was not their fault, the attorney said, but their reputations at their respective schools were damaged beyond repair. They would be much better off at other schools.

The two other teachers nodded and left. Levine, his blood percolating, told the lawyer that not only would he fight, but he did not want such an appeaser to represent him. If the union could not find someone else, Levine said, he would find his own attorney and send the union the bill.

A second lawyer called Levine at the union's request. He seemed young, but he had experience with tenure cases. They began the formal grievance process—a letter to the principal, another letter to the superintendent, Otty Norwood.

Downey seemed genuinely bothered by the decision he had made, and Levine's reaction. He tried to explain. "I think you're too smart to be in high school," he said. "Eventually you'll get bored with teaching and become a bad teacher." He told Levine he had seen this happen with bright instructors. After a few years they realized they were clever enough to get by with minimal preparation. They stopped making lesson plans and used the same tests and exercises year after year. Some left teaching. Some stayed and gravitated toward less demanding courses where their ennui would not be so noticeable. Either way, the students were denied their best efforts.

By the time a committee had been formed to hear the case it was July, warm and humid. The committee consisted of four school board members led by Jane Orans, a strong woman with firm views on the need for quality instruction at the high school.

Levine sat at one table in the school board meeting room, facing the four board members. With him were his wife, the union president, and his attorney. On the other side was a table with Norwood, Downey, the two assistant principals who had evaluated Levine, and the school district attorney. Levine was not worried about money or getting another job. It was his reputation he wanted rebuilt. As the superintendent and his attorney presented the district's case, his anger grew. What they presented, he thought, was unbelievably flimsy and contradictory. He was allegedly both too lax and too demanding. This was why he had been put through such nonsense?

When the district finished its case, Levine took over, interrupting his attorney to make points and demanding the union chief keep silent. He questioned Downey, who took the interrogation with great cheer. When Levine caught him in an inconsistency, the principal smiled and said, "Touché."

Levine's lawyer displayed the excellent Regents test scores of Levine's students. He asked the evaluators how, given this record, they could say he was not a quality teacher. As instructed by the school attorney, they declined to elaborate on their negative evaluations. One assistant principal said simply, "I stand by what I wrote."

Some of the questions from the board members indicated they had doubts about the Downey decision. But Norwood stood fast, and his influence was crucial. "I just don't see a case for keeping him," Norwood told the committee. "And as you know, under state law, without the recommendation of the superintendent of schools, the board is not empowered to grant tenure. And I won't do that."

Orans regarded him coolly. "Otty," she said, "that may be true. You might not give him tenure no matter what we do. But our next superintendent would."

Teachers rule high-performing high schools. The strong instructors have support from parents, whose power defines such institutions. Such teachers cannot be significantly disciplined except in extraordinary circumstances. The elite high schools that emerged in the postwar era, at a time of rising power for teachers' unions, proved themselves no better equipped to discipline their faculties than the weakest urban schools.

Union agreements—buttressed by the widespread feeling that teachers at elite schools were doing good work—were designed to help protect good teachers like Levine. But they gave similar protections to weak teachers. The inability of the best-equipped schools to do anything about this suggests that the problem demands a political solution, as troublesome as that may seem. The compromises forced on school administrators by such rules never end, as Levine discovered after the Orans committee reinstated him.

Mamaroneck's science department head had assumed Levine was gone and had given his upper-level physics courses to other teachers. When the newly tenured Levine reappeared in September, he was assigned general science courses for ninth graders, and not just any ninth graders, but the most distracted, least motivated in the class. Levine took it as a refreshing change of pace. He had to prepare for only one course given five times a day. He liked the challenge of reaching the unreachable. What better way to show he was not the arrogant, awkward martinet described at the tenure hearing?

For Downey the change was not so pleasant. Levine's AP Physics course had been given to a teacher who seemed qualified, at least on paper. Unfortunately, the man did not want the course. He had not had to prepare lessons at that level in years. "You can force me to take this class," he told Downey. "You can force me to be in the classroom. But you can't force me to teach it."

Principals who tried to bend veteran teachers to their will risked being forced into months of counseling and hearings and other aggravations. Downey had not been able to discharge a probationary teacher with few social graces or allies. How could he expect to persuade a veteran teacher to take a physics course he did not want? Aware that he was beaten, Downey asked Levine to take back the physics course. Levine agreed. The two men shared a mutual feeling of respect mixed with resentment. They had to share power in this system, but neither of them liked it or wished to be reminded of it.

By elbowing his way onto the faculty, Levine was forever to be regarded by some of his colleagues as pushy and rude, and he did little to correct this impression. He remained quick to tell other teachers where he thought they were wrong. Most administrators, and many faculty, gave him a wide berth. When he made a point at a meeting, others rarely followed up on what he said. Sometimes, he thought, it was as if he were talking to himself.

Yet in the spring of 1992 Coffey picked Levine to be the science department chair.

TIME WARP

Sue Burcroff taught science at Mamaroneck and knew a great deal about time. She was a tall woman who wore large glasses and pinned her long brown hair back in a bun. She had grown up on a farm in southern Pennsylvania. The pace of life had varied then, fast when the peaches and apples in her parents' orchards had to be harvested, slow when winter left the branches draped in snow.

She had been accustomed to leisurely rhythms when she was a high school student. The book work came easy to her. The regional school did not expect much of its students. Few of her classmates pursued their educations after high school. No one in her family had ever graduated from college.

But when she arrived at Pennsylvania State University, she found that time was alarmingly compressed and that she was falling behind. She was majoring in zoology. Concepts and vocabulary piled up. The volume of work was much more than she had ever encountered, more than her high school teachers could have imagined. Each semester she teetered on the edge of failure. For a while she thought that she was just stupid, a farm girl risen above herself. She wondered if it was right for her to ask her parents to spend so much money on a dullard.

Then she learned that time, if manipulated properly, also had the power to save her. From her first semester at Penn State she was rarely away from science. She worked in the research laboratory to help pay her tuition. She had regular, after-hours contact with the concepts that frustrated her in class. Biology professors got to know her and patiently answered questions. They encouraged her not to quit.

Slowly, almost imperceptibly, she began to understand. The jargon seeped into her everyday conversation in the laboratory. The concepts jelled as she went about her chores. In her junior year she began to see the interdisciplinary connections that helped zoology make sense. In her senior year she got an A in Histology, the study of tissues. When the professor asked her to teach the laboratory section of the course in her last semester, she felt transformed. Teaching had become her calling.

Burcroff earned her master's in biology and found a job in a country school in Cincinnatus, New York. For more than a decade she prodded farmers' children who, she thought, deserved the same chance she had had. She worked for the New York state office of the National Education Association for two years and then, beginning a second marriage, moved to Westchester in 1979 and saw a notice of an opening at Mamaroneck.

The APPLE program needed a new science teacher. Dee DaBramo, APPLE's first director, interviewed Burcroff while he lay on pillows strewn on his office floor. Other APPLE faculty sat in chairs, waiting with professional interest for the applicant's reaction to DaBramo's favorite interview question: "What are you going to do the first time a kid says, 'Go fuck yourself'?"

Burcroff was perched on a stool, feeling like the class dunce. She thought DeBramo was excessively weird, but his question was a good one, more complicated than it sounded. "I guess it would depend on the circumstances," she said. "I can't tell you precisely what I'd do. In some cases I would be really offended, but in other cases I might not be. It would depend on who the kid was."

It was the answer he wanted. Flexibility and self-confidence were essential at APPLE. Burcroff was hired and stayed fifteen years in the program, coaxing a love of science out of discouraged children whose upbringing had been very different from hers. When the high school's regular science department lost a teacher, she agreed to teach one regular biology class, which was why she was in the room when Levine, the new science department chair, tried out another of his unpopular ideas.

Coffey, as principal, knew Levine was a gadfly who always had questions, but the teacher also cared about children and wanted to make the department better. Colb, on the other hand, thought Levine should never have become a teacher at all. Although Colb became superintendent long after Levine's tenure hearing, he shared some of the feelings that had led the principal and superintendent then to try to get rid of the physics teacher. He thought Levine took perverse pride in being contentious and went to great lengths to demonstrate his contempt for most of his colleagues. But Coffey was willing to take the risk and put Levine in charge.

For years Levine had been unhappy with the ninth grade general science course. It was an indigestible stew of factoids and pseudo-labs. With no Regents test to give it direction, no one thought the course was very good and no one wanted to teach it. The counselors dumped the least motivated students into it. Teachers struggled through the year while maneuvering for a change of assignment. Levine had not forgotten that he had been given five such classes after he fought off dismissal. What a dumping ground they seemed to be, for both indifferent students and unpopular teachers.

Academically weak ninth graders, it was thought, needed a year to mature before they could be talked into taking Biology. Levine thought that was nonsense. They could start Biology immediately if the course were designed properly. The more he thought about it, the more it seemed to him that the problem was time.

American educational researchers had for several decades been suggesting new ways to organize the school day and the school year. They were mostly ignored. The fifty-minute class period and the two-semester course were too tightly wired into

American life to be discarded on the basis of a few professors' fieldwork.

But the academic critics kept trying. John Carroll, an educational psychologist at the University of North Carolina at Chapel Hill, showed in 1963 that intelligence as usually measured had a time element. "Highly intelligent people will learn faster," he said. "For other people it will take more time to learn, but they will eventually learn." Daniel L. Duke, a professor of education at the University of Virginia, said, "Everyone learns at a different pace. What we have done is held time constant and varied our expectations, when what we need to do is hold our expectations constant and vary time."

Several Virginia high schools stretched algebra into a two-year course after discovering that many students lost interest in mathematics when forced to absorb too many new ideas too quickly. In San Mateo, California, history teachers at Aragon High School stretched an AP American History course into three semesters. Strong students had time to enjoy the subject, spending a full month re-creating the Constitutional Convention. Weak students discovered they could absorb more than they had thought possible.

At Wakefield High School in Arlington, Virginia, educators adjusted time in another way. They reduced the number of courses in each semester and increased the time devoted to each course— two hours a day of English, for example. It was part of a "block scheduling" concept developed by University of Virginia professor Lynn Canaday, so popular that Canaday's answering machine was obliged to tell callers it would be several months before he could accept any new consulting jobs.

Time stretching was part of the message of Theodore Sizer's Coalition of Essential Schools. It advised that teachers act as coaches, not lecturers, and help each student proceed at his or her own pace. *Washington Post* columnist William Raspberry wondered why schools could not treat their slower students as his newspaper treated him. His office's new computer system was making him feel as clueless as any high school freshman, but his bosses acted on the assumption that he would eventually learn if given enough time.

Like most classroom teachers, Levine had little time to read educational research journals. He was not familiar with the growing academic interest in the pace and structure of learning. But his job as a physics teacher was to coax children to examine problems from new angles, and it seemed to him the two-semester ninth grade science course could be revitalized by simply stretching it over three semesters.

At a department meeting, he suggested a year-and-a-half Regents biology course for the academically weak ninth graders being herded into general science. "It will be a slower track, but it will be the same course, and they'll take the Regents test the other kids take at the end," he said. "We'll just stretch it out."

As usual, most of his colleagues did not like his idea. Biology was too difficult, they said. It required a great deal of reading, memorization, and discipline. "What about earth science?" one teacher said. It was also a Regents course, with a somewhat easier examination at the end of it. That would not work either, other teachers said.

Levine understood their point. The old system worked fine for faculty. The students spent time in a science class, as mediocre as it was. Most of them passed and did not have to endure the frightful tension of a Regents test. Everyone was happy. There were no complaints.

Burcroff, however, saw where Levine was heading. She had seen what APPLE students could do if given enough time and personal attention. Levine was suggesting, she thought, a way that every child might benefit from the new national emphasis on raising educational standards. The standards movement was, like all educational fashions, pleasing to contemplate in the abstract but full of poisonous assumptions that could make schools even worse than they were. States and school districts were raising their standards without expecting some students ever to reach them. American children were brought up to assume they were born smart, or not smart, and that was that. In the Asian cultures Burcroff had studied, it was not inborn abilities but effort that was thought to be important. If Americans could change their thinking in that direction, it would make an enormous difference. Teachers at Mamaroneck, for instance, would no longer assume that certain students did not have the intellectual ability to learn biology.

Levine decided to create a new course called Earth Science Plus. Burcroff, Chris Ward, and he each taught one section of the new course in the fall of 1993. They had a total of sixty students, including all of the special education students in the ninth grade. Some counselors worried that failure in this demanding course would ruin their students' chances of surviving the transition to high school with some shred of self-esteem. To prevent this, the three teachers emphasized vocabulary. Each student had to understand the nomenclature. They looked for weak spots in comprehension and used different strategies to reinforce those points.

By the fall of 1994, with only a semester to go before the Regents test, the original group had shrunk to forty students. Levine resisted the temptation to collapse them into two sections. He was at Mamaroneck High, and thus he had enough money to maintain three sections of just thirteen or fourteen students each. For the last semester, all three classes were given to Burcroff for the final drive to the Regents examination.

Burcroff's one advantage, she thought, was that her students liked the idea that they were taking a test usually reserved for "smart" kids. They also appreciated the extra time they had with her. Chris Byron, a fifteen-year-old freshman, noticed that in his other courses teachers would hand out assignments but offer little help. Burcroff often stopped at his desk and asked if there was anything that was not clear. She was friendly with everyone and emphatic when she had to be. The students trusted her.

As the January 1995 Regents test grew near, she pushed harder. The examination would be nearly three hours long. She was concerned that no matter how well her students knew the material, they would not be able to concentrate for that long.

The American education system, including the Mamaroneck schools, had concluded that children in the television age could not be expected to think about one subject for more than twenty minutes at a time. Lessons in elementary school were often designed to last no longer than that. Middle school teachers varied their routines. Now, in the ninth grade, Burcroff's students were being required to grind through a long, complicated multiple-choice test requiring considerable reading skill and a long attention span.

She drilled them with old test questions. She told them to pace themselves. She had an extra proctor assigned to the test so that anyone who wanted to go out and take a short walk could do so. She gave each student a Tootsie Pop, a gesture her students considered wonderfully cheesy. She intended it as a reminder that they keep their energy level up.

Thirty-six of her students took the test. Nineteen of them passed with a score of 65 or higher, and all but two scored more than 50 percent, meeting the minimum requirement for graduation. The best score was an 83 registered by a fifteen-year-old ninth grader named Shannan Faulkner. The girl's horrible science grades in middle school had made her wonder if it was realistic for her to pursue her interest in becoming a teacher herself. But she had taken her time during the test, mulling over her answers as she liked to do.

Burcroff was pleased that so many had passed a test the old system would not have allowed them to take. But she was also upset. So many other students in other schools were allowed to slide through, no one counting on them for much. What happened to them in places that did not have Mamaroneck's tolerance for experimentation, and the resources to keep class sizes small?

As soon as the examination was over, she noticed, the class went slack. They appeared to have much less interest in their work. The change in mood gave her a sense of the awesome motivational power in a test they knew to be difficult, written not by her but by the State Board of Regents.

Several of the students who had just missed the 65 percent cutoff said they wanted to try the test again in May. Most of them spent the second semester in a special introductory biology course to prepare them for Regents biology the next year.

At the beginning of the three-semester experiment, Burcroff had not been wholly convinced of its wisdom, even if she was more enthusiastic than anyone else Levine spoke to. She was not certain she wanted so much effort bound up in the results of a test.

Toward the end she realized that she had not prepared her students as well as she should have for the shock of the long examination. If she had begun to give them longer tests months before the Regents, they would have been more prepared. An adjustment of their internal clocks might have made her pep talks and candy less necessary.

But it had worked for more students than she had expected. Some who considered themselves academically hopeless now thought they could do anything. That was an exaggeration also, but it was taking them in the right direction. No matter what their scores, each of them drew courage from having completed a high-standard course. All of them took a third year of science, and all but one a fourth year.

A school like Mamaroneck, she thought, had time and talent and equipment assembled for the children of its most driven parents, who were, not coincidentally, usually the best students. But the same resources could be used to help the less motivated. The atmosphere, if used properly, could give them a sense that they too were part of the academic tradition, that the peer pressure for excellence applied to them as well.

Just how much could she accomplish, she wondered, if she could harness the notion of playing the same game as the smart kids?

EXTRA HELP

For Debbie Schoeneman, a slim blonde in the class of '95, high school was a carefully scheduled affair, with appointments recorded in the black-covered weekly planner she had bought at the Corner Store in Larchmont. Talking very fast, following up every detail, she was elected president of the freshman, sophomore, and junior classes. She was coeditor of the *Globe*. She became a leader of the Safe Rides Club. She acted, danced, and choreographed in PACE. She ran the Cove, a Friday night dance club at Flint Park.

But she occasionally had trouble with mathematics, so she decided to hire a tutor, becoming part of a trend that has been spreading throughout elite schools, involving one family after another as fears of losing the college race grow.

One of the less obvious flaws of the ability grouping that dictated many assignments at Mamaroneck was the strain of dealing with students like Schoeneman who did better in some subjects than they did in others. The usual academic sorting did not work for her. She was in accelerated English and social studies classes, pulling in grades above 90, so she was put into accelerated mathematics too. This was not only because the counselors assumed that a student good in one subject would be good in others, but because once the school had scheduled the honors English class for one period, it was easiest to put its students into the same honors mathematics class in another period.

When Schoeneman did not do well in honors mathematics, she was moved down to the middle-level mathematics class. That was too easy; she scored at the top of the class. When she was returned to the honors sections, she found herself in trouble again.

She hated comparing test scores. She could not understand why she was sailing ahead of the boy at the next desk in English and social studies, and falling 10 or 20 points behind him in mathematics. Cliff Gill, the stentorian algebra teacher, told her to persevere. One day when she was having a particularly difficult time in class, he made a promise: "Miss Schoeneman, you think this course is tough? Miss Schoeneman is too busy organizing the world to consider the importance of my question. Yes, this course is tough. But you'll see that has some advantages. On the Regents, everyone in this class will get a 95 or a 100. You should all get a 95 or a 100 *on a bad day!* . . . Well, maybe not everybody. But at least you will all get a 90."

Months later Gill posted the Regents results on the door of his classroom. He identified each student with a number. Schoeneman approached the list with some eagerness. She ran her eye down the indentification numbers. She found hers and read the score: 89. It was a respectable grade, but it made her sick. Only one other score on the list was lower, an 86. She spent the rest of the afternoon weeping on her back porch and dipping into a carton of Ben & Jerry's Chocolate Chip Cookie Dough ice cream brought over by a friend.

She decided she needed help in mathematics, but with so many activities she had no suitable time slot to see a teacher during the school day. She secured her parents' permission for a mathematics tutor and hired one at $60 an hour.

There is nothing new about American children, particularly the wealthier ones, paying for extra academic help. In the nineteenth century, instructors in foreign languages and science visited mansions on Beacon Hill or Fifth Avenue to help young people struggling with day school lessons. The use of tutors had spread to the upper edges of the American middle class by the middle of the twentieth century. It found its way to an entirely different clientele in the 1960s, when many colleges organized tutoring programs for inner-city children. Even an untrained undergraduate, it was thought, could provide enough enrichment to coax a ghetto child to do his homework and take school seriously.

Schoeneman's generation was the first in which significant numbers of middle-class students in public schools hired outside tutors. The surge of tutors was foreshadowed by the appearance of SAT preparation companies, such as Princeton Review and Kaplan, and an assortment of franchises promising to help children with any subject at any grade level. In Maryland's Montgomery County, Los Angeles's San Gabriel Valley, the lakeshore towns north of Chicago, and dozens of other communities with college-bound children, learning centers appeared in shopping center storefronts alongside pizza parlors, bakeries, and dry cleaners. Most of them charged $35 to $50 an hour for their services. Elementary school students needing help with reading and arithmetic produced much of the business, but there were also tutors for high school courses. Demand for French declined, but Spanish tutors were hot.

By the mid-1990s, when Schoeneman and several of her friends began to seek tutors, the private teaching business was in a growth spurt. Sylvan Learning Centers had five hundred outlets around the country. Huntington Learning Centers had one hundred offices offering reading, writing, and arithmetic lessons. Their shopping center offices resembled classrooms, with two or three students at a time working with a tutor.

The number of private individuals tutoring in students' homes also increased. Many of them were former teachers who had retired or taken time off to raise their children. Some were still working full-time in the classroom and earning extra fees after school. Usually, but not always, they dealt with students who were not in their regular classes. Some parents wondered about paying teachers to save the pupils they apparently were not reaching in class.

Were they being paid twice to do the same job? Some schools attempted to ban their own faculty from tutoring students from their own schools.

Tutors advertised by word of mouth and with notices in community and school newspapers. Some tutors pinned photocopied advertisements to supermarket bulletin boards with vertical strips at the bottom, each with the tutor's telephone number to be torn off for easy reference.

In parts of the south, midwest, and west the rise of private tutoring came late, but the New York suburbs were so accustomed to the practice that by the mid-1990s it was fodder for satire. The *Scarsdale Inquirer,* a community weekly, led its 1994 April Fool's edition with a report that the school board was about to hire a personal tutor for every child at the high school. One parent was quoted suggesting the program be retroactive. "My thirty-year-old still can't spell," she said.

The editors of the Scarsdale student newspaper, the *Maroon,* amused themselves with what they called a typical student's evening schedule:

4:00– 5:00	Math Tutor
5:00– 6:00	Chemistry Tutor
6:00– 6:10	Dinner
6:15– 7:15	English Tutor
7:15– 8:15	History Tutor
8:15– 9:15	Spanish Tutor
9:15–10:15	SAT Prep
10:15–11:15	Achievement Tutor
11:15–12:15	French Tutor

In a more serious *Maroon* article, Scarsdale students defended tutoring. The school had a complex class schedule with free time in the middle of the day for library study or extra help from teachers, but often a student's free period did not coincide with her teacher's. The school's math center, designed to provide tutoring, was often crowded and unable to provide the hour a week of undivided attention that a private tutor promised in exchange for money.

Elite public schools may be thought of as tax-supported private schools, but the growth of tutoring reveals how different public and private school services can be, even in these affluent neighborhoods. Mamaroneck High had few classes with more than twenty students, but Rye Country Day School, just two miles away, could offer for tuition of $14,250 a year an average class size of only fifteen, and had fewer scheduling barriers to keep students from consulting their regular teachers.

Schoeneman dealt directly with her tutor. She scheduled appointments and chose which assignments to discuss. The tutor helped prepare her for the tenth grade geometry Regents test. In the ninth grade Gill may have been too demanding for her taste, but her tenth grade classroom teacher had not been demanding enough.

Coffey worried about Schoeneman. Why would someone so capable of exploiting every school opportunity think she needed a tutor? "Why don't you just go after school and talk to your teachers?" he said.

"I don't have time after school," she said. "I'm in performances, and I do all kinds of crazy stuff, so it's very good for me to know that at the scheduled time I will have this person to myself. Especially with math, I feel very comfortable with one person working with me one-on-one." If she did not have to face a tutor at least once a week and show what she could do, she might fall back, and it would be even more difficult to catch up. She sought a tutor only in those few cases where her teachers were weak or unable to communicate effectively with her, the rest of the time seeking out helpful teachers like Levine or biology teacher Barbara Lapine at lunch and in other spare moments.

Despite its growing popularity, the notion of American students paying for extra help scratched at a sore spot—the fact that public schools were created to give all children an equal chance at an education. Some educators said tutoring was nothing more than a security blanket for the overly anxious. They said students would learn just as much if they did extra homework during the time they would otherwise be seeing their tutors. Was it right, they asked, for other students to be left with the feeling that they could never compete against children with wealthy and indulgent parents?

Eric Rothschild, the Scarsdale history teacher, cringed at what he thought was an erosion of the American commitment to equal opportunity. He compared tutoring to a crowd watching a parade. One person in front stood on his toes to see the band. All the people behind him also had to stand on their toes. No one saw the parade any better. The tutored student could not gain on his peers because they hired tutors too.

Some questioned his analogy: Was education a competition, or an expansion of consciousness? If tutors nurtured deeper understanding of history and science in young minds, why stand in their way?

Advocates of change offered the tutoring controversy as one more indication of the need for more individual instruction in class. If teachers cut back on the time they spent parroting the textbook, Theodore Sizer argued, they would be able to address each child's weak spots.

Many teachers acknowledged that extra time with students like Schoeneman would cost schools money, but it might also enliven the learning process much more than money spent for computers and bigger textbooks. If two extra hours a week with a knowledgeable adult kept Schoeneman on track, why couldn't the schools extend the same privilege to everyone who needed it?

In 1996 California lurched in this direction by committing $1 billion to lower class sizes in elementary schools, promising to pay for extra teachers who could be brought in to make sure there were no more than twenty pupils per teacher. It was a slapdash, poorly organized program, which led many schools to divide gyms and cafeterias into makeshift classrooms in order to qualify for the money and the new staff. Experts warned that without the right training, the new teachers—many without credentials—would not be able to help their students learn to read as well as they could.

But no one doubted that the extra time spent with each student was an idea worth exploring. With a growing number of retired people looking for worthwhile pastimes, with college students looking for pocket money, and with high school students seeking public service credit, some educators asked how much would it take to organize a national tutoring corps to help millions of high school students in less favored neighborhoods who, like Schoeneman, needed a little extra help.

BRAIN COMMUNES

The school building opened in 1964 and shows some wear. Its flat brick facing and metal frame windows have a spiritless prefabricated look. The concrete windowsills reveal water stains. Weeds jut up around the maples in the front courtyard. The abstract sculpture in front has a kitschy *Star Trek* look.

This is the Thomas Jefferson High School for Science and Technology, a symbol of a moment of high excitement, fueled by panic, in American education. In 1983, two years before Jefferson was reborn as a school for young techno whizzes, a federal report entitled *A Nation at Risk* warned that the public school system was disintegrating into mediocrity, particularly in the sciences and engineering, where national survival was at stake.

Several businessmen in northern Virginia decided to fund a special high school for science and mathematics. With the cooperation of the state and the Fairfax County public schools, they created one of the strongest public schools in the country. Eleven other states have opened science and mathematics schools, in their cases providing room and board so that they attract exceptional students from hundreds of miles away.

Jefferson and schools like it are a special category of the elite. They were created by law, not by accidents of geography, wealth, and real-estate marketing, and they illustrate most vividly what makes an elite school other than affluent, aggressive parents. Most, if not all, of their students are selected not because they live in the school's neighborhood but because they have passed an admission test, similar to and sometimes identical to the SAT or ACT required of college applicants. Eighth graders who want to enroll in the Illinois Mathematics and Science Academy (IMSA) in Aurora, Illinois, for instance, average 1184 on the SAT, 282 points above the 902 national average of high school seniors four years older than they are.

The public room-and-board schools are a relatively new breed, but many special schools have a long history. New York City high schools like Stuyvesant and the Bronx High School of Science became selective schools several generations ago. Boston Latin, Lowell High in San Francisco, Walnut Hills High in Cincinnati, Franklin High in New Orleans, University High in Tucson, and several other selective public high schools have long traditions. They were created by local educators who wanted the same critical mass of young intellect that communities like Chagrin Falls, Ohio, and Palo Alto, California, achieved through real estate promotion and political tradition.

Among the more than 30 special schools in the country, Jefferson may be the most interesting and in some ways the most surprising. No school is more ambitious, but at the same time its administrators question that ambition and look for ways to turn what parents conceive as a manufacturer of top college applicants into a nurturer of imaginative thought.

Although it has only 800 seniors and juniors, Jefferson in 1996 gave 1,931 AP examinations, second only to the 2,082 given at Stuyvesant High in Manhattan, a special school with nearly twice as many students. Ninety-six percent of Jefferson's AP students had passing scores of 3 or higher, compared to 91.5 percent at Stuyvesant. In 1995 Jefferson had 112 National Merit Semifinalists, the most in the country for the fifth year in a row. Its average SAT score in 1994 was 1343, 49 percent higher than the national mean.

Yet its principal, Geoffrey Jones, a cheery steelworker's son, frowns at the glorification of such statistics. He argues that AP tests and science fair ribbons are not the way to motivate students. He has one of the strongest AP programs ever created, and it does not make him happy. He prefers Jefferson courses such as Computer Architecture, Elements of Artificial Intelligence, and Supercomputer Applications that go beyond AP Computer Science. His mathematics department ventures beyond calculus to multivariable calculus and linear algebra. He sees his pre-engineering, research labs, and technology department as a model for high school education a century from now, with courses in DNA biotechnology, microprocessor system design, principles of automation and robotics, and quantum mechanics.

Jones says Advanced Placement is designed for the convenience of colleges and high schools who want to accelerate students along very narrow tracks. His school, he argues, should nudge young minds out of these ruts and stimulate creativity and interconnection.

High-performing schools such as La Jolla and Paul D. Schreiber High in Port Washington, New York, have established national reputations for producing winners of science competitions, like the Westinghouse Science Talent Search. Jones' students have had similar success—ten Westinghouse finalists, more than any other Washington area school. He does not discourage their work, but he does not encourage it either.

"The notion of competing against one another for the best science project is absolutely the opposite idea of what we want to do," he said. "The notion should be, what can we learn from each other and how can we work collaboratively to develop each other's ideas? How can we celebrate what we are learning and feel good about this process rather than always having a winner and loser?"

His message is: Einstein is dead. It is not the lone genius but the laboratory team that has produced most of the new thoughts and inventions of the last half century. A company looking for scientists is not going to hire the Westinghouse prize winner and ignore the students who came in second and third. It is going to hire all of them, Jones says, and expect them to work together and take advantage of what each has to contribute. A school that prepares such students is not a brain farm, but a brain commune, promoting intellectual progress through joint effort.

Jefferson began as an ordinary-enrollment school in 1964 and was reopened as a school for science and technology in 1985. That year it received eight hundred applications for its first class of four hundred. In 1995 it had twenty-seven hundred applications to fill the same four hundred ninth grade slots, forcing a winnowing process as brutal as Yale's. The first cut, down to eight hundred applicants, was made on the basis of middle school grades and scores on a test similar to the SAT. Then the admissions staff looked at activities, portfolios, and other signs of talent in cutting the eight hundred down to four hundred twenty who were admitted, the assumption being that about twenty would not accept admission. School board policy forbids consideration of race, sex, or family income in the admission process. Only 40 percent of the student body is female. Jones would like to admit more girls, he says, but not enough of them apply. It is still hard to interest many fourteen-year-old girls in a school so wedded to science and mathematics.

Other schools devoted to science and mathematics include the Bronx High School of Science, Brooklyn Technical High, and eleven state boarding schools: IMSA in Illinois, the Alabama School of Mathematics and Science in Mobile, the Arkansas School for Mathematics and Sciences in Hot Springs, the Indiana Academy for Science, Mathematics and Humanities in Muncie, the Louisiana School for Mathematics, Science and the Arts in Natchitoches, the Maine School of Science and Mathematics in Limestone, the Mississippi School for Mathematics and Science in Columbus, the North Carolina School of Science and Mathematics in Durham, the Oklahoma School of Science and Mathematics in Oklahoma City, the South Carolina Governor's School for Science and Mathematics in Hartsville, and the Texas Academy of Mathematics and Science in Denton.

Most are not much bigger than private boarding schools. IMSA has 600 students in three grades. The Alabama School has 257 students in just two grades, eleventh and twelfth. The public boarding schools usually spend two or three times as much per child as regular public schools, about $18,000 per student at IMSA and $14,000 at the Alabama school, mostly because of the cost of food and shelter.

A regular school that loses a student to a special school not only has one fewer star to inspire its other students, but also receives less state money. This irritates local school boards, state legislators, and other interest groups. Sharon Voliva, legislation chairwoman for the Illinois Parent Teacher Association, told *The Wall Street Journal* that she thought the creation of IMSA was a mistake. "There doesn't need to be two separate systems, for the elitist and for the common," she said.

Neighborhood rivals of nonboarding special schools like Jefferson feel similarly shortchanged. The staff of Langley High School in McLean, one of the strongest schools in the country, miss few opportunities to point out that teachers at Jefferson are paid 7 percent more for handling a student body nearly devoid of academic weaknesses. Biology teachers at Langley say that their students must read about recombinant DNA in a textbook, while Jefferson students have studied the real thing in gels supplied by one of their corporate sponsors.

In 1995 Alabama Governor Fob James Jr. said he wanted more funds for the state's regular schools and cut the budget of the Alabama School of Science and Mathematics by 15 percent. The school had opened in the old Dauphin Way Baptist Church four years before, using the former church Sunday school for classrooms. It was jarred by the cutbacks, but a foundation supported by Alabama corporations such as International Paper and the Olin Corp. found enough money to maintain the forty-five-member faculty and the heavy dose of physics, chemistry, and biology classes.

Some of the special schools have been criticized for using state money to produce graduates so heavily recruited that they reject state universities in favor of the Ivy League. In retaliation, state universities are increasing their own recruiting efforts, offering lucrative merit scholarships that many special school graduates find hard to refuse. Jennifer Jenkins, a spokeswoman for the Alabama School, said more than half of its graduates go to Alabama universities. For the North Carolina school in Durham, the figure is 72 percent, a measure of the quality of in-state schools such as Duke and the University of North Carolina at Chapel Hill.

The North Carolina High School of Science and Mathematics was born in 1980, the first of the state boarding schools for science and one of the most successful. The faculty took over the old Watts Hospital, an empty hulk with hidden rooms and old pathology laboratories that inspired tales of medically interesting ghosts.

Like other science academies, the North Carolina school prides itself on an active program in the arts and music. Joe Lyles, one of the art teachers, recalled standing in a corridor trying to recruit visiting students in 1980 and being approached by a teenager who asked if he employed right-brain stimulation techniques in his lessons. "Of course I do," Lyles said, not having any idea what the boy was talking about. Lyles has since educated himself. He starts his course with an exploration of brain science and human perception of shapes. This appeals to a classroom full of future doctors, molecular biologists, and computer engineers.

One hundred miles west of Durham in Winston-Salem the state has set up the even more unusual North Carolina School of the Arts, a boarding school that accepts two hundred fifty students from as far away as California for intensive work in drama, music, ballet, and other disciplines. Other arts schools, such as the Duke Ellington High School of the Performing Arts in Washington, D.C., and the La Guardia High School of the Performing Arts in New York, are less numerous than the science schools and depend more on auditions than SAT scores in deciding whom to admit.

But many science schools have their artistic side. The hallways between classrooms at Jefferson are decorated with student oils and pencil drawings and photographs. Art teacher Don Okazaki's classroom feels like a dark loft in Soho, with paintings covering the windows and odd mobiles hanging from the ceiling. Students work on oils and portraits between physics and computer classes. Many talk of music and math and science and art all blending together and how they might combine all of them in a career in computer graphic arts.

In Jones's perfect world, there would be no college recruiters trying to force students like that to decide on a major and present a transcript full of AP scores and prizes and grades. He would like to take the concentration of young minds and turn it into something that defies the image of the elite high school, emphasizing not individual achievement but imagination and cooperation and defiance of conventional wisdom. Instead of having grades and scores on examinations, he says, such students would "internalize a sense of excellence" and "know when they have learned something well enough and when they haven't.

"If they go off to a job and they are forever dependent on the boss coming by and saying they've done a good job," he says, "they are not going to be effective contributors to the workplace and they are not going to be leaders."

His students, as attractive as they find such thoughts, still sign up for hundreds of AP tests and fret over their college applications, a culture of prize-loving achievement not different from that at New Trier or Gunn or Mamaroneck, just more concentrated, a chemistry experiment in progress.

CONCLUSIONS

BY ANY OTHER NAME

On April 2, 1995, Debbie Schoeneman got her letter from Tufts. It said she had been put on the waiting list, the worst possible news. She had applied to twelve schools and Tufts was one of those she thought would admit her without question. The letter meant her sense of what each college thought of her was terribly askew. As she drove back to school she considered the possibility that she would be rejected by all her top schools and find herself surrounded by corn and soybeans at Oberlin College, her least favorite of the dozen.

She was reluctant to consult her guidance counselor, Diana Marx. There was a wide generation gap. Marx was sixty-seven and a year away from retirement after ten years as a counselor at Mamaroneck and seventeen years as a counselor and English teacher at the Hommocks. She was a friendly woman with the intelligence and determination to graduate from Brooklyn College with a Phi Beta Kappa key by attending night school while raising two children. She had had many successes in persuading colleges to accept marginal students. But Schoeneman and some other students did not feel connected to her. Two of Schoeneman's friends assigned to Marx had already hired, with their parents' strong support, private college counselors. Schoeneman said she was afraid Marx might have written her off as a socializing blonde with unrealistic academic ambitions. It was sometimes, she thought, like talking to somebody's grandmother, a monologue in which nothing she said seemed to register.

Schoeneman's unhappy struggle with the SAT widened the gulf. She took the Preliminary Scholastic Aptitude (later Assessment) Test in the fall of her sophomore year. She grimaced when she opened the envelope and saw she had gotten a 1090. Everyone told her she needed to break 1300 to have a chance at the most selective schools. Her first attempt at the SAT in the fall of her junior year yielded only a 1190. She saw no creative aspects to the exercise, and resented the way her male friends, such as Lewy and Hafetz, breezed through the SAT as if it were a sixth grade arithmetic quiz, while she studied twice as hard and did worse.

In the spring of Schoeneman's junior year, she took her second SAT and scored a 1260. She tried again in the fall of her senior year and got a 1290, a 610 on the mathematics and a 680 on the verbal. She was not going to break 1300. She gave up.

After the first SAT, Marx told her that she was unlikely to be accepted to Brown or Penn and should not bother to apply to Cornell or Wesleyan because it would just mean more rejections. Washington University might be too academic, Schoeneman remembered being told, but Marx thought she ought to apply to Emory because it was both academically challenging and fun. Marx strongly recommended Oberlin despite all the contrary signals Schoeneman was sending. "It will be great for you," Marx told her. "My grandson went there and he loved it."

Instead of hiring a private counselor as her friends had done, Schoeneman sought help from another Mamaroneck counselor, the sweetly upbeat Nick Kourabas. He knew that despite her relatively mediocre scores, she had been running the school for four years and would impress admissions officers. "Yeah, sure, apply to Cornell," he said. "Apply to Wesleyan too. Someone might like you there."

Mamaroneck's student-counselor ratio was the envy of

Kourabas's friends in the New York City schools, where he had once been a very unmotivated student at Stuyvesant High. As a Mamaroneck counselor, he needed to keep track of only one hundred sixty students, compared to three hundred or four hundred per counselor in New York. The teachers' association did not like him saying it, but he thought he had a reasonable workload. He could spend useful time with each student. Counselors varied in quality. Some did not deal well with certain kinds of students. Some had bad years. Some were distracted by family problems. Each tried to cover for the others when they could, without making too much of a fuss about it. Schoeneman was, in essence, a student who did not need a counselor, so any help he gave would be unlikely to offend anyone.

On the afternoon Schoeneman got the Tufts letter, Kourabas was one of the first people she encountered when she returned to school. "This is ridiculous," he said. "We've got to call them." Mindful of protocol, he suggested Schoeneman ask Marx to contact Tufts and see if they had made a mistake. Marx remembers seeing Schoeneman and sharing her consternation. Schoeneman recalls the moment differently: the counselor telling the student not to worry and the student restraining an impulse to be rude. Both remember that Marx agreed to call Tufts in the morning and see what she could do.

Schoeneman arrived early on April 3 to make sure Marx followed through. On the way she passed Coffey's office. He had heard what had happened and called her in to soothe her. If Marx had not called yet, he said, come back and he would call Tufts himself.

Marx was engaged with another student and had not yet made the call. Schoeneman returned to Coffey's office and sat while Bunny Pulice, Coffey's secretary, fetched Schoeneman's file. Coffey looked for points to emphasize when he called the admissions office. He leafed through a copy of her Tufts application. Something in the counselor's recommendation bothered him. "I didn't know you played soccer, Debbie," he said.

Schoeneman found this amusing. She was a skilled modern dancer, but team sports were not her strength. She had played one season of soccer when she was ten but was so inept she gave it up. The same thing happened with field hockey. Her many athletic friends, delighted to discover a flaw, often reminded her of this.

"I don't play soccer," she said. "Why?"

He read her a sentence from Marx's recommendation: "To quote Debbie's soccer coach, 'She is one of the top one percent of female athletes I have ever seen.' " There were words about rock climbing, something else Schoeneman did not do. The recommendation said nothing about her string of class presidencies. There was nothing about her editorship of the *Globe* or presidency of the Cove dance club or seat on the Safe Rides board. This was the report Marx had sent not only to Tufts, but to Brown and Penn and Wesleyan and Cornell and other schools high on Schoeneman's list. The applicant's political and journalistic activities were noted elsewhere in her application, but an admissions officer would have found it odd that her counselor did not mention them. Some might have even wondered if the student's claims of extracurricular stardom were genuine.

Coffey sent Schoeneman off to class and called in Marx. "There is a problem here, Diana," he said. Marx was thunderstruck. She would later recall it as one of the most distressing moments in her career. Almost immediately, she realized what had happened.

Her husband Stan had died suddenly of an aneurysm the previous July, just as they were planning their fiftieth wedding anniversary. When she returned to school in August to begin preparing college applications, she was still reeling from his death. She had to prepare recommendations for forty seniors. The counseling office secretary had gathered the files, but in collecting material for Schoeneman, some papers from an adjoining file had mixed in. Lisa Schroeer followed Schoeneman on alphabetical lists of Mamaroneck senior girls. She was a dark-haired athlete, particularly talented in soccer. Wellesley accepted her early. Somehow Marx had placed comments that related to Schroeer in the recommendation for Schoeneman.

Devastated and embarrassed, Marx apologized to Coffey and to Schoeneman. Coffey called Tufts and several other colleges to make sure they knew of the error. But it was late in the process. Many schools had already sent their letters.

Schoeneman found to her surprise that she was much calmer about the error than almost everyone she knew. She had reported the facts as dispassionately as possible to her *Globe* friends. By the end of the day the parent grapevine was vibrating with rage. Several mothers told Sandy Schoeneman, a psychologist, that they thought she should sue. Morris Schoeneman, a physician, called Coffey and concluded the principal had everything under control.

They waited for the rest of the letters, each a ticking bomb. Brown rejected her. Penn rejected her. But on a pleasant spring afternoon, standing in her front hall, she opened an acceptance letter from Wesleyan. For a while she thought that was where she would go. It had a lovely campus and an innovative curriculum, if somewhat isolated on the back roads of Connecticut. At the last moment she decided instead to go to Cornell, which also accepted her despite Marx's warning that her scores were too low. Marx said later that she would have told Schoeneman that her later SAT scores in the 1200s moved her into contention for Cornell, but by that time Schoeneman had stopped seeing Marx.

The parents outraged by the recommendation mistake organized no protest. The girl had gotten into a school she wanted, a balm for any number of sins. In a culture ruled by that singular obsession, botching a college application was easily forgotten once college admission was achieved.

Mamaroneck, like other elite schools, was not judged by how well it educated every child, or how often it exposed its students to lifelong avocations, or how well it connected its lessons to what was happening in the world. If its students were admitted to colleges and universities that they and their parents found pleasing, then no more questions were asked. Diana Marx's error had been a minor one, committed in good faith, but even if she had been as venal as Lady Macbeth, few would have cared once her anxious client got into the Ivy League.

EXAMINED LIVES

Samuel Telesford had no desire to go to Cornell. He wanted only a regular diploma, an emblem of his hard work in adjusting to a new country, and by June 1995 his goal was in sight. Although it was unlikely he would graduate on schedule with his class the following June, his grades were improving and college seemed within his reach.

He received a 94 in Dale Zheutlin's Art Foundation course, where he showed talent for color and composition. He received an 87 in Health, a course he had previously failed, and a 95 in Changing Times, Phillips's cinematic examination of postwar America. In that course, among other assignments, he received an A for a neatly written 169-word summary of the film *Wall Street*.

His English and social studies grades from Team 9 were lower, but he had done more work for them. His writing improved. "Be more specific, be more specific," Esposito had said. By the end of the year, Telesford would earn an 81 from Borsellino for the social studies portion of his grade and an 86 from Esposito for English. He loved a crowd, so his presentation on the Japan internment camps went well. The result was not as electrifying as the girl in Restaino's class who brought a duffel bag to her presentation and asked her classmates how they would like having to leave everything behind but what the bag could hold. But Telesford explained clearly Roosevelt's fear of West Coast riots and the Supreme Court's unwillingness to take action.

Some of Borsellino's multiple-choice tests were tricky, but Telesford thought he was beginning to understand how to pass them. His essays were literate and easy to read. His wide-looped penmanship was very different from the difficult-to-decipher scrawl of the American-born boys in the class.

It was the autobiography project of which he was most proud. It had worked its way into his imagination. He had to address his own life—the trip from the Canal Zone, the contrast between warm Panama winters playing soccer and chilly Mamaroneck nights watching television with his mother, his feelings about God and school and friendship. Esposito let him use the computer in his classroom to write the chapters. Telesford came at lunch and after school to work on the collection of essays he called *Turtle Power.*

One noon period he was in Esposito's room while the Team 9 teachers were in Borsellino's room arguing about the final examination. Word of their success was beginning to circulate. Educational consultant Pat Carini and her associate, Mary Hebron, had collected glowing student evaluations of the Japan project. The test scores indicated the students were absorbing the Regents material as well as always. Several students on the lower end of the scale, like Telesford, were understanding things they did not ordinarily understand and showing an interest in topics they did not ordinarily appreciate.

But the team did not want to lose its edge. Cronin and Ahearn wondered how to handle one of the essay questions that would likely be on the Regents test:

1. The excerpt of the poem below expresses the author's view about imperialism.

   Take up the White Man's burden,
   Send forth the best ye breed—

Go, bind your sons to exile
To serve your captives' need;
To wait, in heavy harness,
On fluttered folk and wild
Your new-caught, sullen peoples;
Half-devil, half-child.
>>> —Rudyard Kipling, "White Man's Burden"

—Explain the attitude toward imperialism reflected in the quotation.

—Identify a specific society and discuss 2 ways the attitude expressed in the quotation affected the history of that society.

The question had been used on previous Regents tests. Ahearn thought it was too obscure, demanding more literary interpretation than knowledge of nineteenth-century colonialism. The subtleties were lost on this generation, and the answers accordingly were weak. "That question was widely misinterpreted by the kids," Ahearn said.

"Not everyone who did it did it wrong," Cronin said.

Ahearn looked stubborn. "I don't know if I want to do that."

"I got no problem," Borsellino said. They had to make sure their ninth graders, no matter how well they made presentations and wrote autobiographies, could handle the Global Studies Regents test they would take in the middle of tenth grade.

"I think it's a curveball," said Ahearn, whose eldest son had been the catcher on the Mamaroneck varsity.

"So what?" Cronin said.

Borsellino noted that if a student didn't like it, she or he could choose another question. They planned to have six on the final, and the students had to answer only two.

"I really tell you," Ahearn said, "when I was proctoring that Global Studies Regents exam and there was widespread misinterpretation of that, it was dreadful."

Cronin shrugged. Ahearn persisted. "I think it defeats what we are trying to do. I don't think it is ever a good question for the Regents. I think it is a bad question."

"That's because the kids don't read it carefully," Cronin said. "If they don't read it carefully, they get in trouble."

"I know the level of my kids," Ahearn said. "They are going to swing and miss big time."

"But they have a week to prepare."

"Let's be straightforward and ask the question," Ahearn suggested. "But when they go to the poetry, they're lost. I'm not going to throw this at them."

"Well, I want this question."

Borsellino attempted a compromise. "You could ask the question and forget the poem."

"No," Cronin said. "I want that level of sophistication."

Turner-Porter spoke up. "So we give them two questions and let them pick."

"This is harder," Borsellino said. "They might not choose it anyway."

"I got some kids who will," Cronin said. There seemed no way to resolve the argument between those who wanted to stretch academic muscles and those who felt such rigorous exercise might cause injury to the weak.

For their second year the Team 9 teachers wanted to change the direction of the course and deepen student involvement by creating a new category of presentations. Students would be asked to address cultural and political questions in several distinct ways—as researchers, as artists, as scholars, as performers, as cultural consultants, and as authors.

The teachers had already drafted a letter to the parents of the incoming class of 1999. It listed fifteen books, from *Jane Eyre* to *Confessions of a Woman Warrior,* from which to select summer reading. Each child had to read at least three books and keep a journal on what he or she had read. Students who wished the advanced designation on their report cards had to read five books.

For all his worries about the Kipling question, Ahearn was feeling better than he had in twenty-two years of teaching. The students were engaged and excited. The special education students had done work he would not have anticipated. He had not encountered the gaps that he feared might occur in a course with so many units taught by students. The Carini-Hebron report was telling him that the students felt they had learned something worthwhile. The evaluations were so uniformly positive it was almost a relief to encounter those few responses that revealed normal adolescent resistance to adult aspirations. The two consultants presented, uncensored, all negative responses to the Japan unit, of which there were exactly eight out of two hundred eighty student evaluations:

1. "I hate Japan."
2. "I learned that Japanese are sneaks."
3. "The best thing about the Japan Project was getting to the end!"
4. "It was stupid."
5. "The teachers should teach it."
6. "[The worst thing was] learning about another country."
7. "I didn't like anything."
8. "Not informative. . . . I didn't learn much."

Nearly everyone else liked the novelty of helping classmates learn and learning from them. "A few thought that they learned much more this way," Carini and Hebron wrote, "and besides that it was much more interesting than listening to the teacher lecture.

"Some students spoke of the pride they felt about pulling it off and doing a good job even though they were nervous. Others just sound quite delighted with themselves in the teaching role or speaking in public—and relishing it."

The stacks of student autobiographies in D220 suggested a coffee-table book sale at Barnes & Noble. Each report had gone through several drafts, as if it were being professionally published. An art teacher, Diana Taylor, showed them how to decorate the final product. A scanner was made available for transferring family photos to paper.

Pictures of turtles graced the cover of Telesford's autobiography. Inside were a Snoopy cartoon, a Panamanian flag, and pictures of Telesford with his mother and several church friends. He divided it into five illustrative episodes: a boyish encounter with rocks and bees, an ode to a dog that did not want him to leave home, a Panamanian *carnaval,* the way God blessed his trip to America, and a church excursion to Boston.

One Panamanian scene anchored the middle of the work. It had an infectious liveliness, despite occasional misspellings and odd constructions. Just as Esposito had asked, Telesford was very specific:

> Close to where the band plays music, a huge oil truck is now filled with water so that the people can have lots of fun being hosed Down with the water from the truck. It is very hot and the people cry, "water, water," and they are sprayed with the water from the truck to their delight. Music is playing with each other and in groups, sometimes with people they do not even know. . . . As you approach the area of the Carnaval, the music become contagious. The bodies of the people naturally sway to the beat. The colorful skirts of the girls and women twirl in the sunlight. The men's feet make tapping sounds on the pavement. Everybody is happy.

His arrival in America is made smooth and warm by finding a pentecostal church that knows his rhythms. The writing was a marked improvement from his clumsy greeting card a year before:

> When we arrived at the main church outside of Lynn, I was so excited that I could hardly wait to go inside. We all sat in the front, as usual, in a group. I kneeled down and prayed the same prayers that I had prayed before. When the service began, I stood up and started singing. It sounded so beautiful because there were so many other congregations singing with us and we were all singing at the same time. The music was good, but I didn't like the American rhythm that they used. I prefer the Spanish style which has a more "spicy" rhythm. I felt that was the only problem with the service. Other than that, everything was perfect.

At the spring gathering of the Team 9 parents' committee, the teachers displayed a sampling of autobiographies on a table in

D251. Coffey was there to lead the celebration. "I love the whole feel and tone of this room," he said. "I am still positive that the experience of this team this year will be the base of the whole redesign of this high school."

Several students had told Restaino they planned to keep their autobiographies to show to their children. A mother said she did not remember her older children feeling so good about a ninth grade experience, or any child of hers writing so much. A father said the course had proved to him that high expectations would also work for less motivated children. One parent asked why they were not expanding the program into the tenth grade immediately. Coffey said that was what he wanted, and perhaps have some more disciplines added to the mix. There were reports of similar programs about to be attempted at other elite schools. Judy Fox had planted the idea at Scarsdale. Great Neck North was within a year of beginning a program, after four years of study.

Restaino knew how lucky he and Esposito had been to find enough teachers willing to take on the freshman class. The sophomore class would be harder, for there were no more easy converts in the English department. Restaino would have to preach the new gospel quietly and patiently, and see who came around. They had gone further than most schools could, by virtue of their financial resources, faculty talent, and—at least in this case—enthusiastic parents. High-achieving schools could reach their low-achieving students if they found something that connected to their lives. Restaino pointed to the autobiographies. "This is not just catharsis," he said. "It is craftsmanship. They have gone through many, many drafts, and my contention is you cannot do that in an essay on the Peloponnesian War."

Some students might thrill to stories of ancient Greek battles, but most would be far more likely to think about form and grammar and vocabulary and narrative drive if allowed to examine their distaste for school or their love of mountain climbing or their suspicions of older siblings or their memories of *carnaval*. "If you make a big deal out of that," Restaino said, "that the unexamined life is not worth living, then I think they jump to it."

MOVING ON

It rained heavily the day before Hopkins and Sarlo were to graduate in June 1996. Although the skies had cleared by 4:00 P.M. when the ceremony was supposed to begin, the traditional venue—the football field—was still a bog. Coffey passed the word that the graduates and their families would have to stuff themselves into the Post auditorium.

Kristie Wilbur, a lacrosse all-star on her way to the University of Michigan, was among the graduates, and her parents were not happy about the last-minute change. There was no room in the auditorium for Jim Wilbur's parents, who were sent off to watch the ceremony on television in a classroom that was locked until Sandy Wilbur intervened.

The air inside the auditorium was sticky hot. Hopkins wore a dress shirt and tie under his black robe. At times he thought he was going to faint, but it had been a splendid year for him and he was happy to celebrate. He was, without any dispute, the class valedictorian, with a 97 average. There had been a glut of applications for early admission to Harvard and only two Mamaroneck students had gotten in, Hopkins and his friend Julie Kalos. He took AP Calculus BC, the more difficult of the two calculus tests, and AP Physics C, the more difficult of the two physics tests, scoring 5s in both. He was editor-in-chief of the *Globe.* He finished his monograph on the Second Amendment, something he was proud of, though the *Concord Review,* chronically short of funds, had to hold off publication that year, frustrating his hopes of seeing the essay in print.

His AP Spanish class had been a joy, the result of the enthusiasm of the teacher, Monica Silva-Lisa, and the presence of many native speakers. Even AP European History, considered by some of his friends to be a memorization marathon, turned out fine. His academic load, even with four AP courses, was not as daunting as it seemed. He worked hard in Spanish and calculus and history, but floated through Russian History and Literature with Ehrenhaft and Phillips. Hopkins told friends that Phillips graded on a scale of 1 to 10: If you got a 1, that meant a 91. His major paper for Phillips was a six-page biography of Vitus Bering, who Hopkins said was Dutch. Phillips noted on the cover page when he returned the paper that Bering was Danish, but he still gave Hopkins an A-plus.

AP Physics turned out to be less rigorous than expected. Hopkins thought Levine was an excellent teacher—clear and vibrant and quick to find ways to illustrate difficult concepts. But he graded the course with a system he called pass-drop. He urged deep thought and hard work throughout the year but let students escape with no grade at all if they did little work and had no chance of passing. Hopkins, who hated grade grubbing, at first liked this system and thought pass-drop would give them all a chance to show that the best kind of learning was for learning's sake. By the middle of the first semester, he had to acknowledge that less noble motives held sway. Most of his classmates had put aside their physics to concentrate on courses where a low B or C might show up on their transcripts.

Hopkins's duties at the *Globe* and his other AP courses were mounting. Despite his good intentions, he found himself slipping into the habit of saving all his physics homework for a free period just before class. He still got a 5 on the test, but his classmates' grades showed the consequences of giving the course a low priority.

Of the fourteen Physics C students who took the AP test, seven failed the mechanics portion and nine failed the electricity and magnetism portion. Since they were all seniors, the scores came too late to have any impact on their university applications. All that the colleges knew was that they had done well enough to get a grade of "pass" in the first semester of a difficult course. Levine felt let down but shrugged it off as the price of coaxing as many people into AP as possible and making them all take the examination.

Mamaroneck graduation ceremonies were less austere than most. Students were allowed to decorate their mortarboards. Most pasted words or designs on the tops of their graduation caps to signify their loyalties and tastes. Hopkins had a white spiral, a mark he and seven friends had decided was their symbol. He added the initials GMB for the Green Mountain Boys in memory of his previous summer's trek up the spine of Vermont.

He had conferred with the two salutorians, Kalos and David Buchwald, about their speeches. They decided to make a single presentation, an allegory of a tiger, the school mascot. Rachel Lissy, the elected class speaker, would provide whatever humor the occasion required. Hopkins spent graduation morning practicing his part of the speech in front of a mirror. When the time came, it went well, although he lost his place briefly and was disappointed that the trio's attempts at dry wit did not amuse the sweat-soaked audience.

The graduates occupied the first ten rows of the auditorium, facing the stage. In the eighth row with the other Ss sat Sarlo, wearing a light dress under her black robe. She wondered when she was going to lose her composure.

She and her eight closest friends, Meaghan Fanning, Christy Kingham, Brooke Leahy, Emily Osborne, Clare Tucker, Malitta Westrick, Kristie Wilbur, and Katie Williams, had bought a two-page ad in the yearbook celebrating their years together. They took the title of one of their favorite songs, Bruce Springsteen's "Glory Days," and placed one of the nine letters on top of each of their mortarboards. Sarlo had the Y in "Glory," plus her lacrosse jersey number, 7, and the coded "h4tb," meaning "hope for the best."

Sandy Wilbur was as pleased with the circle of friends and with the outcome of a Mamaroneck education as her daughter was. Kristie, she thought, might have gotten a better academic foundation at a boarding school. Mamaroneck's emphasis on sports seemed a bit too much to her despite Kristie's great success. The college competition seemed irredeemably ruthless and some parents, she thought, used professional contacts and the promise of major donations to get their children into the universities of their choice. But Kristie was going off to Michigan with a good start in Chinese, a load of AP credits, and a confidence in herself fortified in part by the Glory Days gang.

Sarlo also thought she had had a very successful year. Her average for the two terms was 87, higher than it had ever been. She had liked each of her teachers and had worked hard, while making time for a final round of outings with her friends. She was elected homecoming queen. She won two $500 scholarships. She played well on a lacrosse team that made the playoffs.

Her favorite course in her senior year was Gender Issues, a literature class exploring femininity and masculinity. It was taught by Ileen Gottesfeld, an emotional woman with long curly hair who was so enthusiastic about her subject that she left herself open to student parody. Opinions of Gottesfeld varied, but Sarlo connected with her immediately. Few Mamaroneck students had thought through the nature of female-male differences more thoroughly than Sarlo. She spoke up, did the reading, and often stayed after class to engage Gottesfeld in further discussion. In writing conferences, Gottesfeld said the same things about Sarlo's run-on sentences and fractured vocabulary that Scotch had said, but Sarlo thought Gottesfeld was nicer and more helpful. The teacher was also a tough and precise grader, so Sarlo's 89 seemed a compliment.

Sarlo's grade in Economics was only an 82, but she loved the course. Ahearn was interesting and amusing. Her other courses were of a familiar sort—lightweight versions of traditional categories. Her non-Regents Trigonometry course drew only ten people. Sarlo was the most motivated and received the highest grade, an 85. Conceptual Physics explored practical aspects of science.

When the teacher told the class what questions would be on the examinations, Sarlo was one of the few to listen and take notes. Her grade, a 90, was again near the top. Tannenbaum took her for a fourth year of graphic arts and used her, as promised, as a teaching assistant, with few responsibilities. He gave her an 88, the same grade she received in Phillips's Changing Times.

Even after taking a new mortgage on their house, the Sarlos could not afford to send their daughter to anything but a state-subsidized school. For a while she had her heart set on Towson University in Maryland. The campus was beautiful. It was warmer than New York. She wanted to become a teacher, and it had an excellent education department. But she could not get off the waiting list. She decided to attend the State University of New York at Oneonta, a three-and-a-half-hour drive over the Catskill Mountains. Oneonta would cost $12,000 a year, $3,000 of that tuition. Sarlo would have a class in work-study skills to help adjust to college expectations. She could try sociology as a possible major and enroll in American Sign Language to fulfill her language requirement. She had a slight hearing loss anyway, and the skill might be useful if she pursued her plan to become a teacher.

She was finishing her high school career with a series of celebrations of family and friends, her first priority. She was not bothered by the differences in her and her friends' lifestyles. The nine of them reflected the socioeconomic pattern of the high school: six affluent girls with college-educated parents and three less-affluent girls whose parents, if they acquired degrees as Sarlo's mother had, did so later in life.

As the graduation ceremony reached an end, Sarlo's feelings for her friends nudged her close to the emotional edge. She marched briskly across the stage to collect her diploma. She made it safely back to the gym. But when she saw Williams crying, she let herself go.

She loved all her friends, both the book smart and the street smart. They would all have good lives if they used well what God had given them. She did not think her practical skills and talents were any less valuable than the academic quickness some of them displayed. That was why she resented teachers and counselors who put her in a slower, weaker, less motivated category before taking the trouble to find out if that was best for her, even if she did not respond cheerfully to every challenge.

After the ceremony, most of her friends went to the Shore Club with their families for dinner. It was $50 a plate, too much for Sarlo, Tucker, and Williams. They adjourned to the Williams house, where Katie's mother had laid out a delicious spread. A couple of beer kegs were there to lubricate the celebration. Sarlo watched her parents soak up the delight of having a daughter graduate from the splendid school they had also attended. Dawn Sarlo smiled and cried and congratulated everyone. John Sarlo shook hands and took pictures.

Sarlo did not think her friends going to Dartmouth and Michigan and Duke and Georgetown had any real advantage over her. Given a choice, she would take her parents and her life every time. But she wished she had been able to have more classes with the book smart. Some of them could make her feel stupid with just a word, but she still liked having them around. There was no better way to cut through a dense lecture or unscramble a complicated homework assignment than to have a friend around who understood it. It was easier for someone her age to explain things. Teachers and textbooks were sometimes incomprehensible.

In the same way, she thought her book-smart friends needed her. With their noses pointed at their computer screens, they sometimes failed to detect people's thoughts and feelings. They needed her to explain how all the ideas in their heads worked, or did not work, in the real world.

She was grateful for their friendship and the lessons they had learned from each other. But, she thought, there could have been more. If they had been placed in the same classes, buttressed by Mamaroneck's energetic teachers and good libraries and diverting pastimes, they might have significantly enriched the memories they were about to take with them to Georgetown and Duke and Michigan and Dartmouth and 180 miles over the Catskills to SUNY Oneonta.

GROWING TOGETHER

By the fall of 1996, Samuel Telesford had made substantial progress.

He was preparing for the Regents test in American History that would guarantee his passage on to college, where he wanted to study the culinary arts.

Omari High, invited back to the APPLE program after his difficult year in White Plains, survived early struggles with tight deadlines and stayed at Mamaroneck. He rose to starting fullback on the football team, scoring several touchdowns, and managed to graduate, although the APPLE faculty pushed him hard right to the end.

Team 9 likewise prospered. When Ehrenhaft retired as English department chair in 1996, Restaino took the job. He had to give up one of his Team 9 classes, but Ahearn and Landrum picked up the slack. By any measure, the interdisciplinary program was a success. Parents had moved from polite uncertainty to applause. The graduates of the team's first year did well in their tenth grade classes. Each year the ninth grade presentations grew more accomplished and the meshing of English and social studies less awkward. The threat of teacher burnout remained, for each class required a different approach. There was no more time or money for preparation than there had ever been. But many of the rough edges were gone.

Word spread to other schools of Mamaroneck's reconstruction of the ninth grade. Coffey and team members received requests for information. A program to place Mamaroneck seniors in internships and encourage exposure to the working world developed under Coffey's guidance. Other experiments began, encouraged by a new superintendent, Sherry King. As the superintendent of the Croton-Harmon district in northern Westchester, the curly-haired King had followed the principles of the Coalition of Essential Schools, of which she was a national leader. The Mamaroneck school board, still leery of Theodore Sizer and his admirers in the coalition, hired her when Mary Anne Mays left to become chief of staff of the National Alliance for Restructuring Education in Washington. The Mamaroneck board appeared to like King more for her résumé than for her reputation as a reformer. She had taught at Scarsdale, had been an assistant principal at Bronxville, and knew how elite schools worked.

Even as it experimented, Mamaroneck continued to sharpen its more conventional tools. The school gave 340 AP tests in 1996, up from 299 in 1995. Expressed as a ratio of tests to the size of Mamaroneck's graduating class (see Challenge Index), the strength of the AP program increased from 1.165 to 1.417, putting it among the top one hundred public school programs in the country. An extraordinary 98 percent of the 240 graduating seniors in 1996 took the SAT. Their mean verbal score was 542, compared to a national mean of 505. Their mean mathematic score 543 compared to a national mean of 508. Eighty-two percent of the class members were admitted to four-year colleges, including six to Michigan, five to Cornell, four to Washington University, and three to Dartmouth. Eleven percent went to two-year colleges.

Mamaroneck had reached a level of excellence where it could even ignore state rules. Mamaroneck allowed some advanced students, like Hopkins, to skip economics, required for graduation in New York, in favor of high-voltage offerings like AP European History. Asked about this, social studies department chair Richard Ciotti smiled and put a finger to his lips.

Such genial independence, just short of arrogance, summarizes the elite public school. State and national rules and standards are made for others. Normal hurdles are too low and ordinary yard-sticks too short. Scarsdale did not bother awarding a state Regents diploma. La Jolla's principal chided San Diego administrators for allegedly trying to dumb down his South San Diego students. New Trier insisted on keeping its level system even though the huge evaluation team it spent $40,000 to bring to Winnetka said it was not a good idea.

Such schools have given the upper levels of American high school instruction unprecedented rigor and complexity. Any parent can confirm this by comparing her child's AP homework with what she remembers of her own high school assignments. United States victories in international science and mathematics competitions demonstrate superiority even on an international level.

High-achieving schools have proved to a certain extent that healthy teacher salaries can help produce good schools, although the success of poorly paid teachers at many elite schools in California (top salaries of $55,000 compared to $70,000 in Illinois and $90,000 in New York) suggests that money is not the only reason. Elite schools have shown that smaller classes with rigorous lesson plans produce understanding and learning. They have illustrated the power of involved parents, even if they are sometimes a very blunt instrument, and even if no one has yet determined how to create ambitious parents if they do not start that way.

The forces that motivate students at these schools include youthful curiosity (rarely given the credit it deserves), desire to please parents, eagerness to keep up with friends, and interest in gaining admission to a good college, this last motive making many educators rightly uncomfortable. College choice is often dictated by fashion, marketing, and financial resources rather than a sense of what each university has to offer. Although admission to some colleges, on the average, leads to higher incomes, the differences are small and over a lifetime do not make up for the higher expense of higher status schools.

There may be a way to shift American culture to a different track, where university admission is no longer a nearly universal dream, but I cannot think of how that can be done. If yearning for the college of one's choice, despite its drawbacks, is such a potent force, perhaps the best thing to do is not to fight it but harness it. Going to college has become as pervasive a goal in American society as graduating from high school was a half century ago. It may be true that this is wasteful and distracting. Future plumbers and gardeners may not need college training, and it may be a misuse of funds to encourage them.

But the money is going to be spent. In 1996 President Clinton announced a plan to make two years of college as universal as high school, and provide funding to support students who wanted all four years. He said he wanted to give everyone a chance at the higher wages that almost invariably come with a college degree. Given the apparent popularity of this idea, it might be wise to consider other reasons, having to do not with paychecks but with the motives of teenagers, that make this a worthy enterprise.

It is difficult to spend much time in elite schools and not come to the conclusion that making college a goal for everyone would give more children a motive for paying attention. Remove the lust for college, and the scores and grades and academic energy at Mamaroneck would drop precipitously. If the day comes when college is as woven into the social framework as high school is today, there will be unforeseen, perhaps damaging consequences, but I think the high schools will be the better for it. If college becomes a realistic goal for nearly all students, might they not be better focused on the lesson at hand?

Granted, they will be victims of a marketing scheme, just as high-achieving high schoolers are now. Many educators rightly worry about that, but perhaps their concern is overdone. To take a noneducational example, American consumers do not have to go to health spas to lose pounds or join the Book-of-the-Month Club to improve their conversation, but it is probably good for them to do so no matter how much they have been swayed by cynical advertising campaigns.

College for everyone might accentuate the notion that learning is for learning's sake. Future plumbers would know that they were not applying to Grinnell to improve their billing procedures, but to ensure they had explored all of life's options and gained an appreciation of art and literature and history to enrich their hours off the job. Employers might be more motivated to hire blue-collar workers whose bachelor degrees denoted maturity, persistence, and intelligence.

Elite high schools have deepened the educations of their most willing customers. The next test is how well they sell their intellectual wares to those who are resisting the pitch. Can they inspire slower, less motivated students as well as children on the honor roll? At Mamaroneck and a few other schools, the use of mixed ability classes for some students and classroom cocoons for others has yielded encouraging results. Also intriguing have been the suburban school programs bringing students from urban neighborhoods.

Such efforts are, unfortunately, exceptions. As wary of class distinctions as Americans are, their public schools still operate on the principle that the book smart and the street smart should not be given the same chance to learn. This two-track system might make political sense in schools with sharp differences in family background and achievement, but its use in suburban schools where there are no socioeconomic differences appears to stem not from sound educational research, but from the ancient need to see ourselves as better than others. Many of the byproducts of this system, such as rules keeping eager students out of AP courses, are utterly senseless.

In the 1980s I spent time at Garfield High School in East Los Angeles, a school as different from Mamaroneck as a Volkswagen bug is from a Mercedes SLE. Garfield's two calculus teachers, Jaime Escalante and Ben Jimenez, and several AP colleagues discovered that their low-income Mexican American students learned what their teachers expected them to learn. The school set the standards high and large numbers of students responded, creating the strongest academic program ever in an inner-city school.

What intrigues me is the thought of what Garfield would have done with the allegedly mediocre students denied the opportunity to take AP courses at schools like Mamaroneck, Scarsdale, New Trier, and Millburn. Their energy and eagerness would have won them instant admission, no questions asked. It is hard to argue they would have done any worse than the Mexican American children who passed these same tests with high scores, yet at their own schools, elite exemplars of high standards, they were denied the opportunity.

That is why I am so suspicious when I hear educators talk about softening what they consider destructively high expectations. Many teachers at Garfield thought Escalante was pushing his students into crippling fatigue and disappointment. Instead, his graduates went on to the engineering departments at USC and Harvey Mudd College and made splendid careers.

There was a tendency on the part of many Garfield teachers, all of them intelligent and well meaning, to equate difficult homework and long examinations with unnecessary stress. Why force such nice young people to grind themselves down, some teachers asked, when they will have a chance to learn these subjects in college anyway? My answer is that if they do not become engaged with these disciplines in high school, how can anyone be sure they will ever go to college? Why are hard courses bad and easy courses good? Could it be that one of the reasons so many American children hate high school is because it is often too easy and becomes boring and irrelevant? A dumb and repetitive lesson is unlikely to get anyone very far, and students know it.

The same thought occurs to me when I encounter parents or teachers at elite high schools worrying about the pressure of college applications and difficult courses. They are concerned about stress, but stress comes in different forms. Some schoolroom demands are silly. My thirteen-year-old daughter Katie was frantic recently over a mistake she made on a chart. She feared an erasure might make the teacher think she was messy and disorganized. It was the sort of mindless standard—margins must be one inch, ink must be black, each paragraph must start with a topic sentence—that students still find in high school, to the shame of the teachers involved.

Standards that make sense—learning the causes of the Civil War, the parts of the inner ear, the formula for the area of a circle—intrigue most students. Those taking difficult courses are often busy, but that is not the same thing as being unhappy. Lessons that reveal how the world works are irresistible. There may be a limit to how many truths a student can absorb in a day, but I have yet to find the student who feels he or she has reached it.

The nonprofit group Public Agenda surveyed thirteen hundred high school students nationally and found 65 percent thought they were not trying very hard and 75 percent felt they would learn more if pushed harder by better teachers. A record 35.6 percent of college freshmen surveyed by UCLA in 1996 said they had often been bored by their high school classes.

What adds unnecessary stress to high school are parents who demand that a child focus on biology when what he really loves is history, or teachers who criticize a composition without suggesting how it can be improved, or department heads who keep a student out of a difficult but interesting class because of disappointing grades the year before. Elite schools should be the least likely places to find such misapplications of education, and the least afraid of nudging a student who is not moving very fast.

Hopkins and Sarlo were very different students who shared a sense of what they and their friends had missed for lack of the stress some educators consider so poisonous. Hopkins recalled his interest in Russian history and in physics, and how little he and his friends did in those courses because so little was demanded. He thought teachers could demand more work without losing the fun of it. Students could be pushed more and loopholes closed, he thought, if teachers wanted to.

Sarlo recalled courses that never rose above the level of eighth grade refreshers, augmented with videos to keep everyone entertained. The teachers did not care as much about such classes as they did about their higher-level courses, she thought. They favored the better students. At the end of high school, she felt she had not learned as much as she could have.

Both Sarlo and Hopkins acknowledged it was their fault they did not do more. Their best efforts should have been, as they often were, motivated from within, not because a teacher piled on homework. Some educators say that some students cannot grasp this until they sample the pap of a low-level course and come to realize they don't like it. To this way of thinking, courses with few demands help expose the real learners, but unless the system keeps the doors open to the most demanding learning experiences, the moment of self-discovery is likely to lead only to frustration.

American teenagers in elite public schools usually know how to handle pressure. They find breathing spaces in books and CD-ROMs and computers and sports and music. Their greatest joy in high school is the friends they find there, who share with them the oddities and beauties of a life of study, without saying so aloud. If the most ambitious schools do not find ways to nudge all of them toward the truths that enliven adulthood, who will?

EPILOGUE

The Mamaroneck High School class of 1997 graduated on a ninety-degree day that left everyone in the football stadium longing for a breeze. The graduates included Samuel Telesford, his dream realized, his diploma waiting for him on the stage at the fifty-yard line.

Also graduating, in a way, was Jim Coffey, who had announced his resignation. He was fifty-seven and had done much that he was proud of, but the demands of the job continued to grow. His innards were telling him he had had enough. He remembered his idol, Ted Williams, deciding to retire after standing on second base and realizing, for the first time, what a long way it was to third.

Once the word got out that Coffey was leaving, his friends and admirers in Westchester and Connecticut began to offer him counseling jobs. He missed working directly with students. He was not quite ready for retirement, and a return to his old life appealed to him. Penny Oberg, the newly appointed head counselor at Greeley, was particularly insistent that he join her back where he had first explored the mysteries of elite school students and their parents.

Near the end of the graduation ceremonies he rose to give his final remarks before the graduates came up. He reminded himself that the other speeches had lasted longer than expected. Both he and his audience were hot and tired. After a few words of thanks, he uttered a favorite phrase—"a hug is worth a thousand words"—and sat down.

Telesford heard him. It occurred to him what a pleasant contrast the warm day was to his first chilly night in his new country. When the black-robed graduate's name was called, he did not hold back. Upon accepting his diploma, he embraced Coffey long and hard, with the muscular joy of a man who had arrived at a place he really wanted to be.

AFTERWORD

A GUIDE FOR STUDENTS
AND PARENTS:
CHALLENGE QUANTIFIED

Nearly every professional educator will tell you that ranking schools is counterproductive, unscientific, hurtful, and wrong. Every likely criteria you might use in such an evaluation is going to be narrow and distorted. A school that stumbles one year may be fine the next.

I accept all those arguments. Yet as a reporter and as a parent, I think that in some circumstances a ranking system, no matter how limited, can be useful. Below are the two hundred forty-three public high schools that I consider the most ambitious institutions of their kind in the country, ranked by their success in coaxing students into challenging courses, certified by a rigorous series of national examinations.

Many schools not on this list do wonderful work. They salve wounded spirits, inspire jaded intellects, and take young people places they have never been before. But when it comes to coaxing high school students into the most demanding classes, the ones I list are at the top among schools with normal enrollment systems—those that admit at least half of their students without requiring them to show high test scores or grades. I have included magnet schools that may draw the majority of students from outside their neighborhoods but do not admit them on the basis of scores or grades. A handful of special high schools, discussed in chapter 29, use grades and/or tests to select all of their students. They are exceptional places but are organized so differently from most American schools that they do not belong on this list.

I use the Advanced Placement (AP) test in determining the quality of these schools. It is not perfect, but at the moment it is the best standard measure of curricular strength in the United States. The International Baccalaureate, which coexists with the AP in a few schools, also tries to pull secondary schools into the upper reaches of many disciplines, but it has not yet spread very far in this country.

To calculate the index number for each school, I have divided the number of AP tests given in 1996 by the number of students graduating from each school in June (or in a few cases May) of that year. Large high schools have no immediate advantage over small ones, other than the fact that school boards are sometimes reluctant to fund AP classes in small schools. Using the graduating class as a measure of school size levels the playing field somewhat for schools that draw from low-income neighborhoods with heavy dropout rates. The strength of each AP program is measured only against the number of students who are committed enough to earn a diploma.

This is not just a measure of parents' money and education, although those factors have considerable impact. The index does not measure how well the students do on the AP tests, but only how many tests they take. A disadvantaged school that coaxes its students into these courses and insists that they take the tests has an opportunity to rank as high as a school full of lawyers' children for whom getting a 4 or a 5 on the AP is almost preordained.

Jaime Escalante's first rule was to let everyone into Calculus who wanted to try it. His second rule was to cajole or bully into the course everyone else who had the faintest chance of success. If at the end of a tough year an Escalante student scored a disappointing 1 or 2 on the test, he saluted the student and welcomed him back for another try the next year. Many of his students acquired new confidence in themselves by the mere act of sticking with the course and taking the test. When they took the course a second time, they were more prepared for calculus's odd vocabulary and complex thought structure. Many of the least eager students at the beginning of the year found that they did much better than they had expected. In 1987 two thirds of the 129 Garfield AP calculus students scored 3, 4, or 5, despite the fact that the school had more students taking the test than all but four schools in the country.

Like Garfield, a few schools on this list—including North Hollywood, Midwood, Eastside, Riverside and Jordan in Durham, and Riverside University High in Milwaukee, have provided extraordinary challenges for students with modest family backgrounds. Some of the schools in Florida and Utah would not be as high on the list if it took into account how students scored on the test. But those states and some others have decided to subsidize test fees and other AP costs to encourage more students to enroll. Educators like Escalante think that is a good idea.

Some teachers rightly complain that the AP course and test are not ideal. Some scholars argue that AP, and the overall educational philosophy of the country, is wrongly tied to the curriculum of selective enrollment colleges. A few schools have found ways to go deeply into certain subjects by means other than AP.

Parents should not immediately doubt the strength of a school that does not have a strong AP or IB program, but they should look at such schools very closely. Consider two schools whose AP programs fall short of expectations. One is Darien High School in Darien, Connecticut, a famously affluent community slightly smaller than the Mamaroneck district but with the same high standardized test scores. In 1996 the school had 169 graduating seniors, but gave only 151 AP tests, for a challenge index of 0.893. AP History teacher George Sykes said some students were not encouraged to take the test. This takes the pressure off both the students and their teachers, and happens far more often than it should. Many Darien students were also kept out of the AP courses because of gatekeeping procedures like those described in chapter 17.

A second school in a wealthy area, Shawnee Mission East High School of Shawnee Mission, Kansas, ranked even further down the scale—160 AP tests and 402 graduating seniors in 1996 for an index of 0.398. The school did not bar any students who wanted to take its AP courses, but it did not expend much energy encouraging them to take the test. Counselor Chris O'Neill estimated that less than half of the students in AP American History took the test in 1997. Principal Angelo Cocolis said that the school's students still score at the top on standardized tests, but research indicates that that is more a measure of their family backgrounds than the quality of the curriculum. A school that shies away from AP tests, based on classroom learning rather than standardized norms, seems to me to be reluctant to challenge its best students and its best teachers.

If those teachers and students shunned AP as an unfair measure of their skills and effort, that might be a factor to consider, but they raise few such objections. Instead, the usual excuse is that too much AP test taking will lower the school's passing rate, or put youthful egos at risk, or drain energies better used to enjoy the last few months of high school before the college grind begins. Such reasons appeal to some people, but not to me. Schools that do not encourage their students to stretch themselves are not doing their jobs.

This index does not provide as nuanced a measure of challenge in public schools as I would like. For instance, it obscures the sins of a very few schools, such as Millburn and Scarsdale, that have so many motivated students that they can bar some of them from taking AP courses and still rank at the top. It gives more credit than I would like to schools that have a few students taking many examinations and many students taking none at all. Nor does the index celebrate as much as I would like the lengths that schools such as Shaker Heights, Lynbrook, and Stevenson go to in encouraging students to test their limits.

The best schools, in my view, give very high priority to challenging young people and are willing to accept the dangers of failure. Educators who teach AP courses risk being judged by a test they do not control. Students who take the courses have committed themselves to the highest measurable level of American secondary education, and all the effort and worry that entails. They may be motivated by desires to look good on college applications and get a fast start on their medical careers, but there is no real harm in that. One way or another, it leads them to a classroom where the deepest wonders of language and science and history are exposed.

APPENDIX

The Challenge Index:
America's Top High Schools

The index measures each school's effort to challenge its students by dividing the number of AP tests it gave in 1996 by the number of graduating seniors in May or June of that year. The list includes all U.S. schools with more than 200 graduates that achieved an index of 1.000 or more, and as many smaller schools as could be found that met that standard. Only public schools that selected no more than half of their students through examinations, grades, or other academic criteria are included. If you know a school that should be added to the list, please contact Jay Mathews at mathewsj@washpost.com or through Times Books.

1. Stanton College Prep (Jacksonville, Fla.)	4.090
2. Jericho (N.Y.)	2.903
3. Wheatley (Old Westbury, N.Y.)	2.862
4. Millburn (N.J.)	2.744
5. Richard Montgomery (Rockville, Md.)	2.464
6. Brighton (Rochester, N.Y.)	2.418
7. Indian Hill (Cincinnati)	2.400
8. Scarsdale (N.Y.)	2.396
9. H-B Woodlawn (Arlington, Va.)	2.342
10. Manhasset (N.Y.)	2.256
11. Greeley (Chappaqua, N.Y.)	2.207
12. North Hollywood (Calif.)	2.198
13. Gunn (Palo Alto, Calif.)	2.075
14. Saratoga (Calif.)	2.057
15. Andover (Bloomfield Hills, Mich.)	2.033
16. Palos Verdes Peninsula (Rolling Hills Estates, Calif.)	1.998

17. Stevenson (Lincolnshire, Ill.)   1.994
18. University (Irvine, Calif.)   1.986
19. Princeton (N.J.)   1.972
20. La Canada (Calif.)   1.970
21. Sunny Hills (Fullerton, Calif.)   1.968
22. Bronxville (N.Y.)   1.963
23. La Jolla (Calif.)   1.961
24. Great Neck North (N.Y.)   1.934
25. Irondequoit (N.Y.)   1.920
26. Eastside (Gainesville, Fla.)   1.896
27. Pittsford Mendon (Pittsford, N.Y.)   1.876
28. Miami Palmetto (Fla.)   1.856
29. Lyndon B. Johnson (Austin, Tex.)   1.853
30. Orange (Pepper Pike, Ohio)   1.849
31. New Trier (Winnetka, Ill.)   1.841
32. Weston (Mass.)   1.827
33. Cold Spring Harbor (N.Y.)   1.826
34. Edina (Minn.)   1.826
35. Chagrin Falls (Ohio)   1.821
36. Tappan Zee (Orangeburg, N.Y.)   1.801
37. Mountain Brook (Ala.)   1.786
38. Ridge (Basking Ridge, N.J.)   1.780
39. Southside (Greenville, S.C.)   1.771
40. Briarcliff (Briarcliff Manor, N.Y.)   1.769
41. Mira Costa (Manhattan Beach, Calif.)   1.738
42. Langley (McLean, Va.)   1.716
43. Enloe (Raleigh, N.C.)   1.702
44. Valley Stream South (N.Y.)   1.696
45. Hillsborough (Tampa, Fla.)   1.689
46. North Hunterdon (Annandale, N.J.)   1.685
47. Highland Park (Ill.)   1.666
48. Westwood (Mass.)   1.659
49. Los Angeles Center for Enriched Studies (Calif.)   1.658
50. Amherst Central (N.Y.)   1.655
51. Fort Myers (Fla.)   1.650
52. Duxbury (Mass.)   1.622
53. Jordan (Durham, N.C.)   1.620
54. Rye (N.Y.)   1.619
55. Coral Gables (Fla.)   1.583
56. Edgemont (N.Y.)   1.580

57. Pittsford Sutherland (Pittsford, N.Y.)   1.578
58. Shaker Heights (Ohio)   1.571
59. Roslyn (Roslyn Heights, N.Y.)   1.555
60. Great Neck South (N.Y.)   1.551
61. Grosse Pointe South (Mich.)   1.550
62. Hall (West Hartford, Conn.)   1.547
63. Fountain Valley (Calif.)   1.547
64. Oceanside (N.Y.)   1.535
65. Williamsville South (Buffalo, N.Y.)   1.518
66. Solon (Ohio)   1.515
67. Miramonte (Orinda, Calif.)   1.505
68. Lower Moreland (Penn.)   1.505
69. Wayland (Mass.)   1.500
70. Rye Neck (Mamaroneck, N.Y.)   1.479
71. Lincoln (Tallahassee)   1.478
72. Highland Park (Tex.)   1.475
73. Westwood (Austin)   1.469
74. Van Nuys (Calif.)   1.458
75. Lake Brantley (Fla.)   1.458
76. Ardsley (N.Y.)   1.452
77. Farmington (Conn.)   1.448
78. Mamaroneck (N.Y.)   1.433
79. Port Richmond (Staten Island, N.Y.)   1.432
80. Kennedy (Bellmore, N.Y.)   1.430
81. Glen Ridge (N.J.)   1.425
82. Niles North (Skokie, Ill.)   1.423
83. Edison (Fresno, Calif.)   1.418
84. Hewlett (N.Y.)   1.418
85. Bethlehem Central (Delmar, N.Y.)   1.402
86. Lewiston-Porter Senior (Youngstown, N.Y.)   1.395
87. Memorial Senior (Houston)   1.394
88. Palo Alto (Calif.)   1.390
89. Plant (Tampa, Fla.)   1.376
90. Glenbrook North (Northbrook, Ill.)   1.371
91. Byram Hills (Armonk, N.Y.)   1.370
92. Clovis West (Calif.)   1.370
93. Lynbrook (San Jose, Calif.)   1.364
94. Plainview-Old Bethpage JFK (N.Y.)   1.358
95. Nova (Fort Lauderdale, Fla.)   1.357
96. Park City (Utah)   1.356

97.	Glass (Lynchburg, Va.)	1.353
98.	Kings Park (N.Y.)	1.345
99.	Cardozo (Queens, N.Y.)	1.336
100.	Asheville (N.C.)	1.335
101.	Long Beach Polytechnic (Calif.)	1.334
102.	Plano Senior (Tex.)	1.333
103.	Westlake (Westlake Village, Calif.)	1.330
104.	McLean (Va.)	1.324
105.	Riverside (Durham, N.C.)	1.312
106.	Bloomfield (East Bloomfield, N.Y.)	1.309
107.	Churchill (Potomac, Md.)	1.304
108.	Herricks Senior (New Hyde Park, N.Y.)	1.304
109.	Lynbrook Senior (N.Y.)	1.303
110.	South Side (Rockville Centre, N.Y.)	1.300
111.	Beverly Hills (Calif.)	1.296
112.	Riverside University (Milwaukee)	1.293
113.	Long Island City (N.Y.)	1.291
114.	Oak Park (Agoura, Calif.)	1.288
115.	Torrey Pines (Calif.)	1.287
116.	Mainland Regional (Linwood, N.J.)	1.285
117.	Cerritos (Calif.)	1.284
118.	Northwest Guilford Senior (Greensboro, N.C.)	1.282
119.	Sherman Oaks Center for Enriched Studies (Reseda, Calif.)	1.279
120.	Corona del Mar (Newport Beach, Calif.)	1.278
121.	Glenbrook South (Ill.)	1.275
122.	Livingston (N.J.)	1.271
123.	Barrington Community (Ill.)	1.271
124.	Vorhees (Glen Gardner, N.J.)	1.271
125.	West Potomac (Fairfax, Va.)	1.251
126.	Oyster Bay (N.Y.)	1.250
127.	Yorktown (Arlington, Va.)	1.249
128.	Grimsley Senior (Greensboro, N.C.)	1.246
129.	Arcadia (Calif.)	1.245
130.	Watauga (Boone, N.C.)	1.244
131.	Southwest Guilford (High Point, N.C.)	1.243
132.	Auburn (Ala.)	1.243
133.	Garden City Senior (N.Y.)	1.239
134.	Oakton (Vienna, Va.)	1.238
135.	Harborfields, (Greenlawn, N.Y.)	1.235

136. Tenafly (N.J.)   1.230
137. Monta Vista (Cupertino, Calif.)   1.225
138. Taft (Woodland Hills, Calif.)   1.224
139. Valhalla (El Cajon, Calif.)   1.222
140. Lexington (Mass.)   1.221
141. Eleanor Roosevelt (Greenbelt, Md.)   1.217
142. Lawrence (Cedarhurst, N.Y.)   1.213
143. Hinsdale Central (Ill.)   1.213
144. Aragon (San Mateo, Calif.)   1.209
145. Bellaire (Houston)   1.208
146. Williamsville East (East Amherst, N.Y.)   1.207
147. Deerfield (Highland Park, Ill.)   1.202
148. Clarence Central (N.Y.)   1.200
149. Grosse Point North (Mich.)   1.198
150. Williamsville North (N.Y.)   1.193
151. Riverside (Greer, S.C.)   1.192
152. Calabasas (Calif.)   1.189
153. Cleveland (Reseda, Calif.)   1.189
154. Wilson Magnet School (Rochester, N.Y.)   1.188
155. Niceville Senior (Fla.)   1.187
156. New Hartford Senior (N.Y.)   1.186
157. Firestone Senior (Akron, Ohio)   1.186
158. San Marino (Calif.)   1.185
159. Midwood (Brooklyn, N.Y.)   1.185
160. Mission San Jose (Fremont, Calif.)   1.182
161. South (Torrance, Calif.)   1.180
162. Wootton (Rockville, Md.)   1.180
163. Campolindo (Moraga, Calif.)   1.179
164. Smithtown (N.Y.)   1.177
165. Chantilly (Va.)   1.176
166. Los Altos (Calif.)   1.174
167. Paul D. Schreiber (Port Washington, N.Y.)   1.171
168. Calhoun (Merrick, N.Y.)   1.169
169. Madison (Vienna, Va.)   1.168
170. Piedmont (Calif.)   1.166
171. Libertyville (Ill.)   1.164
172. Bountiful (Utah)   1.163
173. Syosset (N.Y.)   1.163
174. Centreville Secondary (Va.)   1.160
175. East Islip (N.Y.)   1.158

176. West Springfield (Va.)   1.158
177. Whitman (Bethesda, Md.)   1.155
178. Ithaca (N.Y.)   1.147
179. Leland (San Jose, Calif.)   1.144
180. Strath Haven (Wallingford, Penn.)   1.142
181. Valley Stream Central (N.Y.)   1.141
182. Maine Township South (Ill.)   1.141
183. Brea Olinda (Brea, Calif.)   1.138
184. Clements (Tex.)   1.138
185. Ridgewood (N.J.)   1.132
186. West Orange (N.J.)   1.130
187. Marshall (Fairfax, Va.)   1.129
188. Westlake (Austin)   1.127
189. Los Gatos (Calif.)   1.121
190. Longmeadow (Mass.)   1.118
191. Von Steuben Metro Science Center (Chicago)   1.116
192. Santa Monica (Calif.)   1.112
193. Alta (Sandy, Utah)   1.112
194. Marina (Huntington Beach, Calif.)   1.112
195. Fremd (Palatine, Ill.)   1.109
196. Niskayuna (Schenectady, N.Y.)   1.109
197. Laguna Beach (Calif.)   1.107
198. Irvine (Calif.)   1.103
199. Northport Senior (N.Y.)   1.103
200. Chamblee (Ga.)   1.102
201. Okemos (Mich.)   1.100
202. Bennett (Kingsport, Tenn.)   1.099
203. Atlantic Community (Delray Beach, Fla.)   1.098
204. Massapequa (N.Y.)   1.097
205. Newton South (Mass.)   1.096
206. Sweet Home (Amherst, N.Y.)   1.095
207. Pearl River (N.Y.)   1.094
208. Foothill (Santa Ana, Calif.)   1.094
209. McQueen (Reno, Nev.)   1.092
210. Robinson (Fairfax, Va.)   1.090
211. John Jay (Cross River, N.Y.)   1.087
212. Commack (N.Y.)   1.083
213. Fox Lane (Bedford, N.Y.)   1.080
214. Aliso Niguel (Aliso Viejo, Calif.)   1.077
215. Burlingame (Calif.)   1.074

Alphabetical Guide to High Schools in the Challenge Index

Bountiful: 172
Brea Olinda: 183
Briarcliffe: 40
Brighton: 6
Bronxville: 22
Burlingame: 215
Byram Hills: 91
Calabasas: 152
Calhoun: 168
Campolindo: 163
Cardozo: 99
Centreville Secondary: 174
Cerritos: 117
Chagrin Falls: 35
Chamblee: 200
Chantilly: 165
Chapel Hill: 220
Churchill: 107
Clarence Central: 148
Clements: 184
Cleveland: 153
Clovis West: 92
Cold Spring Harbor: 33
Commack: 212
Conestoga: 221
Coral Gables: 55
Corona del Mar: 120
Coronado: 224
Croton-Harmon: 233
Deerfield: 147
Duxbury: 52
East Islip: 175
Eastside: 26
Edgemont: 56
Edina: 34
Edison: 83
El Camino Real: 231
Eleanor Roosevelt: 141
Enloe: 43
Esperanza: 230

Evanston: 235
Farmington: 77
Firestone Senior: 157
Foothill: 208
Fort Myers: 51
Fountain Valley: 63
Fox Lane: 213
Francisco Bravo Medical Magnet: 237
Fremd: 195
Garden City Senior: 133
Glass: 97
Glenbrook North: 90
Glenbrook South: 121
Glen Ridge: 81
Grapevine: 229
Great Neck North: 24
Great Neck South: 60
Greeley: 11
Grimsley Senior: 128
Grosse Pointe North: 149
Grosse Pointe South: 61
Gunn: 13
Half Hollow Hills West: 216
Hall: 62
Harborfields: 135
H-B Woodlawn: 9
Herricks Senior: 108
Highland Park (Ill.): 47
Highland Park (Tex.): 72
Hillsborough: 45
Hinsdale Central: 143
Hewlett: 84
Indian Hill: 7
Irondequoit: 25
Irvine: 198
Ithaca: 178
Jericho: 2
John Jay: 211
Jordan: 53

ACKNOWLEDGMENTS

Diane Cleaver was my agent for sixteen years until her sudden death three years ago. She devoted herself energetically and unselfishly to me as well as many other authors. She tweaked us when we needed it and offered the insights of someone who not only had a splendid sense of the publishing business but knew words from her other lives as an editor, essayist, and novelist. I never worried about what was going to happen to my books while Diane was around. I miss her very much, the only consolation being that she left me in the hands of her fine colleague, Heide Lange.

This book was not my idea, although I have found the writing of it so intriguing that I have begun to pretend otherwise. Peter Osnos, then the president of Times Books and now publisher and chief executive officer of PublicAffairs, first suggested that I investigate the world of elite public education, my only contribution to the conversation being a quick realization that it was an interesting idea and had never been done. Peter and Steve Wasserman, then a senior editor at Times Books and now the editor of the *Los Angeles Times Book Review,* guided the book through its early stages, then handed me over to Peter Bernstein, the new publisher of Times Books, and Peter Smith, the editor who found several ways to clarify and sharpen the manuscript. Times Books publishing associate Salma Abdelnour and copy editor Patricia Romanowski were also invaluable to me.

Joe Mathews, Anna Wilde Mathews, Aric Press, Jason Vest, John Schwartz, and Anne Wheelock, author of *Crossing the Tracks,* read the manuscript and made helpful suggestions. Nearly every person interviewed for this book was given relevant portions to check for errors, and one of them, Mamaroneck High School English Department Chair Philip Restaino, gave the entire manuscript one of the most detailed and helpful critiques I have ever had.

I received generous support from the Mamaroneck Union Free School District board, particularly Penny Oberg, Douglas Kreeger, Bradford Stein, Ellen Freeman, and Benson Bieley, superintendents Mary Anne Mays and Sherry King, and most importantly Mamaroneck High School Principal James V. Coffey. I am also indebted to five recent graduates of Scarsdale High School. They are my son Peter Mathews, who first introduced me to the rituals of parenting at an elite public school, and four seniors who worked on the book as my interns under Scarsdale's senior options program: Nan-Ting Kuo, Emily Bell, Peter Schwer, and Sonia Inamdar. My editors at *The Washington Post,* Tom Dimond, Paul Bernstein, Doug Feaver, Richard Paxson, David Ignatius, Jo-Ann Armao, Robert G. Kaiser, and Leonard Downie, Jr., were, as usual, understanding and supportive.

Conversations and events that I did not hear or see have been reported as the participants remembered them, with emphasis on those elements found in more than one account. Any mistakes remain my responsibility.

INDEX

ABOUT THE AUTHOR

JAY MATHEWS is an education reporter for *The Washington Post* and a winner of the National Education Reporting Award. Mathews served as the *Post*'s bureau chief first in Hong Kong and then in Beijing and Los Angeles. This is his second book on American high schools. Mathews and his wife, Linda, have three children and live in the suburbs of Washington, D.C.